GW00455390

A

CHRONICLE OF SMALL BEER

TO DECIMA

Great-great-niece of the diarist

A
CHRONICLE OF SMALL BEER

The Early Victorian Diaries of
a Hertfordshire Brewer

by

Gerald Curtis

With a Foreword by F. G. Emmison

PHILLIMORE
London and Chichester

1970

Published by

PHILLIMORE & CO. LTD.
Shopwyke Hall, Chichester, Sussex, England

Text set throughout in 11/12 pt. Press Roman

Printed on Dalmore Smooth Wove paper

*Made and printed in England
by Stephen Austin and Sons Limited
Caxton Hill, Hertford*

ACKNOWLEDGEMENTS

I have to thank Mrs. G. N. T. Chastel de Boinville (formerly Miss Hannah Pryor) for kindly permitting me to publish extracts from the journals of her great-great-great-uncle, John Izzard Pryor, and for allowing my daughter Delicia, Mrs. C. B. Q. Wallace to take photographs of the portraits of the diarist and his wife, and also of the house and grounds at Clay Hall, now known as Walkern Hall.

In common with many Essex folk who are interested in local history, I am much indebted to Mr. F. G. Emmison, lately Archivist of our County, for advice and encouragement.

CONTENTS

	Foreword	ix
I	The Pryors	1
II	The Move to Clay Hall	8
III	The Family at Clay Hall, 1829–46 *(1) Louisa, Emma and Juliana*	13
IV	The Family at Clay Hall *(2) Son Alfred*	24
V	The Family at Clay Hall *(3) Dear Fred*	35
VI	John Izzard and Politics	46
VII	Manners and Customs	56
VIII	John Izzard as Deputy Lieutenant	69
IX	The Neighbours	72
X	Social Occasions	80
XI	Local Administration	91
XII	County Business	103
XIII	Visits to London	108
XIV	In Journeyings Often	121
XV	The Church	136
XVI	John Izzard and the Crown	151
XVII	Farming in Times Good, Bad and Indifferent	158
XVIII	Sport	174
XIX	Taxation	180
XX	The Medical Profession	186
XXI	Servants	194
XXII	The Family at Clay Hall, 1847–61	200
XXIII	The Man John Izzard Pryor	213
	Pedigree *facing page*	214
	Index	217

LIST OF PLATES

John Izzard Pryor   facing page   6
                                                        and on front cover

Louisa, Second Wife of John Izzard Pryor   facing page   7
                                                        and on back cover

The South Wing of Clay Hall   facing page 102

The Brewery House, Baldock (front view)   facing page 103

The Brewery House, Baldock (rear view)   facing page 118

The Residence of Vickris Pryor, Baldock   facing page 119

FOREWORD

To be asked to write this foreword is a pleasant privilege, all the more so as my maternal ancestors for centuries were yeomen and farmers in Hertfordshire—at its West End. The diary now published relates to its East End—an area, as indeed the whole county, that was virtually unaffected by the growth of London except as a market for its agricultural products (including beer) and even less affected by the industrial revolution.

The diary is that of a brewer—country gentleman—magistrate whose activities were typical of hundreds of his contemporaries. Untypical, however, was his having kept an illuminating diary, and completely untypical is the way in which Gerald Curtis has presented it to the reader. It is rarely that an editor breaks down the high wall of chronology. Even where he is lucky enough to have a multi-coloured wall (and some have to be satisfied with the plainest), little or no pattern is usually discernible. But here he has re-arranged the bricks by their different hues and reconstructed a series of gazebos. The book has no massive introduction: the imposing editorial entrance has been re-set to embellish each of the gazebos. The re-designed structure, its parts skilfully integrated, is pleasing to the reader and profitable to the scholar. This is due partly to John Izzard Pryor himself being an unconsciously good diarist. It is also due to Gerald Curtis being, not an architect nor a country brewer J.P., but a scholar—county alderman—farmer, whose combined attributes have given such a felicitous result.

A glance at the Contents reveals a wide range of the chief subjects, all seen through the eyes of a Victorian, who exercised without qualm his *patria potestas* to break a daughter's romance and inflict an uncongenial calling on a greatly loved son. There is much of travel in the late coach and early railway age; something of holidays in infant seaside resorts; glimpses of a London familiar to Dr. Johnson, and latterly of the still-recollected London of the hansom cab. That climax of Victorian achievement—the Crystal

ix

Palace—is visited with appropriate awe. In the countryside, against
a background of persistent human distress, the farming revolution
shapes the enclosures whose elimination we now witness; and
cholera, which knows no class distinctions, insists that attention be
paid to the drains of rich and poor. Medicine, politics, taxation,
the constant worry of servants, the banishment of drunkenness
from polite society, the change in the times and fashions of food
and drink, the arrival of the bath and shower-bath, the welcome to
the first hot-water bottle—soon to be relegated to oblivion by the
electric blanket—all the details which go to the business of living
come in for mention and make it possible to savour life as it was
lived in the comfortable circumstances of the Early and Mid-
Victorian gentry.

F. G. EMMISON

May, 1970

I

THE PRYORS

For something over a hundred years the British Middle Classes lorded it over wide areas of the earth. From them were drawn, for the most part, the officers of the Navy and Army and the Administrators of the Indian and Colonial Empires. Their origin was diverse: some came from families long established in the middle class; some were unendowed members of aristocratic families; others made their way up from below. But all, leaving aside the Scots and a minute number of Roman Catholics, were members of the Church of England. This, rather than education at a public school, was the hallmark of their class. The emphasis on public school training was a late growth. Neither Clive nor Rhodes was a public school man.

These Anglican families received substantial reinforcement at the beginning of the nineteenth century from the Quaker sect. Halevy, the French historian of the English People, attributes the grave secession which took place at this period to the fact that the Society of Friends which had come into being as a revolt against formality and superstition, had, with the passage of time, become enslaved to both.

'Therefore,' writes Halevy, 'though the sect survived,' many members were repelled and left it, but they took with them much of that spirit of peace and philanthropy for which it was distinguished. Nineteenth century England owed much to these former Quakers.'

Among the many families who deserted the Society of Friends and became Anglicans at this time were the Pryors of Hertfordshire. In 1827 the head of the family, John Izzard Pryor of Baldock, began when he was 53 to keep a day-to-day diary. It might seem late in life to acquire so excellent a habit. But, in fact, he was to fill 33 volumes—many of them Letts' No. 8 Diary—before he wrote his last entry on 15 May, 1861. He thus recorded life during 30 of the 35 years of the Half Reformed Constitution.

1

The motives which impel a man to keep a diary are usually diverse. John Izzard Pryor—he is referred to as such for there have been many John Pryors, but only one John Izzard—evidently did not overlook the possibility of his entries being read by posterity. He often pauses to explain a relationship obvious to any one acquainted with the family. On the other hand, he can scarcely have thought that posterity would share his interest in his digestion; and he was clearly apprehensive lest any contemporary should read his entries. He rarely wrote anything which it would not have done for his wife or sons to see.

His was not the pen of a ready writer. His style was threadbare. He described neither human appearance nor character. Although as a countryman he rejoiced in the beauties of landscape, he was no hand at description. He kept his diary much as he kept his account books, accurately and faithfully in order to present to His Maker 'a true account lest He returning chide'. Since he lived the life of a minor country landowner, he had little to chronicle but small beer.

Despite its limitations, the diary may, nevertheless, be read, as the XXXIX Articles advise the Apocrypha be read, for example of life and instruction of manners. By its means a glimpse may be gained into Early Victorian Halls and Rectories and something learned of the homes from which men were to go forth to rule or influence the world. The services which members of the Middle Class who remained in Britain rendered to their own country in the administration of local affairs are not often recognised. But it can be claimed that the fact that Britain avoided revolution in the XIXth century was as much due to the humane conduct of affairs in the Parish Vestry by Parson, Squire and Farmer, as to the statesmanship of greater men at Westminster. Entries in the diary tell something of these humble, yet supremely important matters.

The diary touches life at many points, and it has been found that considerations of space make it impossible to set it forth chronologically. The entries regarding salient topics have, therefore, been brought together.

But first something must be said about the family history of the diarist. The reader is also referred to the pedigree at the end of the volume.

John Izzard Pryor was born on 30 May 1774, the eldest son of

John Pryor, a Quaker maltster of Baldock in north Hertfordshire. The Pryors are an old East Anglian family. Thomas Priour, the Burgess for Hertford in the Parliament of 1313, had the good fortune to be at Woodstock in 1331 when Queen Philippa gave birth to the son who is known to history as the Black Prince. Edward III was then hunting at Watton in Hertfordshire, and Priour was commissioned to take the good news to him. It was then, and long afterwards, the custom to reward the bearer of good tidings and Edward did not omit to do so. A gift of 40 marks annually, later commuted to a grant of land at Baldock, was Priour's reward.[1]

Thomas Priour's brother John was Sheriff of London about this time, and the family seem to have been of established position in the fourteenth century. Then for three hundred years they disappear from history. They did not profit from the spoliation of the Church. There is no Pryor among the freeholders of the county in the list of 1561; none among the inhabitants of the county assessed to pay £20 in 1590 for the defence of the country; Charles I did not think it worth his while to include them in the list of Hertfordshire gentry from whom a forced loan was to be raised in 1625. Nothing more is heard of them until after the Restoration when various individuals of the name came into conflict with the authorities over the Conventicle Act. For the Pryors were Quakers, and obdurate Quakers; and for the next twenty-five years there was usually one, or more than one, Pryor in residence in Hertford Gaol. Robert Pryor spent eight years of his life, 1664–72, there. Francis, for a third offence against the Conventicle Act, was sentenced to transportation. Incessant contrary winds preventing the ship from leaving Falmouth for the West Indies, the Master came to the conclusion that the Hand of the Lord was against him. He accordingly put Pryor and other convict Quakers ashore. But the Privy Council were not impressed and ordered their re-arrest and consignment by a vessel whose master, as Cussans the Hertfordshire historian drily puts it, was less favoured by Divine Manifestation. Whether Francis ever returned from his West Indian exile is not known.

The Glorious Revolution of 1689 brought better times for Quakers and with the passing of the Toleration Act liberty of

---

[1] *Calendar of Patent Rolls, 1330–34* (1893), p. 74

worship was assured and persecution ended. The foot of the Quaker was now set upon the path of prosperity. In common with many another Quaker family the Pryors began to thrive. The diarist's grandfather Robert, who died in 1744, built up a substantial business as a maltster at Baldock. He married twice. His first wife was Ellen Izzard; his second Elizabeth Taylor by whom he had three children, the last posthumous. John Izzard, the brother of the first wife, acted as guardian to these children, and, when he died in 1759, left them his landed property in Willian, Weston, Clothall and Bygrave, villages near Baldock.

To this land John Pryor, Robert's eldest son, eventually succeeded. It was natural that he should call his eldest son, the diarist, John Izzard, after the family benefactor. John, besides farming his own land, was in business as a brewer and maltster at Baldock. He died in 1819 leaving four sons and two daughters, among whom his ample property was divided. John Izzard, the eldest, took over the brewery; and Vickris the youngest, the maltster's business. The other two sons, Thomas and Robert, became partners in the London Brewery of Truman, Hanbury and Buxton; the former lived at Hampstead, the latter shared a house with his bachelor partners at the Brewery at Brick Lane. The elder sister Elizabeth lived a spinster all her days at Baldock; the younger Martha married Joseph Morris, a wealthy brewer who lived at Ampthill, a small town in mid-Bedfordshire, fifteen miles from Baldock. John Izzard Pryor married Joseph's sister Hannah as his first wife.

Since the earliest days of the sect, for more than a century and a half, the Pryors had been Quakers. Proud family tradition must have told of the sacrifices which earlier generations had made for their faith. Yet John Izzard and his brothers and sisters, some sooner, some later, one and all became Anglicans, Thomas alone excepted; and he died young and his widow became an Anglican. The first to leave the sect was Vickris, the youngest brother. He did so on marrying an Anglican lady in 1809. The last was the elder sister Elizabeth who was baptized at the age of 70 in Baldock church in 1843. John Izzard's membership of the Society of Friends lapsed in 1820 when he married as his second wife Louisa Bell, daughter of the Rev. Robert Bell, sometime Fellow of New College, Oxford. But he did not become an Anglican until 1829.

None of John Izzard's children by his first wife was christened as an infant. Yet all had themselves baptised in the Church of England when they grew up. Within a few years the family had become so wholly Anglican that no one saw anything strange in Juliana, John Izzard's youngest daughter, marrying in 1843 a parson who was also a Pryor.

Until 1829 John Izzard lived at Baldock. Presided over by the parish church with its tower and Hertfordshire 'spike', the town is built on both sides of the Great North Road, the houses standing well back with a strip of green in front of them. The houses themselves are, many of them, as old as the seventeenth century; but there are some red brick Georgian mansions, notably that attached to the Brewery, John Izzard's residence, and that in Hitchin Street belonging to the Maltings, where John Pryor had lived in his day, and where Vickris, John Izzard's youngest brother, was residing at this time. Baldock was too close to the town of Hitchin to aspire to the dignity of an independent market, but it had an economic life of its own centred round the Maltings and Brewery, and the posting inns which provided for travellers on the Great North Road.

In 1827 John Izzard purchased the Clay Hall estate in the parish of Walkern, seven miles from Baldock, and in the following year took up his residence there. It was a small estate, less than 500 acres; but as he owned land in half a dozen other parishes, and the other landowners at Walkern were absentees, his standing as squire of the place was not questioned. Walkern, a village of 700–800 inhabitants, straggled along the west bank of the little river Bean from the hearty, prosperous rectory beneath its elm trees and rookery on the north to the water-mill on the south. The grey stone gothic church of St. Mary stands close to the rectory on the opposite bank of the river. There are three substantial farm houses in or close to the village street, and two long-established and well-built inns. Between these were the picturesque but primitive dwellings of the labouring poor.

Clay Hall—renamed Walkern Hall by John Izzard's grandson-in-law, the Rev. John Cotton Browne—stands above the Walkern valley to the south east of the village. It is not a building of architectural merit. The main block of the house, of Georgian construction, faces east and west, and, as a whole, lacks distinction.

What claims to beauty it has must be based on the small wing added by John Izzard, the upper rooms of which are light and gracious, and on the servants' wing and stables which, although constructed in yellow brick, an unhelpful material, nevertheless contrive, thanks to their proportions and simplicity, to make a pleasing impression.

Despite its architectural shortcomings, Clay Hall, standing amidst its flower gardens, lawns and immemorial trees is a pleasant place. The landscape in which it is set has been created by the care of generations and retains something of the serenity of the lives which went to make it.

Clay Hall, while it ranked as a mansion, was no great 'place'. It had more in common with Mr. Bennett's Longbourn than Mr. Darcy's Pemberley. It was typical of the house where, in many Early Victorian villages, there lived the smaller country gentry, a class which had lately grown with the prosperity of the country, and to which the Reform Act of 1832, with its lengthened voting list, was to give greater importance.

The ruling classes of the English countryside have always been recruited from outside the agricultural community. For we may make bold to say that very few county families have been founded on successful farming. Men who have made fortunes have, down the centuries, invested their money in rural England. As often as not they have been strangers in the country in which they have elected to settle. But the Pryors were old Hertfordshire stock. The improvements in agricultural technique which occurred in the eighteenth century had enabled the country to feed its increasing population. Farmers on good arable land prospered, and all those dealing in the products of the countryside with them. Cobbett in his *Rural Rides* remarked that the Quakers were to the products of the earth what the Jews were to gold and silver. They were a sect of agricultural middlemen. As corn merchants, maltsters, and finally brewers, the Pryors flourished in the agricultural boom. Many another Quaker family, particularly in East Anglia, shared in this prosperity, which owed something to long-continued war; and their names are writ large on maltings, bank, and brewery to this day. The Pryors did not take to banking, but proximity to London, no doubt, assisted the family to find commercial openings there. They obtained a footing in Truman, Hanbury and Buxton's

John Izzard Pryor

(*facing page 6*)

Louisa, daughter of the Rev. Robt. Bell, sometime Fellow of
New College, Oxford, second wife of John Izzard Pryor

Brewery in Brick Lane, and founded two merchanting firms of which one, Cotesworth and Powell, survives to this day.

Readers of Miss Charlotte Yonge's novels, recollecting how strong was the Early Victorian prejudice that trade and gentility could not run in harness together, will enquire to what extent John Izzard, after he had doffed his brewer's apron, was accepted by the neighbourhood as squire of Clay Hall. But there does not seem in Hertfordshire ever to have been a divorce between trade and landed property. Memorials in the village churches to departed City worthies show that commerce and land in the county have been linked for many centuries. Most of John Izzard's neighbours owed their fortunes to trade, banking or brewing, and were still actively interested in them. Mr. Wigram at Benington was a Blackwall shipbuilder; the Chauncies at Great Munden were West Indian merchants; Mr. Abel Smith of Watton Woodhall came of a banking family; while the Murrays at Ardeley had founded their fortunes on the probably none too savoury labours of a Commissary General to the Army. It would have been news to John Izzard that there was anything to be ashamed of in a fortune acquired by trade. The diary shows him personally making repeated calls on a baronet at his smart London address in order to collect an overdue, but not particularly large, bill for beer.

John Izzard reigned at Clay Hall from 1829 to 1861; and the word is advisedly chosen. It was the hey-day of squiredom. Never were there so many squires, and never again did they have things so much their own way. It is the merit of the Diary that something may be learned from it of the life of squire and parson in days when—so it seems to us as we look back—eternal sunshine gilded both Hall and Rectory.

II

THE MOVE TO CLAY HALL

No mention is made in the diary of the purchase of the Clay Hall estate; but on 12 February, 1827, John Izzard wrote: 'Met Mr. Pemberton the architect and builder of Hertford at Clay Hall by appointment to examine the house and to explain to him the alteration I propose making, and also what I intend building in addition on the south west side—of which I made a rough sketch.'

The plans which Mr. Pemberton drew up were closely scrutinised by John Izzard and in one instance at least amended.

March 21, 1827

'Mr. Pemberton adopted some alterations which I suggested relative to the cellar stairs to make sufficient space for a small room adjoining the butler's pantry for the butler to sleep in.'

Here John Izzard was in advance of the times. In 1843 when his nephew Marlborough Pryor built what he described as a cottage ornée at Weston Park, he considered a small recess in the pantry sufficient for his butler. Indeed, it was customary in many country houses until very recently for the butler to bed down in the pantry, his presence there being held essential to the security of the silver.

John Izzard's experiences with architects and builders were such as is the common lot of humanity. The house was not ready for nearly two years, and when he came to the final settlement on 21 June, 1830 he wrote:

'Mr. Pemberton came over this morning, having sent his accounts some weeks since which I had looked over. The sum total was very great, exceeding considerably what I had calculated upon and what I was given to expect. The whole amount was £9,540-10-7.'

While the interminable building proceeded John Izzard busied himself with the garden and grounds. Bernard Darwin in his essay on Country Life and Sport in Early Victorian England remarked that it was an era not of flowers but of the rolling of gravel walks.

Indeed it was a new gravel walk which first occupied John Izzard's attention.

May 1, 1828
'Setting out the wide gravel walk from the shrubbery Iron Gate in a sweep round the lawn on the south east of the house up to the stable back gates.'

February 18, 1829
'Finished the new gravel walk round the lawn next the shrubberies, having a wide border on the shrubbery side for American and other shrubs.'

April 1, 1829
'My waggon from Clay Hall went to London to load back with American plants and other trees and shrubs from Hammonds Nursery, Bagshot in Surrey.'

There is only one reference to flower beds. But with the planting of trees the greatest care was taken.

April 4, 1829
'I had the trees planted singly on the lawn on the south west corner of the house, fronting the shrubbery. First of all I planted sticks and viewed them from the drawing room and boudoir windows so that none should come in a line with each other. They consisted of tulip trees, copper leaved beeches, pyrus orientalis, flowering almond, liquid amber, and cedars of Lebanon.'

Many of these trees still survive.

The furnishing and stocking of the cellar engaged John Izzard's careful attention.

April 1, 1829
'I called at Chas. Perkins in Mark Lane to order a pipe of port to go to Clay Hall as soon as the doors are put to the cellar. Price £84—a discount to be allowed for ready money.'

June 4, 1829
'I rose at 4 o'clock this morning to superintend the getting down of 2 pipes of port at Clay Hall. I had ordered S. Strap my carpenter to have the stallings ready and Green the cooper with the sledge from the Brewhouse. We succeeded very well in putting them down into their proper places in the ante cellar adjoining the arched cellar.'

A pipe of port is 105 gallons and when bottled amounts to 52 dozen. The port bought from Perkins therefore cost 32/3 per dozen.

At length all was ready and on 17 August, 1829 the family moved in to their new abode, Morris and John the two elder sons being left in occupation of the Brewery house at Baldock. A month later Mrs. Pryor gave her first dinner party.

September 18, 1829

'We had a large party to dine and sleep. Soon after 5 our friends began to arrive. First my brother and sister Joseph Morris and sister Elizabeth in their carriage. Brother Robert and Vickris and his wife and their son Richard in their carriage; sons John and Morris in the phaeton and Mr. Handley and Mr. Veasey in his carriage. Mr. Meetkirk came on horseback as he thought the water would be deep in the Cromer road. With our guests staying with us viz. my nieces Eliz. and Martha from Baldock and Betsy Morris from Ampthill together with Mr. Lee and Dr. Bliss and his wife made us a party of 26.

Dinner which was well dressed consisted of 6 quarts of turtle soup from Peacocks, 2 haunches of venison. A fine turbot, a beautiful salmon with the general etcetera of a dinner accompanied by champagne and sauterne hock etc. gave universal satisfaction. The port drunk after dinner was the Woolmer port bought at Sir John St. Aubyn's sale 21 years in bottle. It was highly praised and the party broke up, to their praise be it recorded, without a single individual being tipsy. Took tea and coffee with the ladies and had a carpet game afterwards.'

No doubt the port was excellent. A notebook of John Izzard's records that it was of the celebrated vintage of 1806, that it was stored two years in the wood at Oporto and sent to England for bottling; and that he bought it at £3.13.6 per dozen when Woolmers, a mansion near Essendon, was sold at Sir John St. Aubyn's death in 1821. But whatever its appeals, it is remarkable that John Izzard could not assume that his guests would end their dinner sober. A less appropriate occasion for inebriety it would be difficult to imagine. There were senior ladies present, and some young and innocent ones too; nieces Elisa, Martha and Betsy were hardly 17. There were gentlemen in Holy Orders at the table also. But it would not do to dilate on the assistance to sobriety which their presence afforded. Temperance was not at this time a favourite virtue among the Anglican clergy, and three days later John Izzard's son-in-law, the Rev. John Lafont, (whose presence can be inferred on this occasion) celebrated his daughter's christening with such emphatic hospitality that Morris Pryor was tipsy, and contritely recorded the fact in his farming diary. A later entry shows that neither he nor his parson brother-in-law could be relied upon to stay sober out of respect for the innocence of young ladies. On the facts, therefore, we may share John Izzard's gratification that his house warming dinner went off so well.

The company included his brother-in-law Joseph Morris, the brewer from Ampthill, and his wife's brother-in-law Dr. Philip Bliss of Oxford. Educated at Merchant Taylors and St. John's College, Oxford, Bliss for some years combined the offices of Sub-Librarian, Registrar of the University, and Keeper of the Archives. He was Sub-Librarian to the redoubtable Bandinel who ruled Bodley from 1813–60. Bandinel, who had begun his career as chaplain to the Victory had acquired on the quarter deck a vigour of expression which daunted his colleagues, Philip Bliss alone excepted. 'The two old cronies chatted away together in the Library, regardless of the rule for silence',[1] and in their lighter moments exchanged poetic epistles on their respective attacks of gout.

Bliss was a born bibliophile. At the sale of his library 745 volumes were bought for Bodley and are kept as a separate collection under his name.

Bliss succeeded Dr. Hampden as Principal of St. Mary Hall in 1848. Mallet in his *History of Oxford University* says of him: 'He had mourned over the old traditions which were perishing. But he retained to the last, a certain sweet, old fashioned courtesy and a punctual and orderly devotion to his duties which had not always marked the older ways.'

Another guest, the Rev. Launcelot Lee, was educated at Winchester and New College, Oxford, where he was a Fellow from 1785 to 1826. Travelling in France after the Peace of Amiens, he was taken prisoner on the renewal of hostilities, and was interned at Verdun until 1815. He was at this time Vicar of Wootton, Oxon.

[1] Sir E. Craster, *The Bodleian Library.*

Mr. Veasey was the family lawyer. Mr. Meetkirk, a descendant of a distinguished Flemish family, was squire of Rushden where he resided in his mansion of Julians. Much is heard in the diary of the terrors of Cromer bottom where the Walkern to Cottered road crosses the little river Bean.

Three days later, John Izzard accompanied by his wife, Dr. and Mrs. Bliss and Mr. Lee 'went in the carriage before breakfast by appointment to our Rector's house, the Rev. Jas. Camper Wright. Accompanied by the latter we walked through his pleasure grounds to the church. No one else but the clerk being present, I was baptised by Mr. Wright who performed the rite in a solemn and impressive manner, Mr. Lee, Dr. Bliss and my wife being sponsors. The carriage took us back to Clay Hall to breakfast.'

John Izzard was never confirmed, but this does not seem to have been considered necessary by the rector of Walkern.

October 4th, 1829

'Mr. Wright having given notice that he should administer the Sacrament of the Lord's Supper after morning service—which he did in a most devout manner—my wife and I partook of it, myself for the first time in my life.'

Having become a member of the Established Church John Izzard was now qualified to take the place in the hierarchy of the County to which his breeding and wealth entitled him. He was appointed a Deputy Lieutenant of the County, nominated to the Commission of the Peace, and made a Trustee for the management of the River Lee.

III

THE FAMILY AT CLAY HALL, 1829–46

(1) Louisa, Emma and Juliana

The family which took up residence at Clay Hall in August 1829 consisted of John Izzard's second wife Louisa, his daughters by his first marriage, Emma and Juliana, eligible young ladies, and their brother Alfred, a young man of 18. Their half-brother, 'Son Fred', John Izzard's only child by his second marriage, now 7 years old, was still in the nursery.

Mrs. Pryor was the daughter of the Rev. R. Bell, Fellow of New College, Oxford, of a family which claimed kinship with the Founder of Winchester College. The Bells seem to have had a tendency towards melancholy. Louisa's brother, a surgeon in the East India Company's service, on retirement resided at Cheltenham. But 'from his mind giving way he was obliged to take up residence at Sandywell Park it being an asylum, entirely with his own consent', writes John Izzard who 'found him perfectly calm and collected but for the delusion he suffers under respecting his being a sinner irrevocably doomed.'

Mrs. Pryor's melancholy finds a mention in an entry in Morris's *Farming Diary for 1829.*

December 25, 1829
'After going to church and taking the Sacrament John and I went up to Clay Hall for dinner. A hearty welcome we met with and spent a happy day. The only drawback to my father's happiness is the uncomfortable state of Mrs. Pryor's mind, giving way at times to fits of dejection and despondency which materially detracts from her own happiness and that of those around her.'

Her husband bore with her patiently, merely recording from time to time that his wife 'found herself much depressed', or was 'sadly out of spirits', or 'feels her spirits sadly depressed.'

In June 1845 he took her to a London doctor 'who after hearing

13

her symptoms prescribed for her. He was much struck with the thick coat on her tongue.' His prescriptions did not do her an atom of good. Next month when she was staying at Oxford with her sister Mrs. Bliss and John Izzard went to join her there, he wrote:

'I was sorry to find my wife dejected and feeling very sadly. She would scarcely see me immediately after my arrival, but was very much pleased when she recovered her spirits.'

She used to stay for long periods every year at Oxford with her sister Mrs. Bliss—she was, perhaps, all her life somewhat in love with Philip Bliss. Her long absences from Clay Hall cannot have been entirely unwelcome.

When, however, her husband broke his leg in his 78th year she rose to the occasion. She seems to have been loved by her step-children and was always in request at the lyings-in of Pryor ladies.

Of Emma the diary speaks little. If mentioned, it is because she walked to Sunday School and was not a passenger in the conveyance sent to church. But of Juliana we hear more.

In October 1833 John Izzard took a house at Brighton for a few weeks.

October 25, 1833

'Mr. Bayley the curate of Ampthill has been staying in the neighbourhood of Brighton and we saw him several times. He this day called and requested an interview with me—which I granted. Its purport was to inform me of his love and affection for my daughter Juliana, and request my permission to pay his addresses to her, mentioning at the same time he had reason to think he was not disagreeable to her.

I told him he took me quite by surprise but that it was impossible I could sanction anything of the kind as I considered him by no means in a situation to marry, having merely a curacy and no prospect of preferment.

I was decidedly averse to long engagements, having seen the evil of them in many instances. I desired he would not think of it.

He had previously been invited to dine with us tomorrow to meet my brother Robert. He begged me not to decide hastily and hoped he might have an interview with Juliana. I told him after seeing her and telling her my mind on the subject I should not refuse his seeing her.

October 26, 1833
'My bro' Robert came to visit us, arriving last evening at 9 o'clock by the "Dart".
Mr. Bayley dined with us, and on his leaving after tea, about 10 o'clock I walked with him for half an hour. I told him the more I considered the subject he had mentioned the more decided I was in refusing my consent. I told him I should not alter as he was not in a situation to make an offer to my daughter. I should positively not allow of his visits, as, from the conversation I had had with my daughter, altho' I found he had made an impression upon her, she was disposed, like a good daughter, to be guided by my sentiments. He pressed his suit with all the power he could but I told him it was all in vain. He begged for one more interview with Juliana which I told him must be the last.'

October 27, 1833
'Mr. Bayley took an opportunity of seeing my bro' Robert this day, endeavouring to gain him over to his cause. My brother told him he did not think he was entitled to make the offer, situated as he was without any preferment. My bro' saw Juliana afterwards and told her his opinion—which coincided with my own.'

October 28, 1833
'Bro. Robert returned to London this morning by Snow's "Dart" Coach. I had a little conversation with him in his bedroom before he started at 6 respecting Mr. Bayley. He said he quite thought I had acted right in the matter.
Mr. Bayley wished to see me again today, having written to that effect. I gave him an interview and told him I was quite decided and that this must be the last time I would see him on the subject.'

February 10, 1834
'My wife having received an abominable letter from Mr. Bayley, curate of Ampthill, whilst we were in London, abusing and vilifying me, she showed it to me. I replied to him this day saying if he sent another letter to my wife it would be returned unopened. His object was to send underhand messages to my daughter Juliana declaratory of his determination to persevere in obtaining her for his wife, notwithstanding all my paltry objections, as he chose to call them, and which "he laughed to scorn".
I conferred with my daughter Juliana respecting it, impressing

the propriety of her never having anything to do with him as she well knew my opinion before, but after such conduct as this I thought she could not hesitate a moment. She assured me she would give up all thoughts of him.

I wrote to him my opinion of his conduct pretty plainly. I told him that I had hitherto treated him with respect and civility, but henceforward all intercourse must cease.'

Thus ended Juliana's only romance.

Her lover had been dismissed on the ground that, being a curate, he was in no position to provide for a wife. But Juliana, who was 27, had an income of her own–rather more than £250 p.a., and the prospects of Mr. Bayley getting a living never seem to have been discussed. When some time after, her uncle Vickris, John Izzard's brother, allowed his daughters Martha and Isolene to accept the addresses of two 'young gentlemen of good family but small fortune'–in short, two curates–Juliana must surely have questioned her father's decision. But if she did, it is unlikely that she received much sympathy. In the Victorian Age Father was always right. Miss Georgina Battiscombe, the biographer of Miss Charlotte Yonge, remarks, 'Filial Duty was for Charlotte the Moloch to which everything must be sacrificed; against its claim neither true love nor common sense had any rights.' One thing is certain. John Izzard never had any qualms on the subject. The Victorian father had a sense of infallibility which his descendants do not possess.

Meanwhile Richard Vickris Pryor, Vickris's eldest son, having graduated with honours at Balliol College, Oxford, had taken Holy Orders. His father had bought for him the right of next presentation to the living of Spettisbury-cum-Charlton in Dorset. It was an attractive place with an income of £700, and an incumbent who had the double virtue of being not only old, but in bad health. He lived longer than had been anticipated. However, in 1841 he died, and Richard came into his Rectory.

John Izzard now takes up the tale.

December 2, 1842

'Received a letter from my nephew R. V. Pryor from Spettisbury soliciting my consent to his paying his addresses to my daughter Juliana. I had previously seen his letter to her to which she had returned an answer but which did not arrive at Spettisbury until the day after he wrote to me.'

December 6, 1842
'My daughter Juliana is in a sad state respecting her offer. She thinks she must refuse. The prospect of settling is, from the worldly point of view, most unobjectionable. Everything is in favour of it if she would but find her heart could go with her hand. After giving her my best advice I leave her to do what she thinks will be most conducive to her happiness.'

December 11, 1842
'Son Morris drove up in his gig and dined and spent the evening with us and remained the night.

The conversation rather extraordinarily turned about R. V. P., Morris saying Mr. Randolph, son Alfred and himself intended going to Spettisbury before long to see him. He spoke very much in praise of Richard, little knowing what had been going forward. I was glad Juliana was present to hear him.

She had some private conversation in the evening with Morris. I told him about what had occurred. He gave her his opinion candidly and much in favour of R. V. P. But Julia still thinks her heart is not sufficiently engaged towards him to give him her hand.'

December 12, 1842
'Wrote to my nephew R. V. Pryor. Gave him an invitation to Clay Hall thinking it was right and proper so to do.'

December 17, 1842
'In the afternoon daughter Julia quite unsettled and desirous of writing to put off R. V. P.'s visit, but there being no post she cannot send a letter off until tomorrow which will then probably not reach Spettisbury until after R. V. P. has left for London.'

December 18, 1842
'Daughter Julia decided to have an interview with R. V. P. Had it been otherwise I was to have informed him in London tomorrow.'

December 19, 1842
'Before leaving home this morning for London I went into daughter Julia's room and found her quite poorly and fearful of having an attack of fever. I am to hear from my wife how she is tomorrow. For if she be worse she would prefer R. V. P.'s visit being deferred but, if better, she would like to see him as fixed.'

December 21, 1842
'Breakfasted at 8, and before I had finished received my expected

letter from my wife. She gave a most satisfactory account of Dear Julia, who was quite in good spirits and happy at the thought of seeing R. V. P. return with me in the afternoon.

R. V. P. arrived at the Four Swans at 12 o'clock according to appointment and we had a much more satisfactory interview than I was, at one time, led to anticipate. My carriage met us at Hertford and we proceeded directly, arriving at Clay Hall at 5 o'clock. I was glad to find dear Juliana so much recovered as to look bright and happy.'

December 22, 1842
'This was a most lovely day, brilliant sun with a mild soft air. Dear Juliana made her cousin Richard a most happy man by accepting him as her betrothed husband to the satisfaction of all her family and what, I am sure, will be the case with his family. Letters were despatched to Baldock and Hinxworth with the happy intelligence to the relations there.'

January 5, 1843
'A large dinner party at our house this day, chiefly of the nearest relatives of R. V. Pryor. We sat down 16 to dinner, which was a very excellent one and praised by all, with the accompaniments of a due share of champagne etc. The party all happy and in high spirits. It consisted of my brother Vickris and his wife and son Thos. and daughter Isaline and Mrs. Randolph, with those of our relations staying with us this Xmas viz. Lafont and Eliza and their son Ogle. Morris and his wife, Alfred, Fred, myself and wife, and daughters Emma and Juliana.'

February 3, 1843 (in London)
'I accompanied the ladies in their glass coach to Bond Street to the Jewellers (Turney) and presented my daughter Juliana with a diamond ring price 20 guineas, discount off £20, which she thought very handsome. We drove afterwards to Gt. Pulteney Street to Broadwoods to look at a pianoforte. None that were finished were quite approved of, but they said they should have some very good ones finished in two months time.'

February 4, 1843
'Met the ladies by agreement at half past twelve at Collards, pianoforte makers in Cheapside. Juliana tried several pianos and liked them much better than Broadwoods. Settled to have one

made on purpose for her in two months, price 106 gns. (semi-grand), which is my present to her with stool 2½ gns. and Canterbury[1] 2½ gns.'

February 17, 1843
'Received a letter from my nephew Richard V. Pryor from Spettisbury. He appears not quite satisfied with the arrangements I have made respecting the settlement and money matters. He had hoped to have had a certain sum annually in addition. I wrote to him by return saying I continued in the same mind unless his father came forward to do something likewise. My daughter Juliana had also a letter from him on pretty much the same subject and recommending their waiting until I should alter my mind.'

The Rev. Richard Pryor evidently thought with Samuel Butler—

> How blest the prudent man, the maiden pure,
> Whose income is both ample and secure,
> Arising from Consolidated Three
> Per Cent Annuities, paid quarterly.

February 25, 1843
'We had a full discussion respecting the settlement, a draft of which, as proposed by Mr. Veasey, was read over and agreed to by all parties, viz. to transfer Juliana's money in the Funds £2,000 new 3½% and £6,500 3% Consols into the name of four trustees, viz. John and Morris Pryor on Juliana's side and Arthur and Marlboro' Pryor on Richard's side, for them to receive the dividends and apply as much of them as it may require to pay the insurance for Richard's life—probably about £140[2] per annum—and the remainder, perhaps £100 or rather more, to Juliana herself for her sole use and benefit . . . Afterwards came the providing for the spending income of the parties. Richard's rectory in the gross produces £700 p. ann., out of which he has to pay a curate £100 p. ann. and rates and taxes about £100 more, leaving only about £500 clear with £150 interest he received for capital, £650. This is not enough to keep up Spettisbury Rectory. I proposed giving £150 between us to make up £800. But my brother Vickris declared he could not afford to give anything like it. To make him and Richard happy about it I agreed to give £150 myself

---

[1] A stand with partitions for music.
[2] According to the table in Letts' Diary, this would have brought in £5,000.

during my life which amounts to the same sum I pay to my son-in-law the Rev. J. Lafont for the £3,000 I gave him on his marriage with my daughter Elizabeth in 1825, and which he left in my hands at 5% interest. In order to provide the above amount of £150 I must curtail my own expenses.

The Spettisbury Rectory being only a life interest it was incumbent for me to take care that Richard's life should be well insured, or in case of his death his widow would be very badly off.'

April 4, 1843
'Dr. and Mrs. Bliss called. The latter accompanied my wife and daughter in a glass coach shopping. I went about my own business fixing to meet them at Collards Music Warehouse at 2 p.m., which I did. Heard the new instrument tried which is to be my present to my daughter Juliana on her marriage. The ladies approved of its tones and all its accompaniments.'

April 6, 1843
'Accompanied my wife, daughter and nephew Richard to look at a second-hand carriage at Windus's as Vickris had seen one he thought might suit Richard. I found when we got there it was a very crazy concern and I told Richard that if I was he I would not have it for nothing. Windus asked £150 for it. We came away quite decided not to offer a shilling for it. I recommended our going to Hopkinson, where we saw a very handsome fashionable stilish carriage of Hopkinson's own build and absolutely as good as new. Just the thing we wanted. We waited near an hour to see Mr. Hopkinson. It was a post carriage and had every convenience, valise, Imperial, etc. Richard agreed to have it on Hopkinson agreeing to take £260 and turn it out complete with the arms. It would have been £100 more if built new. The ladies were delighted with it.'

It seems that Messrs. Chalker & Charger's bill in Surtees' *Ask Mamma* was not all exaggeration: 'Verily Sir Robert Peel was right when he said that there was no class of tradespeople whose bills wanted reforming so much as coachmakers.'

April 30, 1843
'On returning home I found my nephew Richard just arrived from Spettisbury, who dined and spent the evening with us. He travelled down post with the Briskza which is to take Juliana and himself on their journey on the 4th after the wedding.'

May 3, 1843

'Mr. Veasey attended with his Clerk Willm. Stockes to attest the signatures of my daughter Juliana and nephew Richard, Vickris Pryor and my own to the marriage settlements—the wedding being to take place tomorrow.'

May 4, 1843

'Nephew Marlboro' Pryor signed the Marriage Settlement as one of the trustees. His signature witnessed by Dr. Bliss.

A beautifully fine day. At half past 10 a.m. precisely we set off for Walkern church in four carriages. In the 1st (a Briskza hired for the tour) my wife, daughter Emma, nephew Richard V. Pryor and Dr. Bliss; 2nd Mrs. Bliss, Mr. and Mrs. Marlboro' Pryor and son Fred; 3rd son and daughter Lafont; 4th in our own carriage my daughter Juliana in her beautiful wedding dress and myself. The Baldock carriages arrived at the same time at the church as previously arranged, viz. eight carriages containing Mr. and Mrs. Vickris Pryor, Mr. and Mrs. Will Gould, son John and his little boy J. Eade, my sisters Elizabeth and Martha, Mr. and Mrs. Felix Pryor, Mr. Arthur Pryor, Mr. and Mrs. Veasey, Mr. Thos. Pryor, Miss Dew and Miss Fanny Gould, Mr. Randolph, Miss Isaline Pryor, who with Mr. Harding and his wife from the Rectory made 36. The ceremony went off remarkably well. The dejeuner was excellent. All in good spirits except at parting with the bride, and the weather was most favourable. The bride and bridegroom set off about half past 2 and by 4 the greater part of the company departed.

The servants had a dance in the evening in the servants' hall, which was well attended and seemed to give general satisfaction. All dispersed before 12 o'clock. A little boy played a capital tune on a dulcimer.

Mr. Harding had the school children in the evening at the Rectory when they had cakes and tea. He had also a party of friends to commemorate the day, many of our Baldock relations taking tea there. Races and games took place, the launch of the new boat, and the evening finished with a display of fireworks.'

The Victorians regarded a wedding as a family event of a markedly private character; only close relations were bidden, and not necessarily all of them. Thus John Izzard, although he had sent him a present, does not seem to have been invited to his nephew Robert's wedding, which took place at St. James' Piccadilly on 22 August, 1844; nor did Julia accompany her husband to his sister Isolene's wedding at Wandsworth in July of the same year. She went home to Clay Hall instead. Thus it was that most of Queen Victoria's children were married in the seclusion of Windsor. Royal weddings in Westminster Abbey are an innovation of the last fifty years. On the other hand the Victorians made a public occasion of the funeral, when the family expressed its sense of its own importance, and the public were expected to testify to their esteem for the deceased. Modern custom appears to be the reverse of the Victorian. The funeral is a family affair; the wedding a public occasion. This tendency has been assisted by the development of the memorial service.

However that may be, there were, according to John Izzard's account, only 36 guests at Juliana's wedding. In fact, he names only 32, including bride and bridegroom; and among them he names as Miss Dew, the lady who had become Mrs. Arthur Pryor in 1841. He forgot his sons Morris and Alfred and their wives. The emotions of the day seem to have been too much for his accuracy.

All the guests, save the family lawyer and 'Our Rector' and their wives and Dr. and Mrs. Bliss, were Pryors, had married Pryors, or were the children of Pryors. No family from the neighbourhood was invited, much less the County.

Nothing is said about presents other than John Izzard's to his daughter. They were no doubt as few as the guests.

The wedding ceremony was necessarily in the morning as the bridal couple had to leave on their 'Wedding Journey' or 'Tour' by Britzka, and needed some hours of daylight in which to reach a suitable resting place. In this case the Wedding Tour lasted some three weeks. On May 26 John Izzard's post contained a good account by 'dear Julia' of their journey home and flattering reception by the inhabitants of Spettisbury and Charlton.

With the following entry in the diary we may take leave for a time of this business-like clergyman and his bride.

March 3, 1844

'I wrote a letter yesterday to my son-in-law R. V. Pryor at Spettisbury in reply to one I received from him on March 1 last soliciting the sum of £100, as he has been put to great expense last year on account of his marriage and felt himself unable to discharge his bills. He had made application to his own father who refused to come forward, but his grandmother gives him £100. For the sake of my dear Julia and to set his mind at ease I wrote to say I would give him £100 but that I would not do so any future time and he must limit his expenditure to his income.'

IV

THE FAMILY AT CLAY HALL

(2) Son Alfred

Despite Sir Winston Churchill's tribute to that noble monarch Alfred the Great, there is to us of the twentieth century something irresistibly comic about an individual of that name, particularly if he lived in Victorian days. To this general rule it cannot be said that Alfred Pryor forms an exception. If, like most Pryors, he kept the noiseless tenor of his way along the cool, sequestered vale of life, he met with a nasty jolt now and then.

He followed his brothers John and Morris at a private school at Bury St. Edmunds, kept by Mr. Charles Blomfield. The school was a well-established institution, having been founded by Charles's father James in 1760. Charles's eldest son was translated from the see of Chester to that of London in 1828 and was the outstanding churchman of his generation.

It is doubtful whether Alfred lost anything by not going to a public school at this time; public schools were at a low ebb, and indeed in this very year there was a rebellion at Winchester where Fred was to go.

January 31, 1828
'Went with son Alfred to Bury. Setting off about 9 o'clock in the carriage to Cambridge. Ordered dinner to be ready on our arrival there at 12. Spent the intermediate time in viewing the great improvements going forward there, particularly at King's College, a very handsome new Gothic screen having been built in the front next the street since I was last there, and a noble hall and Provost's Lodge etc. in very good taste erected on the west side.'

It is not often possible to endorse John Izzard's judgements of taste, but on this occasion we may do so. Wilkins's screen is not without its merits; and if it is not entirely successful, perhaps few of Wilkins's buildings are. (They include the National Gallery,

University College, Gower Street and St. George's Hospital.) When
it is recollected what was perpetrated in other places, e.g. Balliol
College, in the name of the Gothic Revival it is clear that King's
men have much for which to be thankful.

After seeing the sights John Izzard 'proceeded by coach to Bury
and arrived there at 8. After tea accompanied Alfred to school.'

January 31, 1828
'After breakfast went with Alfred to the school. Found Mr.
Blomfield too ill to see me. I therefore settled the account with
his son and partner Mr. Jas. Blomfield and explained to him my
intentions respecting my son remaining only half a year longer
and that I wished him to pay particular attention to the Mathematics, Mensuration, Merchants' accounts, Surveying and the use
of the globes, and to resume his dancing. He is therefore not to
attend at Dr. Malkins (the Grammar School) this half which will
allow him time for his other studies. This plan is pretty generally
adopted for those boys not intended for either of the universities.'

After leaving Mr. Blomfield's Academy at the end of the summer
of 1828 Alfred led the life of a gentleman of leisure at Clay Hall.
We are told that he surveyed the lawn and measured the bridleway
between Baldock and Clay Hall, finding it to be nearly seven miles,
and was sworn in as a Special Constable at the time of Luddite
riots, but there is no evidence of his being usefully occupied on
any other occasion.

In 1833 his father decided that his training as a man of business
must begin.

June 26, 1833
'I accompanied my son Alfred to London this day. Proceeded
to Gt. St. Helens according to appointment at 12. We found Mr.
Foster Reynolds returned from Sweden who, with his brother
Morris, received us very politely. Mr. Smith Jnr. from Hamburgh
joined us a few minutes afterwards.

We discussed several matters relative to Alfred's situation with
Mr. Smith's father at Hamburgh and settled matters satisfactorily.

Alfred goes to Hamburgh with the understanding of remaining
two years if his health permits and no advantageous offer of settlement in business presents itself in England, in which case he is to
be at liberty to leave at the expiration of one year. £1,000 is to be
the sum paid by four instalments if he remains two years, and £500
if he only remains one year.

I invited Mr. Smith to dine with us in Brick Lane, which he accepted. We afterwards went to Lombard Street to secure berths in the Chief Cabin in the "William Jolliffe" Steam Packet which leaves London for Hamburgh on Friday next at midnight. The charge was 7 gns. for every passenger in that part of the vessel.

Alfred and myself then went on board the William Jolliffe lying off the Tower and found the cabin and berths very comfortable. Alfred had No. 13 and Mr. Smith No. 15, close together.

Mr. Smith appeared a pleasant, well-informed man and quite the man of business. I hope Alfred will be happy in such a family. In the evening we looked over the stables (at Brick Lane)[1] as the horses, about 100, were nearly all in.'

June 28, 1833

'At half past 10 Mr. Smith Jnr. came and looked over the Brewery and storehouses with which he was much pleased.

We went together to St. Helens at 12. I paid a cheque on Barnett, Hoare & Co. on Mr. Smith's account for £250 for the first half year's instalment into Mr. Foster Reynolds' hands; and propose paying the 2nd at Xmas next. Agreed to be on board the "Willm. Jolliffe" by 11 o'clock tonight.

Alfred at 2 o'clock went to the vessel with his luggage and saw it safely stowed on board. Alfred and I dined with my brother in Brick Lane and at ¼ past 10 the latter accompanied us in a hackney coach to the Custom House Stairs where we went off in a boat to the "William Jolliffe". It was a beautiful moonlight night, serene; Robert looked over the cabins, berths, steam engine etc. and was quite pleased saying, if he was at liberty he should have enjoyed going to Hamburgh too.

Mr. Smith came on board while we were there and introduced us to the captain. They were to set off about 1 o'clock as the tide would then serve, it being now nearly done coming up the river.

I could not help feeling much at the parting—as did Alfred, but both being of the opinion that it would be greatly to his advantage and improvement, the thought supported us both on the occasion.'

July 8, 1833

'Despatched a joint letter to my son Alfred by post to Hamburgh

---

[1]   The Brewery of Truman, Hanbury & Buxton where Robert, John Izzard's brother, resided with certain of the partners who were bachelors.

written the first page of foolscap by myself, the 2nd by my wife, and 3rd by daughters Emma and Juliana, with a little addition by Fred. Sent it through the post at Stevenage along with a letter from Richard Pryor; paid 2s. each letter, being the postage to Hamburgh.'

January 8, 1834
'Received a letter from Mr. Smith of Hamburg respecting the proficiency my son Alfred has made since he has been with him, with remarks upon his conduct, which is satisfactory with the exception of his being too reserved and silent occasionally.'

August 27, 1834
'Son Alfred being expected to arrive by the Jolliffe steam boat. Morris is to meet him if he arrives as expected.'

September 1, 1834
'I sent the omnibus over to meet Kershaw's coach at Stevenage and we all had the very great pleasure of seeing Alfred returning by it, looking very well, altho' he had encountered a very stormy passage. They were driven out much to the northward of the general passage and were two days longer than usual. He and a few other passengers landed at Harwich where the steam boat was obliged to take in a supply of coals for the engine, the stock being exhausted.
He took coach to London and arrived yesterday evening, the steam boat not getting in until this morning.'

October 24, 1834
'Went on board the "Edward Bankes", lying off the Custom House, a Hamburgh steamer which starts at 4 o'clock tomorrow morning. We looked over the berths in the first cabin and Alfred selected a good one for his passage back to Hamburgh. They were busy repairing some damage done to the head of the vessel, having encountered a violent storm on the 16th and 17th.
Accompanied him to the office 69 Lombard Street where he engaged his berth and paid his passage £5. We spent the evening together in Brick Lane, and about 11 I accompanied him to Bishopsgate Street where I took leave of him, Felix and Henry Pryor accompanying him to the steamer.'

June 10, 1835
'Received yesterday a joint letter from Mr. Smith Hamboro and

son Alfred, the former wishing the latter to stay six months
longer with him without any additional premium but as a visitor—
which is very handsome in Mr. Smith. Alfred seems quite agreeable to remain a few months longer if nothing eligible has yet
presented itself for his embarking in trade.'

April 30, 1836

'Received a letter from Hamburgh from my son Alfred in which
he expresses a strong desire to embark in the Hatfield Brewery if
it can be bought at a reasonable price at the approaching sale.
I replied this day stating my approbation and wishing him to make
arrangements for coming over to England directly.'

May 31, 1836

'Son Morris came up from Baldock by Kershaws this morning to
attend with his brother John (who is staying in town) and my son
Alfred and myself, the sale of the Hatfield Brewery by auction at
the Auction Mart this day.

It was my particular wish that we should purchase the property
jointly if it could be bought at a fair and reasonable price, John
and Morris to have one moiety and Alfred the other moiety, as he
is too young and inexperienced to enter into a concern of that
description alone.

Their experience and knowledge of the Brewery with occasional
attendance on the spot, and Alfred's close attention and residence
there, appeared to me a good introduction for him; and only for
the first two or three years would it require so much attention
from them.

We met at Brick Lane and talked the matter over seriously and
advised with my brother Robert who saw it in the same light as
myself. But I was sorry to find both John and Morris adverse,
particularly Morris who thought a great deal more would devolve
upon him than he could possibly attend to. When we were setting
off for the Mart he appeared most uncomfortable and unhappy.
John did not oppose it so violently but said he had much rather
have nothing to do with it—although we had looked over nearly
the whole of the concern, public houses etc. together. I accordingly was much chagrined to lose a chance that might not occur
again. But as I could not think of embarking on business myself
again, I felt obliged to give it up.

The sale came on. The bidding began at £20,000. I considered it cheap and was tempted to bid as far as £24,300 and then stopped. It was knocked down to Mr. Spurrell for £24,350. We had previously valued it at £25,000.'

June 1, 1836
'I passed a very bad night as I could not but think the property was well bought yesterday. I could not get it off my mind, as, could John and Morris have seen it in its proper light, I think it would not have been disadvantageous to them, and a capital settlement for Alfred. My bro' Robert would have advanced me what money I wanted. The whole affair with working capital would have taken up £40,000.'

June 5, 1836
'I had a good deal of conversation with Morris respecting my disappointment about Alfred. He said he would do all in his power to make my mind easy, as he was miserable when he came to the point about embarking in the Hatfield concern.

I proposed Alfred should be allowed £500 p.a., his board, and the keep of a horse out of the Baldock Brewery until the fourteen years of their lease are expired—it has about three years still to run; for him to take an active part under them in the business; and for some further arrangement to be made at the expiration of that period.

Morris consented so far as he was concerned, and when John returns he is to see him about it. Alfred will board with Morris.'

June 10, 1836
'My wife brought me a letter from Baldock yesterday that Morris had received from Alfred from London, which he thought it right I should see. It was written from the Bridge House Hotel London, where he had arrived from Oxford after seeing his sisters safe by coach to Oxford, and leaving them.

He was unable to return home having, much to his grief, got into a detestable scrape in London with a diseased female. He is now deservedly suffering in consequence. But hopes to get home by the middle of next week.'

June 30, 1836
'A beautiful morning and hot day. Called at the London Bridge Hotel to see Alfred who is recovering very slowly but gets out in

the cool of the day for a short time. His medical attendant thinks he will soon be able to come home.'

July 27, 1836

'Received a letter from Mr. Edw. Smith Junior enclosing one he had just received from his father in Hamburgh wishing his son to speak to me about a sum he thinks I should not object to give him for Alfred's prolonged stay with him at Hamburgh. The hint now given that £250 would be a handsome equivalent for his stay I confess surprises me extremely. I have referred to his letters and also Mr. Smith's which explicitly show that there should be no further money paid; also the offer was certainly handsome and liberal and acknowledged as such.'

August 16, 1836

'I called at the York Hotel, Bridge Street, Blackfriars agreeable to my appointment with Mr. E. Jas. Smith Jnr. whom I found with his letters and papers ready to receive me. After considerable conversation, finding him and his father remained of the same opinion, I told him that, as we saw the matter so very differently, to show him I wished to act in the most honourable manner, that I would leave the affair entirely to any gentleman of honour conversant with mercantile affairs to decide between us; that he might name a person first, and if Mr. Reynolds approved his decree should be final; or Mr. Reynolds should name a gentleman for him to approve; Mr. Smith to tell him his account of the affair and to show him his letters, and Mr. Reynolds to do the same on my behalf.

He did not think, he said, that his father would like the plan. He said he would write to his father by this night's foreign post.'

September 11, 1836

'Received a letter from Foster Reynolds this morning enclosing two papers containing the decision of Mr. Alexander Doorman, who had been fixed upon by Mr. Reynolds and Mr. E. J. Smith for a referee. The result was that he, taking every circumstance into consideration, held Mr. Smith was in justice entitled to receive £250 from me for Alfred's prolonged stay in Hamburgh—but that I was borne out in my objections by Mr. Smith's letter offering to allow him to remain and waiving every pecuniary remuneration.

Mr. Foster Reynolds therefore thought it best to pay the sum at once to Mr. E. J. Smith Jun.'

January 28, 1837

'Son Morris had heard thro' Mr. Fearnley Whittinstall that the Hatfield Brewery would be redisposed of, and said he had a good deal of conversation with his brother John about it. They had agreed that, in case I still remained of the opinion that it was an eligible situation for Alfred, that they would embark on half of it with him—if it could be had on fair terms.'

February 2, 1837

'Went to Hatfield with sons John and Morris, and arrived at the Brewery at 12 o'clock when we found Mr. Spurrell Junr. and Mr. Simpson ready to receive us. We went over the premises, examined their stock of malt and hops, and also the barley in the maltings and the malt on the floors—all of which we found very good. We tasted also the stock of beer in the vats, which was not to be found fault with.

After this we went into the books, debts, loans etc., all paid; but on coming to their sales of beer we found they had very much decreased since the late Mr. Field's time, and since the auction sale of the property in May last, the trade not averaging now 6,000 barrels, whereas at the sale the average for three years was stated to be 7,600.'

February 3, 1837

'Proceeded to Mr. Simpson's office, Bucklersbury No. 18, my bro' Robert accompanying me. Son John soon joined us and Mr. Watney attended for Mr. Jas. Spurrell, his brother-in-law. We went fully into the Brewery Statements and endeavoured to get the stipulated sum (reduced) but would get no alterations in the sum to be paid viz. £31,000. But after difficulty got the time of completion and entry altered to Lady Day instead of midsummer which is much more advantageous. John and Morris have a half share and Alfred the other.'

February 12, 1837

'Arranged with Morris for Alfred to go to Baldock on Tuesday to accompany them to Hitchin market, and to begin to acquire a knowledge of the Brewery Department by getting up to brew with Mr. Tranter and go through the whole process for several brewings; and at other times accompany their clerk Robins to the public houses belonging to the Hatfield Brewery to become acquainted with the publicans.

Alfred is also to board and sleep at my son John's preparatory to taking possession at Hatfield on 25 March next with his brothers.'

February 14, 1837

'Had a long conversation after dinner with my bro' Jo. Morris respecting the Hatfield Brewery, and told him I should be much obliged if he could accommodate me with the loan of £8,000 about which I had previously written to him. He said he had money in the Funds which he would sell out. He eventually agreed to let me have £3,000 on my own account which I propose giving to Alfred to make up his £5,000; and also £5,000 to Alfred on my being security with him. The interest will be 4% and paid half yearly, and we are to pay the broker's charge for the sale.'

February 15, 1837

'Went to see how Alfred was getting on in the Brewhouse as he was to get up this morning with Jos. Tranter and go through a Brewing with him. I found him with his apron on and looking like a brewer. He seemed to like it very well.'

March 25, 1837

'Our engagement for meeting Mr. Jas. Spurrell was fixed for today to pay him the money for the Hatfield Brewery, and the valuations of the malt, hops, beer, horses etc. On arriving in London I went to Messrs. Robarts, Curtis & Co. to receive the £8,000 which I had borrowed from my bro'-in-law Jos. Morris, and afterwards to Brick Lane to receive a check for £10,000 borrowed from my bro' Robert Pryor of which sums I lend my son Alfred £15,000 and give him the remaining £3,000, which with £2,000 of his own makes him £20,000 to take into the concern for his half share. His brothers John and Morris also advance £20,000. The purchase and valuation amount altogether to £34,000 which leaves them £6,000 for the trade and any other purchases that may hereafter be made. We settled the business very amicably and paid the money at Messrs. Templats, Thames Street, solicitors to Mr. Spurrell, our solicitor Mr. Veasey being present.'

March 10, 1838

'Mrs. Vickris Pryor wishing to have some private conversation with me this morning, I accompanied her into their little parlour where she detained me a considerable time telling me she was not satisfied with her daughter Jane's engagement with Alfred, and that her daughter coincided with her in consequence of some particular behaviour of his on Thursday evening coupled with some other "disagreeable" that took place when they were in London last week. She never noticed this to me on their return when I met them at Hatfield respecting some alterations. I thought they were all perfectly good friends.

She said she had appointed an interview with Alfred this evening when she should tell him the affair must be suspended.

I told her I thought it was a pity things had gone so far as for almost the day being fixed for their marriage, and I thought he would be exceedingly excited, but that I wished to keep entirely out of it.

It is a very disagreeable business and how it will end I know not.'

March 11, 1838

'Dined at my bro' Vickris, who is still very poorly and nearly confined to his bed. Bro' Robert was of our party at dinner and son Alfred. It was a very unpleasant business with Alfred, Mrs. V. Pryor and her daughter Jane, the latter being unwell and lying on her sofa above stairs with a bad headache, occasioned by crying and having a bad night.

Alfred had considerable conversation with her and told her if she wished to break off the match—ardently as he loved her—she should be free from her engagement. She could not decide what to do, not liking to break off but yet wishing to put off the marriage for some time longer. I was also present with Alfred and her for a short time and gave it as my opinion that if she thought she could not love him with her whole heart she certainly had better not marry him, altho' things had gone so far. She could not quite decide and so the matter ended.

My bro' Robert said Alfred behaved handsomely in the matter, and wished her to have a few days to decide.'

May 10, 1838

'The company assembled a little before 11 o'clock at my bro' Vickris' house in Hitchin Street and proceeded to church in carriages. The bridegroom (Alfred), Mrs. V. Pryor (the bride's mother) and myself, being three in the first carriage, followed by six other carriages with the bridesmaids and near relations, the bride and her father in the last.

Richard Pryor, the bride's brother, performed the ceremony, the bride getting through very well and looking sweetly. The brides-maids were my daughters Emma and Juliana, her sister Isolene, Miss Harman and Miss Wil Morell.

Returned a little before noon and soon after sat down to an excellent dejeuner with a most liberal supply of champagne pro-vided by my bro' Robert.

Soon after 2 o'clock the young men with some of the ladies went to the Races at Odsey. The bride and bridegroom after having changed their dresses set off in a handsome britzka to proceed to Windsor.'

V

THE FAMILY AT CLAY HALL

(3) Dear Fred

Frederick Bell Pryor was the youngest son of his father and his mother's only child. Yet, in accordance with the stern custom which has been characteristic of the British upper classes for centuries, he was sent from home at the ripe age of seven to face the world in a small academy kept by the rector of the neighbouring village of Great Munden.

We may obtain one glimpse of him at this stage of his existence from John Izzard's entry 10 July, 1830.

'Fine morning, wind south-west. Sent the tilted cart and a common cart to meet Mr. Price's boys at the end of the road two fields beyond Walkern Park Farm. They arrived at Clay Hall about noon, Mr. Geo. Price accompanying them. I also invited three of Mr. Pollard's boys to meet them, making altogether with Alfred and Felix a party of 19. They brought their bats, balls etc. with them and set to work playing cricket, a very pretty sight, most of them being dressed in flannel jackets and white trousers.

I had ordered a round of beef and plum pudding to be ready for them at half past 2 o'clock by which time they had finished their game. They sat down in the billiard room to their repast which they enjoyed and each of them had a glass of wine afterwards. They then adjourned to the kitchen garden to regale upon strawberries, currants and raspberries with which they were delighted. My son Fred was as happy as possible in running about everywhere with them, but is not fond of the game of cricket. The boys played a little again in the afternoon and then had tea and cakes at 6 o'clock for a finish. Mr. Geo. Price dined with us ... Soon after 7 the boys returned as they came, Mr. Geo. Price accompanying them on horseback. They all enjoyed their day thoroughly.'

Mr. Price's academy was designed to prepare Fred for still sterner things. On 8 October 1830 he found himself inside the Winchester coach travelling to school at Twyford.

October 9, 1830

'Proceeded to Twyford in a post chaise at 12 o'clock, three miles from Winchester, found Mr. and Mrs. Bedford at home expecting us. We went over the whole of the establishment, which gave both my wife and myself great satisfaction. Mr. Bedford himself is blind, but a very superior man. There are four masters beside in the school and Mrs. Bedford is a most intelligent and active lady. There are 50 boys and it requires two or three years to get admission. We left dear Fred very comfortable.'

Twyford School still flourishes. During Fred's time there Mr. Bedford made over the headmastership to the Rev. Robert Wickham, whose family have provided the headmasters ever since. Through the courtesy of Robert G. Wickham Esq., the present headmaster, it is possible to give some account of the school as it then was.

Even at this early date Twyford was a genuine preparatory school, boys coming—as did Dear Fred—at the age of 8, and leaving at 14—Fred left when 13—to go to Winchester, but sometimes to other schools. Hughes, the author of *Tom Brown's Schooldays,* a contemporary of Fred's at the school, went to Rugby.

The amenities of the school included (and had for some years) a bed for every boy, albeit in cramped quarters, indoor accommodation for ablutions, ample space for work and play in Upper and Lower School, gymnastic apparatus, and a small football pitch. The fare included small beer brewed on the premises, and at some date in the late thirties was distinguished by the fact that, by special order of Mr. Wickham, meat was served before pudding.

Discipline was maintained by beatings in front of the assembled school. There still exists in use in the school a slate, dating from Mr. Bedford's time, which hangs from the headmaster's throne in Upper School. It is inscribed with three headings. Ineptus, Tardus, and Inurbanus. A boy who had been 'slated' had to write his name in the appropriate column. Inurbanus (Impolite) was regarded as the most serious, and, in Mr. Bedford's days, was punished with beating.

The curriculum appears to have been broader than was general at the time, for besides the classics French, Mathematics and English were taught.

A few letters written by Mr. Bedford's old boys survive which speak of the school with remarkable affection. Clearly it was no Dotheboys Hall. Nevertheless, the present headmaster writes that it would have horrified modern mothers, and the fact that Dear Fred's mother both visited and approved of Twyford indicates that, whatever the general opinion of Victorian womenfolk, there was stern stuff in them.

Here with twice-yearly intervals for holidays at Christmas and Bartelmy (July 16–August 26, there were no Easter holidays) Dear Fred remained until July 1835 when he stood for election as a Founder's kin candidate for a scholarship at Winchester College.

William of Wykeham the Founder, being a priest of piety, left no direct descendants, but he was well endowed with prolific sisters. An absolute prior right of entry to the Foundation had been awarded to Founder's kin by the statutes of the College, which permitted them to arrive when seven years of age, and did not insist on their leaving until they had attained the ripe age of 25. The College was soon encompassed with an ever-growing crowd of Founder's kin. In the reign of the first Elizabeth the number of Founder's Kin Scholars was limited to ten. But they survived until the University Commission of 1857. By this time they had become 'not only a licensed abuse but a standing jest.'

The unofficial test of the genuineness of a boy's claim to be Founder's kin was to try to break over his head one of the trenchers still used in College Hall. If the trencher broke before the head, that proved it. The official test was less exacting. A couple of lines of Ovid were repeated, and a line and a half construed. To the traditional question 'Can you sing?' the traditional answer was given, 'Yes, Sir, All people that on earth do dwell.' The candidate was then held to be qualified to be a scholar of Winchester provided that he obtained sufficient votes from the Fellows. (J. Firth, *Winchester College.*)

It is clear, therefore, that we need not attribute to 'Dear Fred' the 'intellectual eminence and scholarship sublime' of the modern Wykhamist scholar.

John Izzard could well have afforded to pay the full fees for Fred at Winchester, or anywhere else. 'To him that hath shall more be given' was the adage of the time.

July 13, 1835 (at Winchester)

'Engaged seeing Cathedral, and making calls upon the Warden,

Masters etc. of Winchester College and introducing our son Fred
as one of the candidates for admission as Founder's kin. He had
been promised the votes of the majority and principal electors for
several years past.'

July 14, 1835
'Dined at Mr. Wickham's at Twyford.'

July 15, 1835
'The day of election for admission into Winchester College, there
being annually elected two as Founder's kin and as many non-
founders as there are vacancies for, very great interest being
necessary to obtain either.

There were many candidates. Fred was elected first and therefore senior, and a boy of the name of Mills was the other, many
being disappointed. There were also eight elected as non-founders.

It being customary for the parents of the candidates to dine in
Hall on this day, I was much gratified with seeing the whole
ceremony which took place and partaking of the good cheer.

My wife and daughters dined with Mrs. Lee, whose husband is
Sub-Warden and brother of Mr. Launcelot Lee, Fred's God-father
and who voted for Fred. He had the votes of all the six electors.'

July 17, 1835
'We were rather late to dinner but got good places at the
Warden's dessert in his own house. Thence we adjourned to the
School Room to hear Dulce Domum sung in great style, Weippert's
band attending on the occasion and the nobility and gentry of the
neighbourhood present. It was afterwards sung abroad in the Play
ground, and last in the Court in front of the school which is the
finish before the boys go home tomorrow.'

July 18, 1835
'The College boys breakfasted at our inn at half past 6 after
which they all dispersed by different coaches and conveyances to
their homes.

August 11, 1835
'Set off to the West End of the town, after transacting business
in the City and paying in £54.12s. at Williams & Co., Birchin Lane,
to Mr. Wickham's account with the Winchester Bank for Fred's half
year's education etc. to midsummer.'

October 26, 1838

'Received a letter from Dear Fred from Winchester announcing the small pox had made its appearance in the school and that in consequence the boys had been vaccinated, himself among the number. Unfortunately altho' the vaccine had taken full effect upon his arm, spots of small pox had made their appearance about his person. The medical attendant said it was a favourable sort and that he was going on well—added to which he writes in good spirits altho' keeping in a bedroom by himself.

Dear Fred had been vaccinated twice before he went to Winchester.'

October 31, 1838

'Good account from son Fred at Winchester, of his having had the small pox most favourably and that the Warden and the medical attendant thought, when it was safe for him to travel, it would be advisable for him to go home for a fortnight.'

November 10, 1838

'The hounds meeting at St. John's I made my appearance there. A large field. We soon found, but being a cub fox he was unwilling to leave the covert. He at last broke away towards Walkern Village and was soon afterwards killed. Son Fred was on his pony and was in at the death. Mr. Stacy procured the brush for him of which he was very proud.'

November 20, 1838

'Accompanied son Fred to the National Gallery and Hungerford Market. Got a mutton chop afterwards at Joe's Coffee House by the Exchange and at quarter before 2 saw him off by the Eclipse coach for Winchester which goes with a pair of horses to Vauxhall and is then forwarded on a truck by the Southampton Rail Road, a distance of 38 miles, the passengers getting into first class carriages. After alighting at the station they proceed regularly on with four horses to Winchester and Southampton.'

December 8, 1839

'In the evening wrote to Fredk. in reply to the one received from him on Friday telling him how much I was gratified in hearing of his promotion to the office of Praefect of Chapel in consequence of his application to his studies and good behaviour.'

January 22, 1840

'Received a letter from Dr. Moberly, Head Master of Winchester College, giving Fred a very good character for the last half year.'

George Moberley, D.D. (1803—85), Head Master of Winchester 1835—65), deserves to be remembered with thankfulness by all schoolboys (and schoolmasters too) for having instituted Easter holidays at Winchester, a fashion speedily adopted at all other schools.

July 15, 1840

'My knee is in much pain when I move. Tomorrow I had long looked forward to as the day of election at Winchester which I shall be prevented attending.'

July 16, 1840

'Son Morris and Alfred go to Winchester by the railway tomorrow to be in time for the dinner and Domum and attend the Ball in the evening. I had a letter from my wife from Oxford much regretting I would not be of the party.'

July 18, 1840

'Received a letter from my wife this morning from Winchester containing the happy tidings of Dear Fred being elected and placed on the Roll for New College, Oxford, having passed his examination with great credit to himself. It was 2 o'clock on Friday morning when she wrote to send off by yesterday morning's post. She had not seen Fred when she finished her letter but expected him to breakfast with her tomorrow.'

July 29, 1840

'My son Fred and his friend Gunning set off to London to see the cricket matches to be played this week between the Winchester and Harrow boys and also the Winchester and Eton.'

Winchester XIs were seen at Lord's until 1854 when Dr. Moberley, fearing that contact with London might harm his school, forbade their further appearance there.

The University and calendar year being then in step, Fred did not go up to Oxford until the following January and put in some time with a country parson who coached youths for the Universities.

January 17, 1841 (at Oxford)

'Fred slept at New College last night. He hopes to be admitted a Fellow of New College tomorrow, having seen the Warden (Dr.

Williams) who must receive a letter from Winchester first which he expects in the morning.'

Under the old dispensation scholars for Winchester became Fellows, not Scholars, of New College.

January 18, 1841

'The Warden of New College sent for Fred and informed him he had received his letter from Winchester and would admit him a Fellow at 11 o'clock if the Registrar could attend at that time. To which Dr. Bliss consenting they went together to the Warden's lodging when Fred was in the usual form admitted an actual Fellow, taking the appointed oaths and paying his fees £2.11.0.

About two hours afterwards I made my call at the Warden's to pay my respects, but he being engaged I could not see him. I therefore left my card.

We looked over the rooms Fred had fixed upon—the best vacant, two pair stairs No. 2 right in the first Quadrangle. Afterwards we looked at and selected furniture which is to be ready in a week, Fred having obtained leave of absence.'

January 27, 1841

'I this day made Fred a present of my black riding horse (Lofty). Brown is to ride him over to Oxford for him. Fred himself starts tomorrow. I have agreed to allow him £200 per annum besides what he will receive from his Fellowship. It is to include the keep of his horse and all expenditure. I have advanced him £50 for the first quarter.'

'Confound all presents wot eat,' said Mr. Jorrocks. When Fred got the livery stable bills he probably said the same.

October 6, 1841

'After dinner I had a serious conversation with son Fred respecting his College life and habits as I had heard he had told some of his young friends he did not intend to go into the Church. I represented to him that it had always been, and continued to be, the great object of his going to Winchester, and afterwards to New College, to qualify himself for taking Holy Orders, and that his mother and I should be grievously disappointed if he did not make up his mind positively to apply himself to his studies for that purpose; and that he would have nothing to expect from me if he did not. He thought, he said, he should prefer the law. But I set before him the folly of such a course. I trust and think he will take my advice. His mother afterwards had a long conversation with him and told him how miserable she should be if he did not do as I wished. He appeared sorry for having said what he had and will, on reflection, I have no doubt, apply himself as we wish.'

October 7, 1841

'After dinner when we were alone my son Fred told me he had maturely considered what I said to him and the result was he had made up his mind to take the advice I had given him and also his mother, and that he would apply himself in earnest on returning to college next week, give up all thoughts of the law, and prepare himself for going into the church. He was sorry he had given us any uneasiness. I was much pleased with his affectionate manner and told him all should be buried in oblivion.'

February 27, 1843

'My son Frederick Bell Pryor attains the age of 21 years this day . . . We sat down 23 to dinner, consisting mostly of our own relations and our Rector Mr. Harding and his wife. Every one seemed happy and enjoyed the party much. Eight bottles of champagne disappeared at dinner, and I gave the best of wine afterwards. Mr. Harding proposed Fred's health with congratulations on the day to which Fred returned thanks in a very neat speech. We joined the ladies in the drawing room in good time considering the occasion and had some good singing and playing. After tea after the ladies had retired billiards were resorted to and we finished with oysters, lobsters and grilled bones in the kitchen. It was about 2 o'clock before the gentlemen retired to bed.'

May 3, 1844

'This is the anniversary of my birth, and the day of completing my 70th year and in excellent health and spirits, for which blessings I thank Almighty God and trust and hope I am grateful.

I have also this day the gratification of receiving just a line from my son Fred at Oxford saying he was through the Schools, his Final Examination taking place on 1 May to his and my great joy and satisfaction. Also a letter from Dr. Bliss congratulating me on the happy issue of the examination after a very nervous ordeal.'

Until 1835 New College men did not have to submit to the indignity of an examination in order to graduate. They did so by process of time. Nine years later the College must still have viewed Schools as a horrifying and unnecessary business.

Son Fred seems to have taken a Pass degree.

February 21, 1845
'I received a letter from Dr. Bliss in answer to the one I wrote to him. He informs me a Founder's Kin Fellow of New College may possess land to the annual value of £270, which is the utmost the statutes allow. I must act upon it in making some alteration in my will in regard to Fred, and leave him more money and less land.'

It may well be that news of this enquiry leaked and inspired the tradesmen of Oxford to grant Fred the extended credit which blighted his life with debt.

June 24, 1845
'Son Fred arrived a little before 6 in the evening, having ridden from Oxford on horseback the whole distance, starting at 7 in the morning. He rode his black horse to Luton and thence on the young chestnut (Turk) which I sent early in the morning to meet him. Brown remains to bring his horse tomorrow.'

Oxford to Luton is 44 miles; from Luton to Clay Hall is 21.

March 1, 1846
'My son Morris saw Mr. Leonard Proctor out with the hounds yesterday. He asked him whether Benington advowson was sold, as represented in the paper, or not. He said "No, it was not sold." Morris asked him what were their intentions respecting it. He said it would be sold if they could get their price. It was bought in at £5,300. Leonard Proctor said they considered it was worth £6,000, but wished Morris to make a bidding.

I thought if the advowson could be bought at the price it was bought in at, it would be advisable to purchase it for my son Fred to look forward to have at the decease of the present incumbent Mr. Pollard who is 63 years old.'

Benington church is about a mile distant from Clay Hall, which is itself in the parish of Walkern. The advowson was bought for £6,000.

May 12, 1846
'My wife and myself went this day to Henley to be introduced to Col. and Mrs. West and their daughter Miss West, the latter being engaged to our son Fred. We went (from Oxford) by rail to

Reading and took a pair horse clarence to Henley. Fred met us on entering Henley, having driven over the evening preceding, got into our carriage, and accompanied us to Col. West's house, at the end of the town nearest Oxford. He introduced us to the Colonel and his wife, and their daughter Louisa Mary, who Fred looks forward to be united to in wedlock at some distant time. Not having taken orders, and being the junior Fellow of a college, he is not in a situation to marry at present.

The introduction over, I had some private conversation with the Colonel and told him I should not object to the match at a suitable time, but I thought, except the living of Benington should become vacant, he could not marry until he was 30, being now about 25. The Col. who is far advanced in years thought it would be a long time to wait, but if it was my wish he should have no objection to it.

My wife and I were much pleased with Miss West who is about one year older than Fred. She does not come into any fortune until the decease of her mother. We were all very sociable and agreeable together. Partook of an early dinner and returned to Oxford.'

December 20, 1846
'This day, I expect, our son Fred will be ordained (as Deacon) by the Bishop of Oxford, having heard from Fred that he had passed the two first days of his examination very satisfactorily.'

December 19, 1847 (at Oxford)
'The Ordination was to take place at 10 this morning in the Cathedral Choir at Christ Church, and no admission into the Cathedral was allowed on account of the Ordination, which was almost private. A few persons were admitted to the organ loft. Dr. Bliss obtained three places for us, viz. his wife, my wife and myself. No one is allowed to be in the choir besides the Bishop of Oxford, the Archdeacon and the young men who are to be ordained deacons and priests. I was very much gratified at being there, the whole ceremony is so exceedingly improving and impressive. The service is performed most solemnly, the sermon adapted to the occasion, and the Communion Service takes place afterwards, the choir singing the responses, and the organ pouring forth its solemn and thrilling sound. The candidates for Deacon's Orders approach the Bishop first. Oaths are administered, and the

Bishop lays his hands separately on each, pronouncing the awful form of words appointed in the Rubric. Those who are to become priests then approach and the scene is almost overcoming. Not only the Bishop lays his hands upon them but also the Archdeacon and two or more of the canons. The Bishop requests a solemn pause for mental prayer. This drew forth tears from many. After this no one is allowed to remain besides those officiating. We accordingly withdrew and the Sacrament was administered to all the deacons and priests. The ceremony lasted for more than four hours.

To see our son Fredk. amongst the number on so solemn an occasion affected my wife, myself and his aunt Bliss, and I think I shall never forget it.'

But he does seem to have forgotten what passed between him and his son one October evening after dinner at Clay Hall six years before. For, if the truth must be told, Dear Fred was no volunteer, but a conscript priest.

VI

JOHN IZZARD AND POLITICS

John Izzard would have been surprised to learn that in days to come the years he spent at Clay Hall would be regarded as a halcyon time. He would have recalled that in his early years there the air was full of the muttering of revolution, and the night sky at Clay Hall red with the glow of burning stacks.

November 9, 1830

'The newspapers state that on account of the riotous proceedings of the mob lately in London the King and Queen declined dining in the Guild Hall by the advice of the Ministers and a notice was issued to that effect on Sunday evening. Great preparations had been made at a prodigious expense by the City on the occasion. But the measure appears to be a prudent one . . . Stocks still falling, now the 3% Consols are down to 78³/₈ on account of the alarming state of affairs.'

November 18, 1830

'This morning's paper contained the account of the resignation of the Duke of Wellington. The Duke, it appears, has made himself unpopular by declaring his sentiments to be against Reform—for which great clamour is made.'

November 25, 1830

'Very shocking accounts in the newspapers of the Lower Orders of People assembling in different parts of the country, particularly in Kent, Sussex and some parts of Surrey and Hampshire, destroying the threshing machines on those farms where they are used, and in many instances firing the premises.

A great many ricks and barns containing corn having been burnt . . . some other persons are supposed to be at the bottom of the incendiary proceeding besides the agricultural labourers.'

December 1, 1830 (at Oxford)

'Oxford does not escape the general threatenings of an excited mob. Many heads of colleges and active members of the University have had "Swing" letters and several farmers of the neighbourhood. They have sworn in a great many special constables and are prepared should any riot take place. Engaged places in the Oxford and Cambridge coach for tomorrow.'

December 3, 1830
'We rose very soon after 5 o'clock and were both quite ready when the coach came to the door a little before 7 o'clock.

No passengers inside beside ourselves. Stopped the first stage at Thame, being allowed 20 minutes to breakfast. We made a very good one—hot rolls and sausages with good bread and butter with that necessary adjunct at this time of the year—a good fire—made us very comfortable. We reached Ampthill at 2 o'clock.

The same state of dismay and terror pervades that neighbourhood from several farms having been set fire to by wicked incendiaries very near.'

December 5, 1830 (at Clay Hall)
'Sons John and Morris rode over for an hour and took luncheon with us. Threats having been received that some ricks and corn should be fired there (at Baldock), a large number of Special Constables had been sworn in and a strong watch appointed for the town . . . They therefore do not think it prudent to be from home during the night.

It is a most lamentable state for the country to be in. Although great rewards have been offered very few of the perpetrators of these diabolical deeds have as yet been discovered. God grant that they may ere long!'

December 6, 1830
'On Saturday afternoon in consequence of an expected rising of the mob at Stotfold a large force was collected from Lord Grantham and Mr. Whitbread and other places, of horsemen and special constables on foot. Having ascertained the names of the ringleaders they captured 16 of them and sent them off in three post chaises to Bedford Gaol strongly guarded . . . Fires continue to be seen in the distance most nights.[1]

Mr. Pollard our nearest magistrate called upon me to recommend special constables to be sworn in at Walkern agreeable to the Circular of the Lord Lieutenant of the County . . .'

[1] Stotfold is in Bedfordshire and close to Baldock. For the riots, see Joyce Godber, *History of Bedfordshire, 1066–1888* (1969), 418–9.

John Izzard had been sworn a Deputy Lieutenant of the County, and executive control of the special constabulary to be raised in the area would rest with him. The Rev. J. Pollard was vicar of Benington.

December 7, 1830

'I called upon some of our principal farmers to know their sentiments as requested by Mr. Pollard but they do not appear to concur with the recommendation.

Wrote last night and sent a letter this morning to Mr. Wright at Eaton to inform him how affairs were going on in this parish.'

The Rev. Jas. Camper Wright, rector of Walkern, was also a Fellow of Eton College, and often absent from his living on that account.

December 8, 1830

'Attended at the White Lyon at Walkern by appointment to meet the magistrates Mr. Pollard and Mr. Green, who came to swear in those who came forward and were approved as Special Constables. The principal farmers, one and all, declined, as did their men. My son Alfred, my bailiff John Pyke, Aylot the gardener, four of my farm men and my two carpenters were sworn and nine more men from the village.'

December 11, 1830

'Received a circular from Mr. Story, Clerk of the Peace, containing the appointment of gentlemen in different places of the county to superintend the constabulary force now swearing in in most parishes for the protection of property.'

December 15, 1830

'Soon after one o'clock I rode over to Julians to see Mr. Meetkirk respecting special constables to know what was done in their neighbourhood. He was just gone on horseback to Buntingford. I therefore pushed on, overtook him, and rode to Buntingford with him. They appear to have sworn a few in but not many.'

The farmers were naturally reluctant to take sides against their men. In any case the men were making a grievance of tithe which the farmers had to pay.

The Labourers' Revolt was mainly centered on the counties south and south-west of London. Hertfordshire was little concerned, probably because enclosure had taken place many years previously.

There is no more pathetic episode in English history than the Farm Labourers' Revolt in 1830.

The men's grievances were many and almost all legitimate— grievances against the poor law, the game laws, tithe, enclosure, wage rates, machinery, unemployment and dear bread. (Clapham, *Economic History of Modern England.*) But they kept their hands from shedding blood, and what other race would have done so? They were not without sympathisers. *The Times* on December 6, 1830 spoke of them as industrious, kind-hearted, but broken-hearted Englishmen, exasperated by insufficient food and clothing, by utter want of necessaries for themselves and their families. But in spite of such influential support the rebels were harshly treated, 600 being transported to Van Dieman's Land, where some died almost immediately of despair.

'The Commons of England', Cobbett had written, 'have given way in common parlance to the Lower Orders.' *The Times* was right to speak of them as Englishmen. Had John Izzard thought of them as such, he might have turned his mind to investigating the causes of their shocking behaviour. As it was he gave no thought to anything but the suppression of disorder.

By the beginning of 1831 the authorities had gained control of the situation, and a reaction set in in which the rebels were treated harshly. Hertfordshire not being so much concerned as some counties, the Hertford Assizes seem to have dealt with only one serious case arising out of the Revolt.

John Izzard was present at the Spring Assizes as a member of the Grand Jury.

March 3, 1831
'At 11 most of the Grand Jury assembled in the Grand Jury Room and got through our business by about 3 o'clock. Went into court to hear what was going forward there. The two prisoners were then being tried for setting fire to five ricks of corn and hay in the parish of Standon near Old Hall Green. With the confession of one of the parties and corroboration by the other parties the case was clearly made out against them. The jury pronounced a verdict of guilty and the Judge presiding in that court (Judge Garrow) passed sentence of death against them. The jury recommended them to mercy which the judge said he would communicate to the King but held out no hope for them.

The business was over at 5 o'clock and at 6 we dined with the judges at their quarters at the Old Rectory house—about twenty ... The High Sheriff next the judges and his chaplain nearest the bottom. We had an excellent dinner and good wine. The toasts were given very quick after dinner and the company departed soon after 8 o'clock.'

Although the Government might quell the Labourers' Revolt they could not silence the demand for reform, and it continued to be an unhappy country.

November 11, 1831

'Sad accounts of the Cholera Morbus having broken out in Sunderland, which has caused a good deal of alarm which, with the disturbance and riots in many places and incendiary proceedings in others, causes an almost universal gloom.'

John Izzard's diary for 1832 has not survived; and we cannot discover what his views on the subject of Parliamentary Reform were although we may well guess. The only reference to the Reform Act is that contained in the entry of 4 December 1835.

'Went to Mr. Veasey's to fix with him upon some freehold property to be conveyed to my son Alfred for my life, to give him a vote for Parliament for Hertfordshire. This according to the New Reform Act must be of the value of £10 per annum.'

After the passing of the Reform Act rural Hertfordshire relapsed for some years into a mood of political apathy. At the election of 1835 two Tories and one Whig were elected by acclamation without the necessity of a formal election. They were re-elected in 1837. In 1841 the Conservatives felt themselves strong enough to attempt to capture all three seats, and succeeded. But in 1847 they surrendered one of these seats to a Liberal without a fight. The next elections, however, in 1852 and 1854 they contested. The record of Hertfordshire bears out the truth of the generalisation of Norman Gash (in his *Politics in the Age of Peel*) that 'the composition of the House of Commons in the age of Peel was decided almost as much by the elections which were contested as by those that were not.' At the General Election of 1841, which installed one of the most memorable ministries of the century, the electors were only called upon to vote in 190 out of 401 constituencies. Until Free Trade presented itself as an issue, country dwellers could afford to take their politics lightly. Chartism was something they read about but did not themselves experience.

August 16, 1842

'Sad account in the papers this morning of the riotous proceedings of the men in the manufacturing districts in the North, visiting all the mills and compelling the men to turn out and join them. A considerable force of troops sent down by rail towards Manchester to assist the Civil Authorities and Yeomanry in those neighbourhoods to disperse them.'

John Izzard was describing the first occasion on which troops were moved by rail for the purpose of internal security. Regular troops were much more popular than yeomanry. They were better disciplined, more patient, and gentler, and nearly always infantry. Rioters do not like cavalry.

On 8 April 1848 John Izzard wrote, 'A proclamation is in the paper this morning forbidding the assemblage of Chartists and other traitorous and disaffected persons on Kennington Common.'

But so little concerned was he with the crisis that he spent the day analysing his Cellar Book.

His descriptions of elections in which he took part recall that of Eatanswill. The nomination of the candidates took place with much ceremony.

January 14, 1835

'I set off with Lafont for Hertford on horseback and stopped at The Sword in Hand public house at Stapleford where my bro' Vickris and son Morris joined us, having arrived in a gig. They then mounted their horses. We overtook Mr. Smith's party and arrived at the Cold Bath before Lord Grimstone's cavalcade came up. We then formed a very large body of horsemen and with elegant banners and a band of music proceeded through the town to the field by the Plough where preparations had been made for the candidates and High Sheriff. There was great jostling and difficulty in getting near the place from which the Sheriff and proposers and seconders of the several candidates were to make their speeches.'

John Izzard remarks that there was a great deal of speaking. The Tory speakers were well received and applauded. Not so Mr. Alston, 'who cut a very poor figure'. He, needless to say, was the

Whig candidate.   But there was no opposition.   'They (2 Tories, 1 Whig) were declared duly elected and chaired.'

In 1841, however, the Tories decided to contest the election. John Izzard returned from his holiday early in order 'to sign and procure signatures to a Requisition to the Honble. Dudley Ryder to come forward as the third Conservative member for the County' at the next election.

June 19, 1841

'Received a letter from the Honble. Captain Cust soliciting sub-scriptions towards the expense likely to be incurred by a contested election for Lord Grimston and the Honble. D. Ryder. Wrote in reply declining to subscribe.'

June 22, 1841

'Rode over to Stevenage to accompany the candidates on their entry.   The morning being fine there were a number of persons present and music and banners preceded the cavalcade.   They called upon most of the freeholders in the town after which about twenty gentlemen (candidates included) sat down to a cold colla-tion at the White Swan.   They explained their views relative to the present political matters and were heartily cheered.

I endeavoured to impress upon them that a short canvass at Walkern would be very agreeable as the tenantry of the new Earl of Essex would, for the first time, I thought, vote for them, the late Earl being of different politics.'

July 4, 1841

'Rowlatt and Stacey came in after dinner to take a few glasses of wine with us and to fix with me about providing means for some of our voters to go to Hertford with us in a body.'

Messrs. Rowlatt and Stacey were farmers at Walkern.

July 8, 1841

'The polling for the three county members commencing this day, and our appointed place being Stevenage, I arranged to give all the Walkern voters on the Conservative side a breakfast at Clay Hall. Accordingly about 24 sat down to breakfast in the Servants' Hall and I took my place at the top of the table. The provisions were cold, viz. a round of beef, fillet of veal and ham, coffee and tea, and two fine large dishes of strawberries.   We sat down at half past 8, and at half past 9 set off in a body.   I accommodated ten of them in the omnibus and the tilted cart, and the others went in gigs and on horses of their own. Mr. Rowlett and Stacey were amongst them. We were met on making our entry into Stevenage with banners and music, and made a very respectable show to the White Swan where we alighted; and in the course of a few hours registered our votes at the Polling Booth. The voting was nearly 3 to 1 in favour of Grimston, Smith and Ryder, so that Alston I think will stand no chance.'

July 12, 1841
'This day the newly elected members for the County, all excellent Conservatives, after the state of the poll for the County was declared by the High Sheriff to an immense assemblage of free-holders and voters on horseback, were chaired round the town of Hertford in capital style, notwithstanding the showers that fell. Fred went to see it.'

The next contested election did not take place until 1852 when a similar breakfast party was given in the Servants' Hall. On this occasion 'Mr. Rowlatt took the management of them, to see to their polling right at Stevenage.'

There was no ballot at this time and at this stage of the proceedings his duties were probably not exacting. But earlier on it would appear that there was a slight element of doubt as to which way a man would vote. Perhaps not all the tenants of the new Earl of Essex saw the light and voted Conservative. Satisfactory tenants were not easy to replace. Canvassing was not a formality as the following entry will show.

December 29, 1834
'Met Abel Smith Esqre of Woodhall Park who is canvassing the county for Representative in the ensuing Parliament soon after 10 at the Water Mill at Walkern Town and by appointment to accompany Mr. Heathcote and himself in soliciting the votes of the freeholders and voters of Walkern and the adjoining parishes. We called on nearly every one in Walkern and went to Yardly, Moor Green, Wood End, Great and Little Munden and Cottered where it became so dark we could scarcely see. Our canvass was on the whole satisfactory. We separated at the Mill where we met, having had a good day's work from about 10 in the morning to 6 in the evening, trotting away briskly most of the way without taking anything to eat or drink.'

While it is true that the Early Victorians set store on only two meals a day, breakfast and dinner, it is difficult to believe that three gentlemen of their position would spend such an exacting day if nothing was to be gained thereby. It is noteworthy also that their mission was not only to the freeholders who might be expected to show an independent turn of mind, but also to the 'voters', men with other qualifications who were tenants and therefore open to pressure. Even their votes could not be presumed.

It is clear that John Izzard was a good party man; but he found it hard to accept the Repeal of the Corn Laws—'a rash and cruel measure' he calls it. He joined the National Association for Protection at its foundation in 1846 and on 25 January 1850—

'Set off accompanied by my son Morris to attend a meeting of Protectionists at the new Corn Exchange to petition Parliament and also the Queen to take into their consideration the ruinous working of Free Trade which bids fair to reduce to poverty those working in Agriculture by the allowing of corn, and wheat especially, to be imported free of duty which has enriched the foreign grower and impoverished our own, without other countries taking anything like the amount of our exports which the projecters of the Free Trade measure pretended would take place.

The Marquis of Salisbury took the chair. There were many excellent speeches made, one in particular by George Fred Young, which was very much applauded. There were supposed to be nearly 1,000 persons present. A few gentlemen kept away, apprehending there would be a row got up by the mob of Free Traders but all went off well.'

It was at this time by no means certain that the country was wedded to Free Trade; and in 1851 Disraeli had only lacked 14 votes to pass a motion taken as tantamount to a demand for the reinstatement of Protection. This, however, was highwater mark. Conditions began to be easier for farmers who did not depend entirely on corn. An expanding and thriving population resulted in a lively demand for milk, butter, meat, wool and other farm products. In 1853 the Association, to the jeers of the Free Traders led by the Economist, dissolved itself.

Later in 1850 arose another political crisis which excited John Izzard as it did many a greater man.

November 24, 1850
'We dined alone. In the evening I finished reading the Appeal, Remonstrance or whatever it is called of the so-called Cardinal Wiseman filling seven columns of the *Evening Mail* newspaper. He was previously Dr. Wiseman but lately made a Cardinal by the Pope, who has sent to England a Bull appointing a dozen so-called Romish bishops to take titles from several cities and towns in England. It has caused universal condemnation, and addresses from both clergy and laity have been pouring in to be presented to the Queen. For it will not be suffered to take place. The Puseyites may, ought to, be ashamed of themselves.'

December 2, 1850
'A meeting of the clergy and some of the laity at Baldock to protest against the abominable interference of the Pope in appointing Roman Catholic priests with a Cardinal at the head of them.'

John Izzard's reaction to 'Papal Aggression' was typical of his time and class. It resulted in the passing of the Ecclesiastical Titles Act which, however, since it had no penal clauses, remained a dead letter; and in 1871 was quietly repealed. Meanwhile the Puseyites have—to use John Izzard's phrase—continued their activities unashamed.

VII

MANNERS AND CUSTOMS

John Izzard lived in two Englands: that of the stage coach and
the open field, and that of the railways and the hedges and
ditches of modern enclosures. But during his life time there
was more than an alteration in the appearance of the countryside;
the temperament and manners of the British people gradually
changed. Manners were more lively in the coaching era than in the
railway age. It has been contended that the reserve of the Briton
is a recent development due to the national admiration for the
Duke of Wellington of whom it was a characteristic. Reserve was
certainly no part of the make-up of the national hero of a slightly
earlier period, the 'Mighty Seaman' Nelson.

However that may be, John Izzard in his earlier pages records
occasions when emotions were displayed more freely than is usual
nowadays. Not that he was himself a ready 'weeper'; on the contrary he seems to have been a self-composed little man. Only twice
does he mention moments when he was close to tears—at Son
Alfred's departure to Hamburg, and at Dear Fred's ordination as
priest. But his contemporaries were more emotional folk and felt
no shame in shedding publicly the appropriate tear. But this,
surprisingly, was not at funerals with their grisly pomp, the plumed
horror of which he describes with so flowing a pen. It was at
weddings that it was expected that the bride should hold up the
proceedings in order to give vent to her emotions.

Thus on 3 April 1834 when Mrs. Pryor's sister married the Rev.
J. Carter we are told—

'Dr. Bliss performed the ceremony very well and the bride,
excepting a little interruption caused by a few tears, got through
very well.'

A modern description of a wedding would dwell on the appearance of the bride. It would not be necessary to report that the
bride 'got through' it very well. But John Izzard rarely omits to
say so.

56

The emotions of the officiating parson at a wedding were also apt to be too much for him.

On 28 June 1831, John Izzard's niece Betsy Morris married Mr. David Powell.

'The clergyman who officiated was the bridegroom's brother who was so overcome by his feelings as to be scarcely able to go through the service.'

At Morris Pryor's wedding on 21 August 1838 we are told that the bride's uncle who officiated at the altar 'got through quite as well as expected.' But the implications of this remark are by no means clear.

If some licence was allowed to the principal figures at a wedding, some also was allowed to the guests. In 1842 *Punch* began some verses on a wedding—

> The guests have departed who stood at the shrine
> All but Vavasour Pelham who's had too much wine,
> And has fallen asleep, on the table, to dream,
> Reclining his brow in a dish of pink cream.

Readers of *Punch* would have recognised young men of their acquaintance in Vavasour Pelham. But the Pryors may have been slightly ahead of their times. We know from John Izzard's remarks on his house-warming dinner that in 1829 their sobriety could not be guaranteed even on occasions of family state. But by 1837 matters had improved.

September 6, 1837

'I accompanied my wife and daughters to Baldock to attend the wedding of my niece Martha with the Rev. Herbert Randolph.

Richard Pryor, the bride's brother, performed the ceremony in a very able manner. The bride looked sweetly and the bridesmaids all beautifully dressed. We sat down afterwards to an excellent dejeuner a la forchette, a very merry party.

Several appropriate toasts were drunk and the party broke up without anyone having drunk too freely.'

In the following year Alfred was married, and as we know there was 'a most liberal supply of champagne'. Temperance was now so far becoming a Pryor family virtue that John Izzard found it unnecessary to commend the wedding guests for their sobriety. By 1843 when 'Dear Julia' married the possibility of intemperance on the part of wedding guests seems to have become so remote as to cease to deserve any notice.

In the earlier diaries there is reference to drunkenness at dinner. For example, John Izzard and Mr. Carter went to dine with Captain Hampson on 19 Nov. 1829–'A male party (would I could say a gentlemen's party) Mr. Cockayne being tipsy soon after the cloth was removed and some of the others towards evening not much better.'

John Izzard who hated intemperance found it difficult to forgive Thomas Cockayne, greatly as he enjoyed a run with his harriers. When on a second occasion Thomas appears to have succumbed, his name is underlined. No doubt his appearance in this guise in the diary is fortuitous, for he is commemorated in Ickleton church by a window bearing the motto *Vivit post funera virtus:* Virtue lives beyond the grave.

But these were, if not gentlemen's parties, at least male parties. On 16 January 1830 Morris Pryor in the midst of a farming diary recorded a contrite note about a dinner attended by his sisters and female cousins: 'I am sorry to say we rather disgraced ourselves by appearing before those we value most in a state of exhilaration bordering on inebriety.'

Morris's contrition is in itself interesting. Ideas were changing. Within a few years no gentleman could be tipsy in a drawing room without causing offence to the ladies; and ten years before Morris's death in 1871 drunkenness had been banished from polite society. In discussing this phenomenon Surtees gives some of the credit to the diffusion of newspapers which relieved tedium. The old port-wine topings wherewith our fathers beguiled their long evenings, he ascribed to boredom. He also commends the habit of serving champagne at company dinners. This, he holds out as an aid to sobriety, because 'a person who drinks freely of champagne cannot drink freely of any other sort of wine after it.'

John Izzard records the figures for the consumption of wine at Clay Hall from 1839 to 1853. From 1839 to 1848 there was little variation. 56 dozen bottles were drunk annually of which 24 dozen were port and 20 sherry. In a normal year 4 dozen of claret were drunk and 2 dozen of champagne. The remaining 6 dozen comprised madeira, marsala, and brandy. From 1849 to 1853 consumption fell to 42 dozen of which 22 were port and 12 sherry. But growing temperance is not the explanation. There was less entertaining on account of family mourning and the serious accident which befell John Izzard in 1851. Even so, if gentlemen were more sober, there is no reason to find the explanation in a dearth of wine.

John Izzard usually bought his port by the pipe in the wood in London, sent a waggon to London to fetch it, and had it bottled at Clay Hall.

With his sherry he took the greatest trouble. It was, at this time, a sweet wine, as often drunk after, as before, dinner. The dry wine so popular in Britain today was not imported before 1857.

July 8, 1834

'Received a letter from Bro. Robert with the finishing account of the ¼ share of a pipe of Sherry I had in conjunction with him and Mrs. Hanbury which we sent a voyage to the East Indies last year. It came back in June, and, after being fined and bottled, was divided amongst us. My share was 12½ dozen received by Kent last Saturday. Including all expenses it averages £2-11-7 per dozen. I tasted a bottle of it this day and thought it very excellent. Had it packed in vault No. 2 Binn No. 6.'

The dominance of the Peninsular wines was a consequence of the long struggle with France. Brandy which was valuable enough to smuggle, was drunk, war or no war. Champagne as a drink for a festive occasion asserted itself soon after Waterloo. Claret was not much drunk in the houses of the smaller country gentry until 1860 when Gladstone removed the duties on French wines. At the same time, he deprived the South African vineyards of a preferential tariff which had assured them a profitable, if humble, place in the British market. In 1831 John Izzard bought some Constantia and Cape Madeira, both good, he says; but he did not usually do so.

Only once does John Izzard mention that he drank gin—it was not a gentleman's drink—and that was at a shoot to keep out the cold. Rum he bought regularly, but he never mentions drinking it. It was used in making punch, a popular winter drink at Clay Hall. John Izzard's receipt for making punch was 'Good and simple and also easy to remember—

1 of sour — 2 of sweet
4 of strong — 8 of weak

being double of every article from the beginning. The strong, alias spirits being $\frac{2}{3}$ rum and $\frac{1}{3}$ brandy. The lemon juice and spirits prepared any time in the course of the day and the hot water added just before the punch is brought on the table.'

The principal meal at Clay Hall was dinner, which took place at 6.30 p.m. when company were expected, but half an hour earlier otherwise. John Izzard's grander neighbours dined at 7 p.m. or 7.30 p,m. At Clay Hall the male guests would not leave the dining room before 8.30 p.m. at the earliest. They spent not less than an hour over their wine, either at the table, or before the fire. They then adjourned to the drawing room where they would find Mrs. Pryor presiding over tea. Few Neo-Elizabethans would survive this experience with credit.

John Izzard frequently went from breakfast to dinner without any intervening meal. For many years luncheon was a ladies' meal. A hot luncheon at Clay Hall was an event only to be justified in exceptional circumstances. A more usual arrangement was for the guests to 'take a little cake and wine' at noon, and to be regaled with an early dinner at 4 p.m. if they could not stay the night.

During the whole of John Izzard's life at Clay Hall joints were carved on the dinner table either by the host, or his sons, or the senior of the male guests. John Izzard records the first occasion on which he met what was known at the time as Diner à la Russe. He and Mrs. Pryor were invited to dine at Knebworth House on 18 August 1852 by Sir Edward Bulwer Lytton to meet the American Minister Mr. Lawrence. Dinner was at 7.30 p.m., and they started at half past 6 in the clarence. But the water on the road at Aston was too deep for their low carriage to pass through, and they had to go round, not arriving until ten to 8.

'We found the company all assembled in the drawing room and all ready to go into the dining room. We made our apology and were soon ushered into the splendid dining hall. The party consisted of thirteen.

We had a very nice dinner, all carved by the butler at large sideboards, no joint or dish appearing on the table, but being handed round by a number of servants in splendid livery. A bill of fare had previously been handed round the dinner table. The length of the table was brilliantly lighted, plateaus and dishes for the dessert being intermixed with the lights. Wines of a variety of descriptions were continually handed round, the champagne being excellent. The dessert was not equal to the dinner, the grapes and apricots not being quite ripe. The coffee ice was very good. On my left hand was Mrs. Reid and on my right, the son of the American Minister. We were much pleased with Mr. Lawrence whose physiognomy is particularly good and conversation very engaging. On joining the ladies in the drawing room coffee was handed round. Afterwards our host amused the company with a species of mesmerism. After a young lady had withdrawn, he asked the ladies and some of the gentlemen each to name a bird, beast, or fish. The young lady named all the birds right but one. We left soon after half past ten.'

Clearly the superstition that thirteen is an unlucky number was not known in Early Victorian Hertfordshire. John Izzard on several occasions records that he was one of a party of thirteen without making any comment on the fact. Perhaps the most striking entry of this kind is that of 22 June 1852—

'My wife and I dined at the Rectory at Walkern, Mrs. Harding in her invite stating they could only make room for two. We with our host and hostess made a party of 13. We spent a very pleasant evening.'

It is doubtful whether Queen Victoria was aware of such a superstition. She certainly did not approve of it. Sir Frederick Ponsonby in his *Recollections of Three Reigns* states that no notice was taken of it at Court in her reign, but that King Edward was very superstitious about being thirteen at dinner. Evidently the superstition is a newcomer.

It is natural to suppose that Christmas traditions have been handed down unchanged. But such does not seem to be the fact. Early Victorian ideas of Christmas fare were somewhat different from those now current. Readers of *Pickwick Papers* will remember that a huge cod fish and half a dozen barrels of real native oysters formed an important part of Mr. Pickwick's luggage when he travelled on the Muggleton Coach to spend Christmas at at Dingly Dell. Cod and oysters were more prominent on the bill of fare at Clay Hall than turkey, plum pudding and mince pies (the latter are nowhere mentioned).

Christmas Day, 1842

'Our Christmas Party consisted of sons John, Morris, Alfred and Fred . . . viz 13.

A very fine cod, boiled turkey and four very fine ribs of beef, fatted by my brother Vickris, being the choicest of a lot sent up from Herefordshire to tie up, about two months since.'

Christmas Day, 1843
'The party at dinner 11. Cod fish and oysters from Buisses. Spent a pleasant evening. Mr. and Mrs. Harding left at about 11 o'clock and soon after 12 we five men, after the ladies had retired, sat down to a game of vignt et une *(sic)* at which I was a considerable winner—a very unusual thing for me. Finished with oysters and Hatfield ale and broke up about two in the morning.'

The supremacy of the cod was challenged when the development of railways made available a greater variety of sea fish.

December 24, 1852
'Received by rail this day a turbot and lobsters, a crimped cod, and two barrels of oysters from Pitmans.'

Christmas Day, 1852
'Our rector and his wife joined our party as usual for our Christmas dinner. Had a fine turbot with lobster sauce, soup, boiled turkey and roast ribs of beef.'

December 26, 1852
'All met again at dinner, partook of a crimped cod, oyster sauce, giblet soup and a new haunch of small mutton with sundries.'

Plum pudding probably formed a part of the Christmas dinner, but was not considered important enough by John Izzard to mention. It will be noticed that he says nothing about the sweet course.

Every Christmas he gave all the farm men a dinner of boiled beef and plum pudding. It is doubtful, however, whether plum pudding had as yet acquired its present status of a dish which is eaten only at Christmastide. It will be remembered that it formed part of the dinner which he gave to Dear Fred and his little friends when they played cricket at Clay Hall on 10 July 1830.

The giving of presents formed no part of the Early Victorian Christmas except that those in a position to do so, might send items of Christmas fare such as a cod fish, a barrel of oysters, game or poultry or a kild of ale to less favoured members of the community. John Izzard always sent a barrel of oysters to Farmers Rowlatt and Stacey of Walkern.

The following is the first reference to a Christmas present.

December 26, 1844

'Presented six pocket books to my wife, children, and grand-children, writing their names in each. Son Alfred and his wife joined our party this afternoon. All our beds are now fully occupied and every stall in our stables.'

It will be noticed that the pocket books were given, not on Christmas Day, but on Boxing Day, and appear to have been given to his wife, his daughters Emma and Eliza Lafont and her three children.

Next year he gave presents on New Year's Day—

January 1, 1845

'Made presents to my grand children accompanied by a verse of poetry to Marian and Winifred.'

Christmas Day, 1848

'Dr. and Mrs. Bliss, my wife and daughter went in the omnibus to church. I walked but found it rather dirty. I found by my place in our pew a very handsome, or rather elegant Prayer Book, a Christmas present from Dr. Bliss which I shall value much.'

There was no Christmas tree at Clay Hall in John Izzard's time, but regularly every year he used to supply one to Mrs. Malet, the wife of the Puseyite vicar of the village of Ardeley.

Christmas Eve, 1852

'Selected a spruce tree for Mrs. Malet's Christmas family party which she decorates with fancy lamps for the occasion. Their servant came over with a little cart to fetch it.'

If the Early Victorians did not celebrate Christmas as thoroughly as is now the custom, they made much more of a christening than is the practice at present. It was customary for the proud parents to give a dinner to their friends, and particularly to the god-parents on the day of the baptism. The *locus classicus* of this type of celebration is the dinner described by Samuel Butler in *The Way of all Flesh*. A note from the hand of Morris Pryor survives in which he describes the christening of his niece Marian Lafont in September 1829.

'Went to Hinxworth to the christening of little Marian Heathcote Lafont. I was not present at the ceremony, which was performed by Dr. Bliss. Mr. Heathcote was the godfather. The rector after-wards gave his friends a very handsome dinner and a plateau of superb grapes at dessert. We all did justice to his wines which were excellent and given with an unsparing hand. I, for one, took more than was necessary or even desirable—which had the effect of making me somewhat absurd. Oh that rational animals should demean themselves in such a manner as to sink themselves lower than brute creation.[1]

Perhaps it is as well that Christening dinners are given no longer.

About the time that the custom of Christening dinners went out that of family prayers came in. John Izzard had grown to manhood in the eighteenth century, and family prayers were not held at Clay Hall in his time. He first mentions them when staying at Roundway Park with the Colstons.

July 24, 1841

'Breakfasted at 9. The servants came in to prayers, Dr. Bliss officiating, reading previously a chapter out of the Bible, their regular practice.'

G. M. Young, in his *Early Victorian England*, quotes Lord Hatherton as saying that in 1810 only two gentlemen in Staffordshire had family prayers; in 1850 only two did not.

John Izzard does not mention them again until 1856 when he stayed with his nephew Arthur who 'read a chapter in the New Testament and the morning service afterwards, the four children behaving very well.'

This was at quarter to 8 in the morning, and afterwards Arthur mounted his horse and rode to Putney station where he took the train for his place of business—Brick Lane. He returned in the same way at 6 o'clock. 'Daily Breading' had already begun. But for Arthur it was soon to end. These were happy times for brewers, and in 1858 he purchased the Hylands estate near Chelmsford. He was High Sheriff of Essex in 1866 and was appointed a D.L. and J.P.

---

[1] The innocent cause of this shocking occasion was married twenty years later in this church, and became the mother of Ernest Heatley, well known as Master of the Essex Union Foxhounds. His was one of the last hunting portraits painted by Sir Alfred Munnings before his retirement. In his autobiography Sir Alfred drew a charming character sketch of Ernest in the home he shared with his bachelor brother and three spinster sisters.

Attention has already been drawn to the difference between Early Victorian and modern practice with regard to weddings. A description of a wedding in the Chauncy family suggests how the family party became the wider entertainment of today.

June 16, 1842
'Dined at 7.30 o'clock, dressing afterwards to attend the Soiree given by Mr. Chauncey at Dane End to which 150 persons had invitations. The dejeuner took place at Green Elms after the wedding, Mr. Nathaniel Chauncey's daughter being married to a Mr. Maples about 11 in the forenoon at which a large family party attended. The church path and the church were strewed by young girls of the village dressed in white and a substantial dinner given to the poor.

We arrived at 9 o'clock and found the carriages coming in very thick. Dancing began directly afterwards and was kept up with great spirit. Quadrilles and waltzes were the prevalent dances. A most elegant supper was served up in an apartment nearly adjoining at 12 o'clock. Plenty of ices, champagne etc. and dancing resumed until 3 in the morning. We left about half past 2.

An instrument called the Choramcisicon, uniting the organ, pianoforte and harp, being equal to a complete band, was played by the person who owned it.'

This wedding ceremony was accompanied by a certain amount of pomp. But it was probably without any music. Even London weddings do not seem to have been choral. John Izzard describes his son John's (second) marriage to Emily Higgs on 19 August 1851.

'The wedding was to take place at 11.30 at St. George's, Hanover Square. We therefore assembled in the vestry at 11 and the clergyman who was to perform the ceremony and the bride's brother came in soon after. But the bride and bridesmaids were not so punctual. Another elegant bride and bridegroom and their friends and clergyman being in the vestry, and another party being expected directly, the party above mentioned proceeded to the altar first. Soon after the rest of our party made their appearance and took the next turn, the last party being rather fearful that they should scarcely get through at the canonical hour. Dr. Higgs performed the service exceedingly well and the bride behaved admirably. The last party were just in time to get through.

Our party all separated to meet again at the Clarendon, Bond Street, where an excellent dejeuner was done justice to and the health of the happy pair drunk in excellent champagne. Some neat speeches were made. The ladies withdrew about three and the bridegroom soon afterwards as they were to proceed to Brighton by the express train at 5 o'clock and had therefore to change their dresses and prepare for their journey. The gentlemen soon after separated.'

It became the fashion to send particulars of a wedding to the Press for publication early in the nineteenth century. Morris Pryor married Louisa Colston on 21 August 1838, and John Izzard records that 'Dr. Bliss wrote and sent off yesterday the particulars of the marriage for insertion in the *Times* and *Standard,* London Papers and also for the Oxford Papers. I also sent the same particulars to Hertford for insertion in the Herts County Press.'

When Robert Pryor was married in August 1844, notice of the marriage appeared in *The Times.* In addition a card engraved with the names of Mr. and Mrs. Robert Pryor was sent to relatives and friends.

Punch in September 1841 described a card of this kind as follows—

'An enamelled card superscribed with the names of Bride and Bridegroom united together with a silver cord tied in a true lover's knot, in an envelope of lacework, secured with a silver dove flying away with a square bit of silver toast.'

It does not seem that the practice of sending cards of this kind long persisted. It is possible, however, that it has survived in a modified form in the custom of sending a piece of wedding cake to friends and relations not present at the ceremony. It will be noticed that no mention of wedding cake is made by John Izzard.

But if Victorian weddings were celebrated simply, funerals were conducted with a pomp which modern taste finds repellent. John Izzard enjoyed a good funeral as much as the next man, but there were limits to what even he could approve, and they seem to have been exceeded at the funeral of Commissary General John Murray, his neighbour at Ardeley Bury.

December 9, 1834

'The remains of Mr. Murray were buried with great pomp and parade at Ardeley at 9 o'clock at night by torch light, the coffin lying in state previously in the Great Hall in his house.'

Harbord, the historian of Ardeley, states that the hearse surmounted with a state lid of plumes, was drawn by 6 horses, followed by 2 mutes, 10 pages, 4 mourning coaches, and the tenants on horseback, the procession being surrounded by 60 men with lighted wax flambeaux. But the custom of conducting funerals at night was going out; and the last royal funeral to take place in darkness was that of William IV in 1837.

In the following entries from his diary John Izzard describes family funerals which were conducted with a restraint unusual for the times.

January 10, 1839

John Izzard tells of the funeral of his brother Vickris's daughter Martha Randolph (she had been allowed to marry her curate, and died in child birth).

'I set off in my carriage about half past 9 taking Lafont with me to Stevenage where the relatives of the deceased Mrs. Randolph were to assemble soon after 10 o'clock to be ready to proceed after the hearse and mourning coach which arrived at 5 o'clock yesterday afternoon from London. The parties assembled in good time and left at eleven in seven carriages—the nearest relatives first and the different degrees afterwards as arranged in a written paper.

We reached Baldock at 12.30 and entered the church at 1, when the burial service was performed by Mr. Smith in an impressive manner. The vault had been dug under my son Morris's super-intendence directly under the communion table at the extreme east end of the chancel. It was very deep and large enough to con-tain eight coffins. £40 is to be paid to the rector in the present instance and £5 for breaking the ground for every other coffin of the family that may hereafter be put in.

The undertakers from London had very good men who under-stood their business and the whole was conducted with great propriety and decorum. Herbert Randolph and my brother were very much affected when the coffin was lowered into the vault.'

In his account of his brother Robert's funeral April 6 1839, John Izzard details the mourning millinery which it was the custom to distribute to mourners.

'After the undertakers had fitted the scarfs and bands on the relatives of the deceased, I as elder brother took my seat in the mourning coach with my brother Vickris and nephew Henry, leaving a place for Marlborough who was to get in at Radwell. There the other carriages fell in and the servants had their bows, bands and gloves. My deceased brother Robert's carriage followed empty after the mourning coach and then five carriages with the other relatives and also two of my brother's partners, Mr. Robt. Hanbury and Mr. Edward Buxton.'

John Izzard's eldest son John who managed the Baldock Brewery and was, on that account, the leading inhabitant of the little town, died there in 1853. John Izzard's account of the funeral at Norton, three miles away, tells how the townspeople took their part in the ceremony. 'A great concourse followed on foot, behaving very exemplarily, the shops partially closed and the blinds drawn on most of the houses. The Rev. B. Donne performed the last sad ceremony in a very solemn manner. The church full of people. The coffin was lowered into the family vault in the chancel and was placed in the catacomb where the deceased's first wife was buried on the right hand. When it pleases God to take me my remains are intended to be deposited in the next catacomb, in the centre and my wife in the same, being built to contain two each. The third catacomb is for son Morris and his wife.

After the service was over the parties returned to Baldock in pretty near the same order to the residence of the deceased and partook of a luncheon. Some time after the will was opened by Mr. Veasey and read to a few more immediately concerned.'

The wearing of mourning was of much importance, not only for the relations, but also for their servants.

April 19, 1853

'Bespoke mourning for my butler, coachman, footman, of Rust our Walkern tailor. My wife also bought mourning material for dresses of Routledge yesterday at Baldock for all our female servants, viz. housekeeper, cook, two chamber-maids, and scullery girl.'

To the Early Victorian mind omission to wear mourning was an affront to the deceased and family and showed a lack of reverence for the scheme of things as ordained by Divine Providence. Thus it was that when in 1857 the butler at Clay Hall died of delirium tremens, the indoor servants insisted on putting on slight mourning for him at their own expense. John Izzard applauded their action and paid their expenses himself.

VIII

JOHN IZZARD AS DEPUTY LIEUTENANT

Some account has already been given of John Izzard's activities as Deputy Lieutenant during the Luddite Troubles. An entry in his diary shows him carrying out the routine duties of his office.

June 9, 1831

'Went in my gig to Welwyn to attend a Meeting of Deputy Lieutenants for the purpose of swearing in and enrolling the Militia for this subdivision of Hitchin and Broadwater Hundred. 56 men (the quota) were drawn at the former meeting which I attended. 35 were sworn in and enrolled this day, all substitutes but one. 21 exempt, being under height or diseased, on examination by the surgeon. The difficiency *(sic)* from the different parishes were balloted for again this day and will have to attend at the next meeting. Captain Hampson and myself were the Deputy Lieutenants officiating, the former acting in both capacities of Captain of the Militia and Depy. Lieut. Lord Dacre looked in for a short time, but finding we were getting on very well he did not stop.'

Britons believe that their country was without conscription until 1917, but such is not the fact. The ranks of the Militia were filled by conscription limited by ballot and subject to the option of paying for a substitute.

Besides carrying out his duties to the Militia, John Izzard took a close interest in the County Yeomanry, in the North Hertfordshire troop of which his brother Vickris and son Morris were officers. Every summer the troop was embodied for a week, and drilled at Baldock in a field adjacent to Vickris's house in Hitchin Street. At the close of training they were inspected by a colonel from the Horse Guards who, having expressed himself satisfied at the manner in which they had performed their evolutions, caught the next coach to London and always avoided accepting hospitality.

69

It is not clear whether the officer's elusiveness was to be attributed to official scruple, or to his reluctance to have further to do with these rustic warriors.

For a quarter of a century the Yeomanry were of paramount importance. 'The mainstay of public peace', writes G. M. Young in his detailed portrait of the age, *Early Victorian England*, 'was not the constable, but the yeoman, and behind the yeoman, though cautiously and reluctantly employed, the soldier.' Sir John Fortescue, writing on the Army in the same volume, points out how few regular troops were stationed in Great Britain. In 1826, for instance, of 83 regiments of the line, 23 were in Ireland, 4 in Great Britain, and the rest abroad. It was, he says, the yeomanry chiefly which stood between the country and anarchy.

In 1839 was passed the Rural Police Act, and during the following decade police forces were organised in the counties of Great Britain. In 1851 *Punch,* with heavy humour, mocked the Cowbridge Yeomanry. An earlier generation had been glad enough that these amateur soldiers stood between them and the violence of the oppressed Lower Orders, and of a numerous criminal class. Now they could be made fun of for serving their country without ceasing to serve their customers.

Annual training always ended with a dinner given by the Troop Commander, Captain Heathcote (Marian Lafont's godfather), the squire of Shephall Bury, a stern unbending Tory, who could be relied upon to take the chair at any meeting called to oppose innovation. He fought Catholic Emancipation, Parliamentary Reform, Rural Police and Railways—the latter militantly, forcibly preventing a survey of his land.

August 4, 1852

'Captain Heathcote giving a dinner to his troop this day, invited me and several gentlemen to dine with him and them at 4 o'clock after the men had gone through some of their evolutions at Broadwater where they met at 1 o'clock.

Hungerford Colston drove the carriage over and came on the ground at 12 o'clock. Mrs. Pryor, Emma and Juliana were within, Mr. Baker and Fred behind, and Cooper on the box with Mr. Colston.

There were a few short showers but nothing of consequence. We retired from the field at half past 3 and sat down at 4 to dine in a long marquee handsomely ornamented with laurels in festoons and Chinese lanterns suspended. Captn. Heathcote was supported on his right by Mr. Abel Smith and Mr. W. Wigram; and on his left by Lord Grimston and myself.

There were several officers of Lord Salisbury's troop present. My bro' Vickris and son Morris dined as officers of the North Herts Troop and also 50 privates dined. Mr. Heathcote presided in his usual excellent manner, and on giving the toasts spoke pertinently, indeed eloquently, and the whole thing went off very well indeed.'

The rise of Louis Napoleon in the middle of the nineteenth century compelled the Government to pay attention to the question of military manpower. An attempt was made to procure it by improving the terms upon which the Militia served, and trusting to voluntary enlistment to fill the ranks, keeping the ballot as a last resort.

August 14, 1852

'I had to attend a meeting of the Deputy Lieutenants for the County at the Town Hall, St. Albans. Present the Lord Lieutenant the Earl of Verulam, the Marquis of Salisbury Colonel of the Militia, Sir Ed. B. Lytton, Hon. Dudley Rider, Sir Ashley Cooper, Baron Dimsdale, Mr. Solly etc. The business was chiefly to draw up and circulate to the different parishes the forms agreed upon by Government for enlistment in the Militia to supersede, if possible, the having recourse to the ballot.'

That Sidney Herbert's Act was hardly a success may be judged by the following passage.

October 28, 1852

'Saw Major Hampson and had some conversation respecting Volunteers for the Militia as we have had none offer in Walkern parish. The Adjutant and Surgeon attend at Baldock on Thursday next and I am to see the police constable to try and see whether he cannot, by that time, get three or four men to come forward.'

IX

THE NEIGHBOURS

At Clay Hall the Pryors' best friends were to be found among the country clergy and their families. At Baldock, however, John Izzard does not appear to have been on intimate terms with the rector, the Rev. John Smith. There is no mention of Smith ever having dined at the Brewery House. Smith had had the distinction of having deciphered Pepys' Diary, a fact duly acknowledged by Lord Braybroke in his preface to the first edition. His lordship added that he was not personally acquainted with him, a curious state of affairs when it is remembered that Baldock is within a few hours' ride of Audley End, the noble editor's mansion just over the Essex border. Whether it is to be attributed to the hauteur of the Early Victorian aristocracy or to the unsociable nature of the rector is open to conjecture.

Relations between Clay Hall and Walkern Rectory were usually cordial, particularly after the succession of the Rev. John Harding in 1839. 'Our rector' and his lady dined every Christmas at Clay Hall, and the two houses were continually exchanging hospitality. Harding who had been a King's Scholar at Eton and had been a Fellow of King's College, Cambridge for twenty-three years took no part in field sports, but was not without parlour tricks, and was a proficient archer.

February 4, 1839

'I brought a quarter of lamb with me from London. I asked Dr. Hinds, Mr. Pollard and our new rector to partake of it today. A very pleasant evening we had. After returning to the drawing room and taking our tea, Mr. Harding took off many celebrated characters to the life, having talent which to a select few he now and then exhibits in a superior manner.

Mr. Harding excels as a toxophilite, frequently planting his arrows in the centre of the target. I never saw so much certainty in

72

anyone,' wrote John Izzard that summer. 'We persuaded him to remain to partake of our dinner quite in a friendly way, and spent a most agreeable evening together.'

Dr. Hinds, whom John Izzard invited to meet the new rector, was vicar of the neighbouring village of Ardeley. Born in the Barbadoes, he had had a distinguished career at Oxford and had returned to his native island to be Principal of Codrington College. Thence he had come to Ardeley. In 1843 he was appointed Prebend of Castleknock in Ireland by Archbishop Whateley, with whom he had worked at Oxford. In 1848 he was appointed Bishop of Norwich. He took a distinguished part in the Commission on Oxford University. His departure was in John Izzard's view a great loss to the neighbourhood.

The other guest at this dinner was the Rev. John Pollard, rector of the neighbouring village of Benington. His wife was a granddaughter of the third Earl of Harborough. He seems to have been a Whig in politics, a fact which perhaps interfered with friendship with the Clay Hall family.

Dr. Hinds' successor at Ardeley, the Rev. William Windham Malet, was no ordinary country parson. Third son of Sir Charles Malet Bt., a distinguished servant of the East India Company, Malet was educated at Winchester and at the East India Company's College at Haileybury. Having served ten years in the Company's civil service, Malet returned home and sought ordination, at first in vain. In 1836 Bishop Bathurst of Norwich ordained him, and eight years later he was appointed to the living of Ardeley on the recommendation of Canon Sydney Smith.

As a churchman, Malet was an ardent adherent to the Oxford Movement, and John Izzard early detected in him 'something of the Puseyite leaven'. But this in no way interfered with the friendship between the two families. Malet had a large family, and John Izzard's grandchildren and his wife's nephew George Pemberton, the son of a John Company's General, entertained one another constantly.

John Izzard occasionally attended church at Ardeley and found nothing to offend him.

June 29, 1845

'There being no morning service at Walkern I rode over to Ardeley. Mr. Malet gave a good sermon and Mrs. Malet (whose pew I sat in) chaunted delightfully.'

On another occasion he wrote—

'Attended the morning service sitting in Mr. Malet's pew with Mrs. Malet. A very good attendance. The offertory has been adopted there after the sermon, but very little is collected. The practice does not seem adapted to a village congregation. Shook hands with Sir Robert and Lady Murray.'

Bishop Blomfield of London had shocked many of his clergy when in 1842 he had recommended the taking of a weekly offertory. There is no provision in the Prayer Book for a collection at Morning and Evening Prayer. It is only in the service for Holy Communion that directions are given for an offertory. The Bishop suggested the weekly use of the Prayer for the Church Militant and the taking of a collection. This was thought to be Popish.

The true Protestant took a collection, when he had occasion to do so, after the service at the church door.

Sir Robert and Lady Murray with whom John Izzard shook hands (this was a new way of going on, ten years earlier he would have bowed) lived at the big house at Ardeley. Ardeley Bury was the nearest mansion of equivalent rank to Clay Hall, and the Murray family were long the Pryors' neighbours without ever becoming their friends.

Ardeley Bury was bought in 1811 by John Murray, Commissary General in His Majesty's Forces. In 1820 he pulled down the greater part of the brick mansion and erected the existing imitation-medieval residence. On his death the estate passed to his daughter, Susannah, wife of Major Adolphus Cottin, who assumed the name of Murray. John Izzard did not see eye to eye with him; nor did he find the lady's second husband more congenial. He was Sir Robert Murray, tenth Baronet of Dunerne (Fife).

Susannah Murray, a robust personality, is remembered at Ardeley by the path which she made and planted with trees from the drive gates at the Bury to the vicinity of the church, and which still survives. Its course is parallel to the road, and close to it; and the villagers aver that it was so made that her ladyship might go to and from church without making contact with, what the Psalmist describes as, the 'Beasts of the People.'

If she had no love for the people, she had less for the Puseyite parson Malet. In 1849 two niches with elaborately carved canopies were discovered beneath the plaster in the east wall of the chancel.

A son of the vicar made a sketch of them. Lady Murray as lay impropriatrix of the living had certain rights in the chancel, and in any case she did not hold with Popery. During the night following the discovery two of her emissaries broke into the church and utterly destroyed the niches.

Commissary General Murray in 1826 built a vault on top of which he made a florid gothic erection which stood where the vestry now stands. It was erected without a faculty, but it was subsequently licensed, despite Malet's protests, by Bishop Kaye of Lincoln. The villagers always called it the 'Cemetery'. Lady Murray died in 1860, and the estate passed to her surviving son by her first marriage, Adolphus William Murray. At her death her husband Sir Robert seems to have left Ardeley with his son and daughter. Adolphus William's career as squire was cut short in 1864 by Delirium Tremens. With his interment the family vault was full. Some years later, but undoubtedly during the lifetime of Sir Robert Murray, Malet had the vestry built where the Murray gothic erection had stood. Part of the latter, including some inscriptions, were built into the vestry. What happened to the rest of it is not certain. But the villagers tell the story that, when some years ago, repairs were done to the Vicarage, there was occasion to move the stone outside the backdoor. When it was turned over it was found to bear Lady Murray's initials. It was part of the Murray monument. Generations of the humbler visitors to the Vicarage must unwittingly have stood upon it.

When the church was restored in 1872 the architect Butterfield, utilising the sketches, put the niches back into the east wall.

Worship at Ardeley church has been, without interruption, Anglo-Catholic in character since William Malet's day. Thus the Indian-civilian-parson defeated his Protestant patroness all along the line.

That John Izzard did not approve of Major Adolphus Cottin (later Murray), the lady's first husband, is clear.

December 21, 1839
'The hounds meeting at Great Munden I mounted son Fred on the young chestnut, and accompanied him on my old hunter there. Son Morris breakfasted at Clay Hall and joined us. Son John was also there and a big field of sportmen. The day was very fine but the ground uncommonly wet and heavy. Hounds fell back to St.

John's where we found. But the scent was so bad we could not make him out except at intervals. The fox came across from near Benington to Ardeley into the Park where I believe he went to ground. Mr. Murray was very angry with several gentlemen riding about his Park although he himself was with the hounds all day. He went so far as to order the gate to be locked. We left then but heard the hounds half an hour afterwards running in the direction of Benington.'

The Lady's second husband was always unpunctual; whether he was to act as Chairman of the Grand Jury, whether he was escorting his wife to a dinner party, or merely making a call, he was always late, and 'did not seem to think anything about it.' But annoying as it was to wait from 7 until quarter to 8 for the Murrays to come to dinner, this was as nothing when compared with Sir Robert's refusal to support John Izzard's attempt to obtain a grant from Quarter Sessions for the repair of the Walkern Bridge. It was poor consolation to reflect that even had Sir Robert agreed to speak for it, it was unlikely that he would have been in time to do so.

It was fortunate that at Benington Park the Pryors had a more congenial neighbour in William Wigram. He was one of the 23 children of Sir Robert Wigram of Walthamstow, founder with George Green of the Blackwall Ship-building Yard, where were built the celebrated Blackwell Frigates. A bachelor, the patronage he enjoyed as a Director of the East India Company was at the service of his friends, and the Pryors, the Chauncies and the Pollards of Benington had reason to be thankful to him. He was for some years Joint-Master of the Puckeridge Hounds with Mr. Nicholas Parry. But the historian of the Puckeridge Hunt (Michael Berry, London, 1950) says that he was content to leave all responsibility to Mr. Parry. He gave excellent dinners.

August 18, 1849

'Dined this day at Mr. Wigram's. Arrived there at exactly 7, the invitation being for quarter to 7. The party met pretty punctually, the others arriving in a few minutes. Several of them being East India Directors were staying in the house. We had a sumptuous dinner. Turtle soup, venison, turbot and grey mullet, side dishes and grouse. Iced punch, iced champagne, burgundy, claret etc. Left to return home at half past 10.'

The continued existence of the East India Company, long after its effective power had passed to the Crown, may possibly be explained by our ancestors' appreciation of the virtues of keeping some patronage in hands other than those of the ruling aristocracy. When the Company was abolished in 1858, the era of the competitive examination had dawned. The I.C.S. was recruited in this manner for the first time in 1852.

It can be readily understood that country gentry and parsons wanting jobs for their sons would find it much easier to wait on Mr. Wigram at Benington Hall than seek an interview with a bored Marquis of Salisbury in the august precincts of Hatfield House.

November 25, 1847
'My wife had a letter from George Pemberton this morning with the agreeable intelligence that he had waited upon Mr. Wigram at the India House and that he had most handsomely given him an appointment as Assistant Surgeon in India, giving him the choice of the Presidencies. He preferred Bengal, his father Colonel Pemberton being there.

My wife had made application to Mr. Wigram, and he had kindly said that when George had passed his examination and should be elected Member of the Royal Society of Surgeons, if he would then call upon him, he would see what he could for him.'

George Pemberton was the son of Mrs. Pryor's sister whose death from cholera John Izzard recorded in 1827. He spent much of his youth at Clay Hall and married Winifred Lafont.

Entries in the diary and memorials in the churches of the Walkern neighbourhood illustrate the importance of the dominions of the East India Company to the gentry and clergy of Hertfordshire.

On 7 January 1844 came the 'very sad intelligence of the death of William Pollard in India,' son of the rector of Benington, 'while serving with the Army on the banks of the Indus.' Five days later Fred rode over to Green Elms to bid farewell to Reginald Chauncy who was off to India in the Civil Service. On 22 November 1847, Captain George Malet called with his parson brother. 'He was with the army in the disastrous affair at Cabool' is all that John Izzard remarks. But he had distinguished himself in the conquest of Sind, and like so many military officers of his generation was as handy with the pen as the sword, and had written a history of that country. It was his last leave at home. He fell at the assault on Bushire in 1856, a year which brought bad news both to parson and squire at Ardeley, for to Ardeley Bury came grievous tidings of the death of a son of the house John Murray, while serving as A.D.C. to the Governor of the North Western Provinces.

Of other parts of the Empire there is scant mention. We hear of a South African settler ruined by 'marauding Caffres' (John Izzard was his trustee), 'Our rector's' lady's brother dies in New Zealand. John Izzard subscribes to a fund for settling the Lower Orders in Australia. That is all. Whoever was building the British Commonwealth countries at this time, it was not the kith and kin of the Hertfordshire clergy and gentry. But they were to do great things later in the reign. The son of a Hertfordshire clergyman, Cecil Rhodes was born at Bishop's Stortford in 1853.

But to return to Walkern and its neighbourhood. At another mansion in Benington, the Lordship, resided the Proctors, with whom the Pryors maintained but distant social relations. With the Abel Smiths at Watton Woodhall John Izzard was on polite but not cordial terms, as was fitting in their respective social positions. For Watton Woodhall was very grand. 'A good dinner served on plate with venison etc.' he remarks on August 27 1844. 'But the party was rather formal'. 'My wife walked over to Benington with Fred', he wrote eight years later, 'to look over the Rectory. Whilst there Mr. Abel Smith and his daughter, both on horseback, called to pay his respects to the new rector, which was very polite and kind of so distinguished a man.' And also good politics. The Walkern tenants voted for Mr. Abel Smith when the occasion arose.

The Chauncies of Green Elms at Munden, an old Hertfordshire family who had made a fortune in the West Indies, entertained freely and were much liked, but in 1844 Nathaniel Chauncy lost his money. 'I accompanied my wife in the carriage to call on Mrs. Chauncy who is preparing to leave their beautiful residence in consequence of their reduced income from the state of affairs in the West Indies. They are going to reside in a small house near London viz. Carlton Villas, Maida Hill, not far from Regent Park. Mrs. Chauncy bears her reverse of fortune nobly.' A later entry completes the sad, eventful history of Nathaniel Chauncy.

July 10, 1856

'A sad account of Mr. Chauncy, formerly residing at Green Elms, Little Munden, but lately of Westbourne Terrace, having destroyed himself by jumping out of a window on Westbourne Terrace.'

But he was fortunate in that he was able to sell his estate to his brother Charles, from whom it passed to his daughter, Mrs. Surtees.

The Pryors were often bidden to Knebworth House by Sir Edward Bulwer Lytton to witness theatricals. The fact, however, that John Izzard was invited to dinner to meet the American Minister indicates that Sir Edward thought him worthy of a more active role than that of audience, even at the advanced age of 78.

John Izzard and his family were accustomed to go to Hatfield House to the Balls and Receptions which the Marquis of Salisbury gave for the County. But he was never invited to dine there, and he was often critical of the Marquis. He declined to accept his suggestion that he should take his seat on the Bench in order to qualify himself to vote against the resolution to set up a County Police Force. Devoted though he was to the Crown, John Izzard had no marked love of a lord.

X

SOCIAL OCCASIONS

Uninhibited by the rigours of washing-up, the Early Victorian gentry enjoyed to the fullest extent the pleasures of the table. Small social gatherings and large official occasions alike, in their view, demanded the production of an abundance of victuals and a lavish supply of wine. But it would be wrong to suppose that the domestic crisis was unknown at that time. An early entry by John Izzard will serve to correct that impression. Christmastide 1827 'caused very large parties of the Pryor family to meet' in Baldock.

New Year's Day 1828
'This day a party of twenty (Pryors) dined and spent the evening at our house. Mrs. North of Ashwell came to us as a temporary cook, our old cook having taken herself off in a huff.' As will be seen later the Pryors had their full share of domestic trouble.

The description already given of Marian Lafont's christening dinner must not be taken as typical of that now extinct family festivity. On 10 September 1834, John Izzard recorded—

'We dined at Mr. and Mrs. Nath. Chauncey's at Green Elms, Little Munden. Their youngest child was christened in the morning by Mr. Jollonds the clergyman there who made one of the party. We had an excellent dinner, turtle soup, fish etc. and spent a pleasant evening and had a rubber at short whist at which I lost 5/-.'

Another festive occasion recorded by John Izzard was the parson's tithe dinner. On 23 November 1831 he wrote, 'Dined with the principal farmers at Mr. Wright's, it being his Tithe Dinner. Good dinner, good wine and good punch.'

These functions did not continue much longer. An Act passed in 1836 commuted tithe to an annual money payment which varied with the seven year average of the price of grain. The assessment of tithe had therefore become automatic, and the parson was saved from annual and inappropriate contention with his parishioners. He still had, however, to collect tithe himself. But he seems to have thought that he was not now under any necessity of entertaining the tithe payers.

John Izzard always entertained his tenants to dinner in January when they paid their rents. The following entry is typical of many.

January 17, 1845

'Prepared in the morning for receiving my rents. They (the tenants) began to arrive about 1 o'clock and I settled with most of them by 3 o'clock when dinner was announced. We sat down 25, 12 of our own family party and 13 of my tenants including two of their sons. They paid up their rents well considering the depreciation of the price of corn and spent a very happy evening together, enjoying their dinner and some good punch afterwards.'

Both Mr. Wright's Tithe Dinner and John Izzard's Tenants' Dinner took place at 3 p.m., the old fashioned hour for dinner. Even so the guests had to find their way home to their farms up muddy lanes in the pitch dark. No doubt their ponies took care of them.

The dinner after the Horticultural Show at Baldock was but little later. But this took place in the summer, and John Izzard never implies that any one was the worse for his liquor. The following describes one such occasion.

July 31, 1843

'The Baldock Horticultural Meeting being today, W. Bell drove me down in his little carriage. There was a capital show of picotees and carnations and a few dahlias. The melons and other fruit not so good as sometimes. We sat down to dinner at about quarter to 4. I was in the Chair as Mr. Heathcote could not attend, having had his collar bone broken by his horse falling with him in London. There was a very small party, only eight at our table, and about twelve at the Gardeners' table.'

When gentlemen dined alone, without the admixture of farmers, gardeners and such like, 6 p.m. was the hour. During the General Election of 1841 John Izzard wrote—

'Soon after 6, a large party of Conservatives sat down to dinner at the White Swan, about 45. Mr. Heathcote in the Chair. Enjoyed a good dinner and did justice to the several toasts adapted to the

82   *A Chronicle of Small Beer*

occasion from our Chairman, who spoke a great deal, and, had it not been for a song now and then, would have been thought too prolix. We separated in good spirits and quite orderly.'

Mr. Pickwick could have claimed as much when he and his companions left the cricket club dinner at Muggleton. By the time they reached the manor house that description was no longer accurate.

The Early Victorians liked to combine official business with good eating. Regularly every year the Trustees of the River Lee travelled down the river for which they were responsible. In a barge towed by horses it took a very long day to reach London. But the Early Victorians not only had remarkable digestions, they were tireless.

June 29, 1836

'My bro' Robert and myself rose a little before 4 o'clock, took a cup of tea, and set off together in the gig for Ware. Drove to the bridge where the barges belonging to the Trustees of the River Lee soon arrived at 6 o'clock.

The day was propitious but very hot when we were stationary in the locks, some of which we had to inspect, also the tumbling bay at Carthagena Lock. Breakfasted in the Barge off Broxbourne about half past 9. Most of the party lunched heartily about 2 o'clock. I contented myself with some strawberries, and some time afterward a glass of porter. We were 12 hours on our passage. Debarked at Limehouse by Richardson's Timber Wharf, and proceeded in three omnibuses, being rather more than forty of us, to Lovegrove's Hotel at Blackwall (the West India Docks) where we were joined by several more gentlemen. After brushing, washing etc. we sat down about sixty to an excellent dinner, Rowland Alston Esq. in the chair.

There was a liberal supply of turtle soup with lime punch, flounders, soals *(sic)*, small perch, boiled turbot and salmon, and lastly white bait, to which luxury all did ample justice, they being nicely done, brought up hot and eaten with lemon only. After this several haunches of venison made their appearance. Lots of champagne was drunk; I contented myself with little more than one glass, and took sherry as champagne does not suit me. Retired about half past 9, Mr. Robert Hanbury driving us to Brick Lane in his phaeton.'

As John Izzard repeated this trip for some years it does not seem that he found it too fatiguing.

Another example of the Early Victorian tendency to make of every occasion an excuse for a good dinner is to be found in John Izzard's account of the consecration of the new church at Thundridge. Mr. Robert Hanbury, whom we last met driving John Izzard to Robert Pryor's house in Brick Lane after the outing of the River Lee Trustees in 1836, pulled down the old church except for the tower and rebuilt it in the best Victorian Gothic on a new site. It was one of the oldest churches in the country.

November 9, 1853

'Having had an invitation from Mr. Robt. Hanbury to attend at the consecration of a new church he has been at the sole expense of building in the parish of Thundridge in which his house and park called Poles are situated, my wife and I set off in the clarence, reaching the church at 11 o'clock. We found a number of carriages arriving just at the same time. The large company invited had cards of admission and places appointed for them. The church was full at the time the Bishop of Rochester appeared, a large train of clergy accompanying him. A particular service appointed to be read on these occasions was read by the Bishop, and the prayers, Litany and Psalms were read by a clergyman at the reading desk, and the Communion Service at the Altar, after which Mr. Faithful of Hertford preached an excellent sermon—all very composing. The Bishop afterwards, with part of the congregation attending him, consecrated the churchyard. Mr. Hanbury gave the invited guests— say fifty at least—a sumptuous luncheon, at his house half mile distant at half past 3.'

But these were all functions on what may be described in modern jargon as 'County level'. Even the business of the parish pump was always liable to end up in a dinner.

April 5, 1847

'I rode down to Walkern to attend the annual vestry for examining Church Wardens' accounts and other parish matters. It took us from 12 to 3 o'clock, and at half past 3 Mr. Harding and I stopped and joined the church wardens and some of the parish-ioners at dinner at the White Lion, eight of us altogether.'

Evidently they got on well together. For all the high society he kept, John Izzard continued to find pleasure in the company of his humbler neighbours.

The following entry gives some idea of what attendance at a County Ball entailed.

December 28, 1843

'Dined at half past 5 and at 20 minutes to 7 set off in the carriage with my wife to an entertainment given by Lord Salisbury at Hatfield House to which we had received an invitation for 9 o'clock. We went with our own horses to Welwyn and there posted on, having previously engaged horses. We entered the house at 20 minutes to 10 and were graciously received by Lord Salisbury, Lord Verulam and his lady and a large party going in at exactly the same time. A large party were assembled by 10 o'clock. Soon after, dancing commenced. Quadrilles principally, a little waltzing, and at last country dances. There was tea and ices in a room thrown open about 11 o'clock. At 1 o'clock the company descended into the great marble hall where the guests partook of a handsome supper, all standing. The soups were hot but everything else cold. Abundance of champagne and other wines. One with a little patience could partake. The hall was lighted up with Chinese lamps suspended high, and numerous lamps and wax candles on the tables. Many of the first families of the county were present. The band of the Hertfordshire Militia of which Lord Salisbury is Colonel performed. The ladies were beautifully dressed. White was the favourite colour with lace, diamonds and jewels. Black and blue coats were most worn by the gentlemen, with white waistcoats; some dressing in scarlet hunting coats. Sons John, Morris and Alfred were also there and the wives of the two latter. We left at quarter past 2, getting to bed about 5, and had a profound sleep until 11 o'clock this morning the 29th.'

John Izzard at this time was nearing his 70th birthday. No distinction was made at this time between gentlemen's morning and evening clothes. John Izzard was probably wearing a blue coat such as that in which he was painted. The hunting men wore the identical coats which they wore hunting. They must have found them very hot.

John Izzard regularly attended balls until he was well over 80 years of age. The last one he mentions was 'a grand ball' given by his nephew Thomas, son of Vickris Pryor, at the house in Hitchin Street, Baldock, on 1 February 1856.

'This being the day, or more properly, the night for my nephew Mr. Thos. Pryor giving a grand Ball at his house in Hitchin Street,

Baldock, for which 160 invitations had been sent to the gentry of the neighbourhood and some at a distance, my wife and daughter and myself set off in the chariot (taking two ladies' maids) for Baldock to dine with my daughter Juliana at 6 p.m., and afterwards at 9 p.m. started for the Ball.

Everything had been prepared in a sumptuous order. There were nearly 200 ladies and gentlemen present and Weippert's band of musicians. Dancing was kept up until 3 o'clock when a supper with every delicacy took place. We left at half past 3 but dancing was resumed and kept up until near 5 a.m. The train of carriages ranged almost the whole length of Hitchin Street.'

The modern dance band has but a transient existence. Weippert's band which played to Thomas Pryor's guests in 1856 had accompanied the singing of Dulce Domum at Winchester when 'Dear Fred' was elected a scholar in July 1835.

Quadrilles and waltzes were, according to John Izzard, the favourite dances. The polka is mentioned at Marian Lafont's first ball at Hertford Town Hall on 5 January 1847. Marian had 'some excellent partners introduced to her through the kindness' of the tutor at Hatfield House, who was an old Oxford friend of Mrs. Pryor.

Theatricals took place occasionally. Sir Edward Bulwer Lytton put some on at Knebworth House regularly.

November 20, 1850
'To Knebworth to attend theatricals at Sir Edward Buller Lytton's at 7 o'clock. Seats were appropriated for us in the gallery amongst many of the gentlemen and ladies of the neighbourhood. The acting was very good. After the first performance was over the company went to the drawing room where a very handsome supper was laid out on long tables with great taste, and wine and water were partaken of to refresh the company after the great heat of the hall where the performance took place. The epilogue and afterpiece took place with great eclat and the curtain fell about ½ past 12. The first performance was Ben. Johnson's farce *Turning the Tables*. The ladies in particular much delighted.'

Knebworth House seems to have taken but little part in the life of the neighbourhood. Its master was more at home in London, and recruited his actors and actresses from among his London friends.

The theatricals got up by the Malets were genuinely local but seem to have been confined to the male sex. But they were popular and we are told that 'the characters were well supported.'

There is only one reference to Strolling Players, and that occasion was not a great success.

February 25, 1831

'My wife and daughters went to Baldock to dine and stop the night at Mr. and Mrs. Veaseys, as there was a company of Players performing at Baldock and Mrs. V. Pryor had bespoke a play for this evening. *The Honeymoon* was the piece, which went off pretty well. But the farce *Simpson & Co.* was so vulgar that the party from Mrs. Vickris and ourselves were obliged on account of the ladies to make our exit.'

This was six years before Queen Victoria came to the throne. It is, however, relevant to recall that Thomas Bowdler (1754–1825), whose 'peculiar happiness' it was to have purified Shakespeare, was no Victorian, and indeed was already dead. *Simpson & Co.* was, perhaps, strong meat. On the other hand, Son Alfred was to find no difficulty in shocking Mrs. Vickris.

The Pryor young ladies could all ride, but did not often do so. They played no games but they were keen, but not very proficient, archers. In the thirties subscription archery parties were the fashion.

September 19, 1833

'An archery picnic was held this day at Aspenden Hall under the auspices of Mrs. Chauncey of Green Elms, Little Munden, who planned and arranged the whole affair, settling previously with about half a dozen families what they were to provide, bring or send for the occasion, and having first obtained the owner Mr. Holbrook's consent, he residing only occasionally in a few of the rooms.

The morning was beautifully fine and the parties assembled between 2 and 3, archery commencing at 3.

Dinner took place at half past 5 and was placed on three long tables in the great dining room, and some extra tables in a room adjoining. Between 70 and 80 persons sat down to an excellent cold repast, the health of the Chauncey family and Mr. Holbrook being drunk with honours. Dancing commenced at half past 7 and continued until half past 10. Quadrilles, country dancing and

a little waltzing, which made the young folks all very happy. We
returned to Clay Hall just as the clock struck 12.'

If cajoled by an eligible young man they might take a cross-
country walk.

March 19, 1833

'It clearing away after luncheon time, Mr. Don Taylor persuaded
the young ladies to take a long walk. The party consisted of Miss
Bell, Emma, Juliana, Donothorne, Alfred and myself. Before we
got to the Lodge we had a shower, which presently blowing over,
the party were induced to proceed. We went to the handpost on
the Walkern Road and from there to Benington High Wood, nearly
half a mile beyond the Aston Four Want Way [cross-roads] to a
flock of sheep Mr. Taylor had observed in coming to Clay Hall
and wanted to inspect as he thought them good bred ones. After
looking at them he proposed taking the ladies in a straight line to
Benington church over ploughed fields and thro' gaps in hedges
and over deep ditches. Marvellous to relate, he accomplished his
wishes. The land was fortunately dry and with a few rents in the
ladies' clothes and veils, the destined spot was reached. We
showed them Mr. Proctor's fine large Malay fowls and his very
small beautiful bantams. They were much pleased with the latter.
We continued in the same way home across ploughed field and
hedge, the ladies being thoroughly tired with their expedition.'

But, except in high summer, the gravel walks at Clay Hall sufficed
for the Pryor ladies. The roads were too dirty to make walking on
them a pleasure; and the carriage was usually requisitioned for
visits to neighbours.

Elopements are not, perhaps, social occasions, but they must not
go unnoticed.

Not all Early Victorian young ladies were as biddable as 'Dear
Julia'. In December 1833 the disagreeable news reached Clay Hall
that John Izzard's niece Juliana Colston had eloped from Filkins
Hall, Oxon., her father's house.[1] 'No tidings had been heard of her
but it was suspected she had gone off with a young man of the
name of Allen (NOT a gentleman), who had the management of a
farm there for a widow woman. She was always as a girl, fond of
the society of servants and people in low situations. Her fortune,
which is large, left her by her grandfather Mr. Morris no doubt was
the attraction, as she was a foolish, disagreeable girl. It is a sad

[1] In the parish of Broadwell, near Burford.

affair.' Thus John Izzard, and he never mentioned her again although Morris married Louisa Mary Colston, her sister.

Filkins Hall was a long way off, but nine years later there was scandal in Baldock.

February 13, 1842

'The report confirmed of a projected elopement of my bro' Vickris's daughter Isaline. It was discovered just in time. A carriage and four horses were waiting with the person and two companions to take her off to London whence the pair were to have proceeded by Rail Road to Darlington and posted to Gretna Green. The adventurer resided as a lodger at Baldock for some time and had kept up a clandestine correspondence with the lady, who had agreed to the place and was dressed and ready for starting at 12 o'clock at night.'

A fortnight later the young lady was made a ward in Chancery to secure her from becoming, by any chance, wife to her gallant, 'a young man of bad character but of specious and good address.'

Alas! Not even the Court of Chancery can secure matrimonial happiness to the best endowed young lady. In 1845 she married the Rev. E. Burrage, 'a pleasant, well informed young man,' notes John Izzard, but of small fortune. He was, needless to say, a curate. (Three of Vickris's daughters married curates; the fourth was Alfred's bride.) When next mentioned he is 'a most unworthy member of the clergy'. In 1858 'Mrs. Burrage, poor woman, being in great distress wrote begging I would make her a present of £5. Her brothers have taken three of her children to their homes and are paying for their education. She has been most guilty and has suffered severely for it.'

She might have done better with her 'gallant'.

But excitements of this kind were rare. It was a placid life. Contentment had to be found in entertaining, and being entertained, by the nearer neighbours. Only when the moon was full would there be dinner parties when guests came from further afield. A good dinner, an hour or so spent by the gentlemen discussing the port, and by the ladies in a manner not recorded, then tea and music in the drawing room, was the order of the day. None of the Pryors was musical. The star performers of the neighbourhood were Mrs. Malet and Mrs. Surtees of Green Elms.

In summer there were visits to one another's gardens, when

refreshment might be confined to a slice of cake and a glass of wine, or a substantial luncheon might be served, as on June 10 1846—

'A party came to look over my garden and to lunch. I gave them cold fowls and some new pork in a beautiful dish of peas with madeira, sherry and champagne, with all of which the party were happily pleased. Lunched at 2 p.m. as the party were to dine afterwards at Mr. Harding's.

I rode to Weston afterwards, having received an invite to attend the school fete. I was there soon after 6. All the neighbouring clergy were there and a number of the gentry. The boys and girls all partook of tea and cake, had games after and behaved very well.'

It is difficult to decide whom to admire the more. The guests who faced undaunted the prospect of dinner at 6.30 p.m.; or the host, now 72, who mounted his pony after such a banquet. But at least he had no more to eat that day. He rode home at 8 p.m.

There is in the garden at Clay Hall an immemorial oak. Beneath its limbs many a luncheon and dinner party was held in his day.

June 24, 1850

'A party of fifteen at dinner including Mr. and Mrs. Malet, Mr. and Mrs. Harding, and Mr. and Mrs. Donne. The party all very happy. When the ladies withdrew they walked about the garden and shrubbery enjoying the fine moonlight until a little after 9 p.m. when the gentlemen joined them. Soon after we all sat down under the great oak and partook of two bowls of syllabub instead of tea and coffee. We had some delightful singing principally from Mrs. Malet, the full moon shining through the branches of the fine old oak.' (Syllabub is made with cream or milk mixed with wine into a soft curd.)

It would be pleasant to leave the subject of social life in Early Victorian times with this idyllic party. Accuracy, however, demands that attention should be drawn to the hazards which attended dining out at this time. 'The conviviality of the dining room always found a hearty response in the servants' hall', wrote Surtees in *Plain or Ringlets.*

John Izzard had two narrow escapes. On the first occasion, after a dinner at his daughter Mrs. Lafont's at Hinxworth, 'my son John's driver, Grub, ran the carriage against the stable gatepost, breaking the panels and the lamps, throwing both horses down,

one of them into the ditch, and breaking the bar. Fortunately the
carriage was in the act of coming round to pick up the family, and
was empty.'

On the second occasion he was not so fortunate,

July 26, 1853

'Being engaged to meet a large party at Sir Robert and Lady
Murray's, the invitation being for 4 o'clock for archery and 6 for
evening amusements and dancing afterwards, we set off at ½ past
5 in the clarence, thinking the grass would be too wet for much
archery. We found a very large party assembled, and long tables
laid out in the Armoury Hall covered with good things of which
we partook. Dancing followed and was kept up with great spirit
until 12 when supper was announced. We left about 1 o'clock and,
shocking to say, were overturned in our carriage very soon after,
narrowly escaped with our lives. But, thank God, we were mercifully saved without any bones broken, and altho' sadly bruised
were able to get home in another carriage.'

July 27, 1853

'I passed a very indifferent night, my leg being painful. We sent
off an express to Hitchin for Mr. Foster at 6 a.m. He arrived
before 9 and examined all of us that were injured more or less by
the terrible overthrow of our carriage, for which I must attribute
very great blame to our coachman (Beckwith). My wife, daughter
Eliza, and granddaughter Winifred escaped with severe bruises; my
daughter Emma had a narrow escape from injuring, if not breaking
the spinal bone at the back of her neck, and I of having again a
broken leg. We are most sincerely thankful to Almighty God for a
narrow escape from death. If the carriage had gone a few yards
further we would have been precipitated a great depth into the
water. We had great difficulty in getting out from the carriage.
Fortunately not being far from the house there was plenty of help
to extricate us and a spare carriage to take us home, our own being
nearly smashed.

Beckwith the coachman has his shoulder dislocated. The footman escaped unhurt.'

XI

LOCAL ADMINISTRATION

It has often been pointed out that the nation was administered by amateurs through the agency of Quarter Sessions and Parish Vestry. At this time there was hardly anything which a Frenchman or a Prussian would have recognised as an administration. In 1830 out of a Budget of 50 millions, only 6 were allocated to civilian purposes, and this had to cover the cost of the Crown, the civil service, the judges and expenses of collection.

Heavy responsibilities fell upon the Parish Vestry, and upon its Chairman, the incumbent of the parish. It would scarcely be an exaggeration to describe him as a functionary of government. For it was at the Vestry table, or more accurately, in the parlour of an adjacent inn (thither in many villages it was customary to adjourn, vestries being cold and comfortless) that the tremendous problems of Poor Relief were tackled. Even after the Poor Law Amendment Act of 1834 the Vestry still took a considerable part as agents for the Union. For roads, too, the Vestry was responsible. The Highways Act of 1835 substituted a rate for compulsory labour, but the responsibilities of the Vestry remained until 1888. Most of the existing roads in the countryside are on foundations of gravel or chalk put down by pauper labour.

John Izzard took his full share of the burden of local administration. When he lived at Baldock he sat as a member of the Select Vestry which was the governing body of the parish. An early entry in his diary must strike a chill into the heart of the reader who remembers his *Oliver Twist*.

March 27, 1829

'Attended vestry at Baldock called for the purpose of taking into consideration the propriety or necessity of building a workhouse capable of containing and employing all the paupers of the parish, the present one being quite inadequate for that purpose.

Several letters were read from overseers of other parishes where workhouses have been built which had proved a great saving to the parish, and the poor had been better provided for. One also from the Marquis of Salisbury in reply to a letter addressed to him by Mr. Geo. Hicks, strongly recommending the measure which he said has been of great service at Hatfield.

The result was a committee appointed to ascertain where a suitable plot of ground could be obtained and report to a future meeting.'

Each year in March the Select Vestry accounts had to be examined and passed. It was a tedious and chilly business, and every year it was protracted by 'the aggravating and ridiculous manner' in which a leading resident Mr. William Clarkson behaved.

John Izzard thus records the last occasion on which he attended the Baldock Select Vestry.

March 26, 1829

'Attended vestry at Baldock to examine and pass the half year's Select Vestry accounts. Mr. Clarkson kept us above three hours looking over every minutia and comparing the amount with the bills. He could not find anything to declaim against but an error of the casting up which amounted to 2/1½. It was bitter cold in the vestry room in the church and the parishioners were very indignant in being kept so long upon frivolous pretences . . .'

William Clarkson who was a distant relation of the Abolitionist, was a strong, if unpleasant, personality. It is, perhaps, not entirely fortuitous that the only iron railings in Baldock churchyard to escape requisitioning are those around his grave. By his will he left money for the upkeep of his monument with the proviso that the balance be paid to the rector for preaching an annual sermon on the uncertainty of life. Baldock being until recently on a bad section of the Great North Road, modern residents need no such reminders. On the last Sunday in February, however, Clarkson's favourite hymn 'Glory to Thee, my God, this night' is sung in Baldock church in memory of this cantankerous parishioner.

How law and order were maintained in the absence of a police force must always be something of a mystery. The parish constables, selected by the magistrates from a list of persons prepared by the Vestry, seem at Baldock to have been capable of determined action, and elsewhere in the County they cannot have been too inefficient, or there would not have been such strenuous opposition to the introduction of regular police, as will be described later.

January 11, 1830

'Lafont and Alfred breakfasted with Pollard on their way to the Quarter Sessions. The subject of principal interest to them as well as to ourselves was the trial of some of the worst characters of our parish of Baldock. One Lee alias Rags and Ruins for felony, the others for an assault on the constables at the Sun Public House of an aggravated nature. The former, in consequence of having been indicted for similar offences previously, was transported for life. The others imprisoned for different terms.'

January 27, 1830

'Vickris went to London today and I begged him to procure a piece of plate for John and William Little, they having taken Lee alias Rags and Ruins whilst having a stolen fowl in his possession, for which he was transported for life and the parish and neighbourhood rid of its most notorious character.'

It would appear from the fact that the arrest of Rags and Ruins was to be commemorated by a gift of plate, that the constables were men of some status, of a cut above the valiant Mr. Grummer of Ipswich who arrested Mr. Pickwick. At the same time one's sympathy goes out to Rags and Ruins, 'that notorious character', and it is to be hoped that his descendants flourish in the Antipodes.

It was not until he had taken up residence at Clay Hall that John Izzard was brought face to face with the problems of Poor Relief. Baldock was a small town, and there was a number of gentry and substantial tradesmen in the Vestry to take responsibility for decisions. But at Walkern there was only the rector and half a dozen farmers, and they were inclined to look to John Izzard for a lead.

Under the first Elizabeth each parish had been made responsible for its own poor. This was what Disraeli in his *Sybil* described as 'The parochial polity of the country which secures to every labourer a home.' The parish was responsible for seeing that the sick and aged, most of whom had spent their working lives within its boundaries, were not left to starve, and that work and wages were provided for those upon whom the misfortune of unemployment had fallen. 'The poor in a loomp is bad', said Tennyson's

Northern Farmer. It was the merit of the system that the poor were dealt with in 15,000 parishes by their neighbours to whom they were something more than an abstraction. The diary shows that John Izzard and most of his colleagues at Walkern Vestry table were inspired with a genuine sympathy for their unfortunate neighbours.

But in 1834 was passed the Poor Law Amendment Act which made the unit of administration of the law, not the parish, but the Union of several parishes. This Act may be said to have cast a chilly shadow over every cottage in the kingdom. It was implemented in Walkern parish, at least, with reluctance, for it destroyed the parochial polity which gave to every labourer a home. But however repellent it looked from the level of the Walkern Vestry table, the Act did make possible more economical and business-like administration of the Poor Law and was the first step in nationalising responsibility for the poor—a process which has only been completed since the Second World War.

The following entry illustrates the arrangements made to cope with unemployment in Walkern before the 1834 Act.

January 11, 1833

'Attended a Vestry afterwards called to divide the men out of regular work and heretofore barrowing gravel onto the roads, some of them rather loose characters. Adjourned from the church to the White Lyon. It was finally settled that each occupier should employ at the rate of 2½ men to every £50 he was rated at, deducting tithe. The names were put down of all the married and single men of the parish. The names of those out of work were written on pieces of paper, and each drew the requisite number to make their quota right.

As I had three or four men who it was stated did not belong to the parish I had to make up five, some of whom were young fellows of doubtful character. I must discharge some of those at present working with me who do not belong, and employ those I have drawn some way or another as I wished the plan to be adopted.'

January 12, 1833

'Informed Warner the man who assists in the garden that, as several men belonging to the parish were to be sent for me to take on, I could not employ him any longer as he belongs to the parish of Wymondley; told Gayewood the other man who belongs to Benington I would only employ him another week.'

These arrangements were not successful, as 'Mr. Rayment the greatest farmer in the parish', who had only four men in his employ belonging to the parish, whereas he ought to have had a dozen at least, refused to co-operate. He employed men because they had certain skills, not because they lived in a particular place. He had sooner pay rates than employ men who had probably not been out of work without good reason. Moreover, John Izzard admits that the 'arrangement, like most plans, had its concurrent evil, in making the men indolent and slovenly in their work and from the knowledge that they must be employed, conduct themselves as they would.'

It was resolved, therefore, to employ the surplus labour 'in the improvement of the roads—not at a degrading, ruinously low rate of wages—the men having been discharged thro' no fault of their own, but so as to enable them to earn the same as they would in the regular routine of farm labour.'

The Act of 1834 put an end to comfortable arrangements of this kind. No more would the unemployed poor be found work in their home parish. Cottage homes would have to be closed, and man and wife with their wailing children would have to trudge off to Hertford, there to live, in separation, at opposite ends of the Poor Law Bastille. No wonder John Izzard, 'our rector', and Farmers Rowlatt and Stacey fought hard to avoid it.

For some years after the Act of 1834 Walkern seems to have been prosperous enough. But in 1842 unemployment began to assume serious proportions. Most of the farmers were prepared to take on additional men and thereby save a rate having to be raised.

November 15, 1842

'I was at Walkern at 10 to attend a vestry called respecting the employment of the poor. I took the Chair in Mr. Harding's absence. All the farmers that attended expressed their willingness to take their quota. But Mr. Rayment and one or two others are deficient. The former is stated to have only one man belonging to the parish in his employ. I undertook to write to him.'

November 17, 1842

'Rode down to Walkern to attend the adjourned Vestry, Mr.

Harding in the Chair. The principal farmers brought the list of the number of men in their employ, but no Mr. Rayment made his appearance. Those present said they must discharge some of their men if Mr. Rayment acted so much in opposition to the rest of the parish. A wish was expressed to give him another chance.

Mr. and Mrs. Harding lunched with us and I walked with the former to Walkern Park to try and persuade Mr. Rayment to employ some of the Walkern labourers. But our labour was in vain.'

December 8, 1842

'Attended a Vestry called for this day as I wished to see the rate for the relief of the poor properly signed by the churchwardens and overseer. Mr. Harding being from home I officiated as Chairman.

Several labourers applied for work, but as Mr. Rayment still refuses to take his share, they, if they cannot get work, will have to apply to the Union.'

Thus, thanks to the obstinacy of Farmer Rayment, Walkern parish came into line with its neighbours, and the poor were abandoned to the tender mercies of the Hertford Union and the Poor Law Amendment Act.

The following entry is typical of several made over the years.

February 23, 1843

'I attended a Vestry at Walkern church to consider about an order of Magistrates to remove a woman of the name of Pegrom and her son aged about two years from Aspenden to Walkern, her father and mother having last lived at Westmill. On searching the old parish chest we found an order of removal in February 1818 for her father and mother to Walkern. Mr. Stacey remembers their having been relieved at Walkern. Therefore we cannot appeal against the order.'

The principle that a person who had become, or was likely to become, a charge on the rates, could be sent back to his home parish, survived the Act of 1834—indeed, it was maintained until 1876, and its ghost walked until recently, since long after it had ceased to be the practice to move the pauper's person, it continued to be necessary to charge the Union responsible; and the maintenance of the accounts provided a harmless, if futile, occupation for scores of Local Government servants. Litigation between parishes—from which Walkern on this occasion wisely refrained—was a God-send to the Bar of the day, and a source of amusement to such of the Vestry as possessed a sea-lawyerly turn of mind.

December 14, 1840

'Attended the Vestry, our rector in the Chair. Agreed to place young Aylott as apprentice to Spriggins at £13—10 or £15, I forget which. The money to be raised by subscription, most of which is subscribed, Mr. Rayment still refusing to give anything.'

The apprenticing of parish children was one of the duties of the Vestry. The old-fashioned preferred to raise money by subscription rather than by rates.

While the Vestry were responsible for the other roads within the parish, the main road connecting it with the world, that which ran south to Watton and north to Ashwell, was a turnpike road, managed by a Trust of which John Izzard was Chairman. Every parishioner was under legal obligation to do six days labour on the roads in the year, or to pay someone else to do so. This duty applied also to turnpike roads. It will, perhaps, not be a surprise to read the following entry.

January 28, 1833

'Mr. Rayment of Walkern Park Farm objected to doing the usual duty on the Turnpike Road between Walkern and Watton. He attended, but the Trustees told him that they could not act in it now being only a committee, but that if he refused to do his duty they would at a general meeting take the necessary steps concerning it. Mr. Meetkirk, Mr. Baker, Mr. Green and myself present.'

However, the Highways Act of 1835 abolished the duty to labour on the roads. The Trustees, therefore, can have had the pleasure of compelling Mr. Rayment to furnish labourers on the Watton road for only one more year.

The road seems to have been prudently managed. The only difficulty which John Izzard experienced was in getting the bridge over which the road passes at Walkern Mill repaired.

April 4, 1848

'I went in the Britzska to Hertford taking Mr. Pollard and Mr. Harding to attend at the Quarter Sessions to endeavour to get an

order for repairing and widening the bridge at Walkern, it being a
County bridge. But the Bench would order nothing more than
£20 without it going through the usual course of being certified by
two magistrates and previous notice given etc. They recommended
it being done by subscription of gentlemen in the neighbourhood.'

April 5, 1848

'Attended a meeting of the Trustees of the Watton Road. I made
a statement of the dangerous state of our bridge at Walkern and
asked for the sum of £20 to be appropriated. But on referring to
our Act of Parliament it was found that the sum of £70 allowed
annually must be laid out on the repair of the Road, and that the
bridge being a county bridge, the County were bound to keep it
in repair. Our best and only plan would appear to be to go through
the usual course of a statement being sent to the Clerk of the
Peace, a month at least before the Quarter Session, signed by two
magistrates, of the state of the bridge; for him to insert it in the
advertisement of the County Business to be taken into consideration by the Bench of Magistrates at the following Quarter
Sessions.'

Until the Local Government Act 1888 brought the County
Council into existence, the County Authority responsible for
Highways was Quarter Sessions. Nothing more is heard about the
bridge. Presumably Quarter Sessions paid for the repairs. Had
John Izzard done so he would certainly have mentioned the fact.

The tolls for the road were let every year to the best bidder. On
one occasion there was some difficulty in doing so.

September 29, 1836

'This being the day appointed for letting the tolls on the Watton
Trust at the Saracen's Head Inn at Ware, I rode over on the roan
horse. A large concourse of toll hirers and a posse of their friends,
some of them most shabby looking fellows, attended. The tolls
were put up at the sum given for them the last two years viz.
£1,105, and a spirited contest apparently took place, and they
were run up to £1,145, the bidding being by £5, when a shabby
looking fellow bid £5 in addition, making in all £1,150. After
the sand had run out of the glass three times he was declared the
lessee.

The other bidders came forward to receive their deposits back,
which all lay marked upon the table when the last bidder who

gave his name as Smith of St. Albans took up his £20 and rushed out of the room. Mr. Cobham who had taken charge of the deposits not being aware of what he was about, it was found he had decamped. He was a fellow employed by some of the parties to run up the others, without any intention of hiring the tolls, knowing the worst would be the forfeit of £20 deposit. But by this manoeuvre he got away without forfeiting it.

The circumstances caused great confusion. The room was cleared and the Trustees came to the determination of putting up the tolls again and making the deposit £50. Some sort of understanding took place between the parties whilst they withdrew and £1,120 was the highest bidding that could be got; and the last Renters were declared the lessees at that sum.'

It is likely that the money raised was used to the best advantage. Sir James McAdam, the son of the inventor of macadamisation of roads, was the technical adviser of the Watton Road Trust.

Sanitation engaged the attention of the Walkern Vestry, probably for the first time in its long history of 1848. In 1827 John Izzard had recorded the death of his wife's sister Mrs. George Pemberton 'after a few hours illness at Nousserabad by that scourge of India, the cholera Morbus.' He little thought that 1831–2 Britain would see an outbreak of this horrifying plague.

November 13, 1831
'Went to church morning and evening. A form of prayer being sent out to the Clergy in all parts of the kingdom to read on account of the apprehended calamity of Cholera Morbus, the same was read morning and afternoon supplicating the Divine Mercy to avert the Pestilence.'

The pestilence was stayed at some distance from Walkern on this occasion, and he wrote—

April 14, 1833
'This being the day appointed for a General Thanksgiving to Almighty God for the cessation of the Cholera, we attended both morning and afternoon service at Walkern.'

But in 1848 cholera returned to the attack, and this time with such virulence that rich and poor, town and country, all felt themselves in the presence of this dreadful antagonist. Indeed, it may be said that the fear of cholera was the beginning of wisdom in Britain, so far as matters sanitary are concerned. Obstruction to measures conducive to public health was swept aside in face of an enemy which made no distinction between the 'Lower Orders' and the 'Quality'. There resulted a series of Public Health Acts, hesitant at first, but after the third visit of cholera in 1854, resolute and business like.

As the disease crept steadily nearer, from London to Hertford, and from Hertford to Baldock, Parish Vestries on instructions from London endeavoured to improve sanitary conditions.

November 6, 1848

'I attended a Vestry soon after 11 this morning to consider putting in force the sanitary measures recommended by Government and sent down to the Guardians of the parishes through the kingdom for warding off as much as possible an attack of cholera. There were only three of us present—Mr. Harding, Mr. Rowlatt our guardian, and myself. We made out a list of names for a committee of inspection, informed them of it, and adjourned the vestry to the 13 November to hear their report.'

November 13, 1848

'Attended a Vestry. The persons appointed last week, having merely taken a cursory view, were at this vestry directed to make a general inspection throughout the village and to give notice that if all the nuisances they remarked were not removed in the course of the week, the names of those who did not comply would be reported. A week was to be given for the removal of general nuisances and a fortnight for the erection of privies.'

Evidently the use of latrines was by no means general at Walkern, and it is likely that Parson Crabbe's description of an earlier East Anglian village might well apply here.

> Between the roadway and the walls, offence
> Invades all eyes and strikes at every sense:
> There lies obscene at every door,
> Heaps from the hearth and sweepings from the floor,
> And day by day the mingled masses grow,
> As sinks are disembogued and kennels flow,
> There hungry dogs from hungry children steal.
> There pigs and chickens quarrel for a meal;
> There dropsied infants wail without redress
> And all is want and woe and wretchedness.

On the other hand, the absence of sanitation may not have been as obvious to the casual visitor as it was to the country priest, and

Walkern may well have appeared, as another English village did, to the kindly American eyes of Washington Irving.

> The trim hedge, the grass plot before the (cottage) door, the little flower bed bordered with snug box, the woodbine trained up against the wall, and hanging its blossoms about the lattice, the pot of flowers in the window, the holly, providentially planted about the house, to cheat the winter of its dreariness, and to throw a semblance of green summer to cheer the fireside; all these bespeak the influence of taste, flowing down from high sources, and pervading the lowest levels of the public mind. If ever Love, as poets sing, delights to visit a cottage, it must be the cottage of an English peasant.
>
> *(Rural Life in England.)*

January 10, 1849

'There have been six deaths by cholera in the Gaol at Hertford and in other places it has become serious.'

October 7, 1849

'Son Morris drove up and dined with us. He brings a sad account of several cases of cholera fatal in a few hours, in Norton Street.'

November 3, 1849

'The cholera still remains very fatal at Baldock, several more deaths in Norton Street having taken place there in the last few days.'

But, within a week, with the advent of frosty weather, the pestilence had ceased its ravages.

November 13, 1849

'Mr. Harding called and brought a paper respecting the Orphan Asylum at Wanstead particularly adapted for taking orphans of parents dying of cholera, and hoping that a subscription might be made on Friday next after the morning service, as it is a day set apart for thanksgiving to God for the great decrease of that scourge which it is calculated has been the death of 15,000 persons in Great Britain.'

November 15, 1849

'This being the day appointed by Government for thanksgiving to be made to Almighty God for the great decrease of the cholera which has carried off many thousands, the day was strictly observed. The working men were set at liberty to attend both morning and evening service at church. Our church, I was glad to see, was quite full in the morning and the congregation very attentive. There was a collection made after morning service.'

That, so far as he was concerned, was the end of cholera. The outbreak of 1854 finds no mention in his diary. He did not, however, forget the importance of sanitation as the entry for 9 July 1856 shows.

'I went down to Walkern to view the proposed plan for making a covered drain in the village from Mr. Rowlatt's to Mr. Stockbridge's. Adjourned to the White Lion where Mr. Harding, Mr. Rowlatt and Mr. Beecroft who had viewed the place agreed to have the drain made. The trustees of the road pay part of the expense, and the proprietors of the houses in front of which the drain runs, pay a proportion likewise.'

The ravages of 'the sickness that destroyeth in the noon-day' had not been in vain.

But before the subject is left it is perhaps relevant to notice the sanitary arrangements at Clay Hall. When the Pryors moved in, there is mention of privies, but not of water closets. On 17 August 1842—

'Mr. Newton of Hitchin came over to examine the water closets which act badly and require setting thoroughly to rights. I inspected the whole from the force pump to the different cisterns. Grove the carpenter is to prepare what is wanted for them by Monday when they commence operations.'

Water closets at this time were defective as the joints of the pipes were not sufficiently tight; foul air escaped, and in many cases there was no window (owing to the window tax) and not even a ventilating shaft as the judges had ruled that this must be taxed as a window.

There is only one other entry on this subject.

June 18, 1849

'I had Geo. Munt the bricklayer over this morning to consult about making a cess pool 10 feet deep and 6 foot diameter on the opposite side of the road to where the drains from the house and offices discharge their contents into the open ditch on the garden side close by the back entrance to the house and stable yard. We propose having a barrel arch across the road through the bank into the pasture field and to have the cess pool in the field and to have a manure pump to raise the sewerage so as to irrigate the pasture.'

The south wing of Clay (now Walkern) Hall built by John Izzard Pryor 1827–28

John Izzard Pryor's residence at Baldock, The Brewery House. The frontage on the High Street

(facing page 103)

XII

COUNTY BUSINESS

John Izzard was usually selected to sit on the Grand Jury at the Hertford Assizes. The duty of this august body, composed of the magnates of the County, was to examine the cases put down for trial and to throw out those in which there appeared to be insufficient evidence to warrant putting the accused into court. Of the Assizes of March 1831 he writes—

'Went in the carriage to Hertford to the Assizes, having been summoned on the Grand Jury. Arrived there at 12 o'clock, just looked into the Great Church where the Judges were attending prayer and the Assize sermon by Mr. Webb chaplain to Baron Dimsdale the High Sheriff for this year.

About half past 12 went into court soon after the judges had entered, answered to my name when called over in the Commission of the Peace and also as one of the Grand Jury. Accepted the invitation to dine with the judges tomorrow, signing my name with many others for that purpose, and putting a shilling in a glove handed round as a check, I suppose, to the names.

There were 26 of us on the Grand Jury. Mr. Meetkirk Foreman with Mr. Daniel the Recorder sitting next him.

I dined with most of the gentlemen composing the Grand Jury at the High Sheriff's table in the Town Hall.'

Surtees in *Handley Cross* describes a Grand Jury going into court 'the rushing in of a white-wanded bailiff exclaiming "Gen'lemen of the grand jury wanted i' kurt" startles a room full of rosy-gilled, John Bull-looking squires, in full cry after various subjects—hay, harvest, horses, hounds—who forthwith . . . scramble into a spacious pen of a box just as the judge is . . . taking his seat for the day. Silence being at length obtained, the commission of the peace is called over, and Her Majesty's gracious proclamation against vice and immorality (is) read, the loose hands nudging each other at appropriate passages . . . The magnates of the Grand

Jury box then answer their names and are sworn, the florid verbiage of the foreman's oath contrasting with the bald plainness of the "you say ditto to that" of the rest.'

Although he was in the Commission of the Peace for the County, John Izzard never took his seat on the Bench. This, however, does not seem to have prevented his attending Quarter Sessions when administrative matters were under discussion. The sort of business which was transacted on such occasions can be seen from that dealt with in October 1836.

'Reached Hertford at 10 and very soon after went into court, Lord Dacre Chairman and the business just commenced.

There was the largest attendance of magistrates that had been known for a long time, several important matters being likely to be discussed.

The first that came was Mr. Lloyd's application for a retiring pension, being late chaplain to the Gaol—not allowed. 2nd Alteration of the gaol to admit more persons working on the treadmill—not agreed on account of the great expense as estimated. Allowing expenses to Inspectors for looking into the state of the weights and measures in the different parts of the country, taking the weights and measures with them. Rates of allowance 10d per diem and 1/- per mile to the different places and back again.'

Four years later Quarter Sessions did, indeed, have an important decision to make, whether or not the Rural Police Act should be extended to the County. It might have been expected that this measure would have been welcomed by the property-owning classes who had had to depend heretofore on the uncertain ministrations of the parish constables Dogberry and Verges. But such was not the case. The Tory view in the County seems to have been that the law-abiding rural areas would be taxed to provide protection to town dwellers.

October 26, 1840

'This being the day fixed for the County Magistrates to decide whether or not it is desirable for the New Police Establishment to take place in the County in lieu of the old Constabulary Regime, a very full attendance was expected. My son John took Mr. Morell and my bro' Vickris in his carriage, they being all magistrates and I took Mr. Veasey in son Morris's briskza as he could not conveniently attend. Mr. Phelips of Briggins Park opened the business and produced his estimate of the probable expense, which he put at between £5,000 and £6,000 or rather more than the County Rate raises at about 3d in the £. Mr. Phelips did not deliver his sentiments very ably, but he had an admirable seconder Mr. Blake of Danesbury who made an excellent speech in favour of the measure. The Marquis of Salisbury in opposition to it broke completely down and cut a poor figure. Mr. Heathcote also spoke against the measure and what he did say was much to the purpose and well delivered. All but acting magistrates were requested to withdraw and a show of hands took place, there being 40 for it and 16 against it, as I heard, for I was one of those who withdrew. The villages and rural areas will have to bear too great a proportion of the expense in comparison with large towns. Before I heard so much as I did this day I was myself against it.'

November 23, 1840

'This was the day for discussing the New Constabulary Police Bill after the Committee had delivered their calculations of the expense attendant thereon.

A report was brought in by the Committee. The expense, according to their estimate amounts to the sum of £5,400 or thereabouts per annum, exceeding the County Rate by about £1,000. The Committee called upon the Court to confirm the resolution passed at the last meeting. But on Mr. Heathcote getting up and showing the very great unfairness of so large an expenditure falling on those parts of the County which did not require the extension of the Police Measure to them, and also the probability that the expense would be infinitely greater than the Committee had stated, he entreated the magistrates to pause before they gave their approbation to so momentous a measure. His speech made a great impression and many who had voted for it altered their minds. After a great deal of discussion a Mr. Tolly rose who had been an advocate for it before, and said that he should move an amendment that the adoption of the measure should be referred for the consideration of the Bench at the next Epiphany Sessions, which was ultimately agreed to.'

January 11, 1841

'A heavy fall of snow during the night which together with the drifted snow of yesterday blocked up the lanes. Son Morris set off on horseback, and Lafont, for the Quarter Sessions at Hertford,

Lafont returned late, took his dinner by himself and joined our circle at dessert. He brings word the adoption of the new Constabulary Force for the County was carried but only by a majority of 4, there being 34 for, and 30 against.'

February 22, 1841
'This being the adjourned Quarter Sessions at Hertford the discussion respecting the New Police Force was expected to be very much opposed, it being very unpopular in this neighbourhood and several other places. I had fixed to attend. The business came on at 12 exactly and a very strong debate it was. The party that had proposed the measure concluded it settled and that the Chief of Police was to be appointed this day; not so the opponents of the measure who presented petitions numerously signed against it. On Mr. Philips making his motion an amendment was moved. After a long debate whether an amendment could be put, the Chairman Lord Dacre decided not. That being the case Lord Salisbury moved that the Court do now adjourn; and on the court being cleared, only acting magistrates voting, the number for the adjournment was 51 and against it 42. Son John and Vickris went up together and voted for the adjournment.'

April 7, 1841
'Received a letter this morning from Lord Salisbury requesting I would qualify as a magistrate to oppose the introduction of the Rural Police in the county. I replied by this night's post, informing his lordship I was sorry I could not accede to his wishes as I had been solicited several years.'

John Izzard makes no further reference to the matter. Evidently the 'Ayes' had their way, and the County Police came into existence. Their early years were difficult. It was not to be expected that magistrates who had resolutely opposed their formation would tend to view their activities with an unbiased eye. The ordinary villagers also were inclined to resent their intrusion. They had got on very well under the understanding, and not too zealous, care of the parish constable. He was, after all, one of themselves. They did not welcome the policeman, this stranger in their midst. He represented a distant and unknown authority over whom not even squire or parson had much influence.

The story of the Walkern village row of 1848 illustrates the lack of understanding and confidence between the Early Victorian police and the public.

January 31, 1848

'A great row took place in the village this evening in consequence of a gang of working men going about with rough music, intending to give a bad woman a ducking. She was a notoriously bad woman, and in the family way, and was saying she would swear the child to someone though she confessed she had been connected with many.'

February 1, 1848

'Three of the policemen that were engaged last night in taking into custody a riotous mob that were parading the village with rough music were very much cut about. Warrants are granted for several to appear before the Bench of magistrates at Hitchin tomorrow. It has been an old custom to go to the house of a notorious character with rough music, as they call it. They say that they should not have made any riot, had not the police set on them. It is a sad business and I think several will be committed.'

February 13, 1848

'We went in the omnibus to church in the afternoon. Fredk. read the prayers and Mr. Harding preached the sermon, but before he began half a score of the labouring men left the church as they thought he had been instrumental in sending some of the rioters to gaol.'

March 2, 1848

'A dismal drizzling rainy day throughout. I went in the carriage to Hertford, arriving at 10. I went into court directly to hear the trial of the seven Walkern men. It came on at 11 o'clock and lasted the whole day, Mr. Justice Coleridge presiding. There were three counsel employed for the prisoners and many witnesses were examined. But all were found guilty except Pettit who keeps a beer shop. The others were sentenced to six months imprisonment, it being a serious matter in the eye of the law to assault the police, and had it been brought in by the jury an assault with intent to commit some bodily harm they might possibly have been transported. As it was the inhabitants considered it a heavy punishment as the police did not behave well and caused them to be much excited.'

XIII

VISITS TO LONDON

For many years John Izzard was accustomed to visit London twice annually in order to receive his dividends at the Bank of England, on his own behalf, and on behalf of relations living at a distance from London, and to make purchases and settle accounts. To the end of his life he paid London tradesmen by cash, and when age and infirmity prevented him going in person, he would send his wife and 'Dear Fred' to do so on his behalf. That great benefactor of the human race, the man who first crossed a cheque, did not do so until towards the end of the diarist's life, and until he had done so cheques had only a limited use.

During the lifetime of his brother Robert, who died in 1839, John Izzard usually stayed with him at the Brewery House in Brick Lane. But he also occasionally stayed with his widowed sister-in-law Mrs. Thomas Pryor at Hampstead. (A block of flats called 'The Pryors' occupies the site of the house and garden.) But Hampstead did not count as being in London.

December 18, 1829

'We all returned to dine at half past 4 as we had fixed to go to Covent Garden to see Miss Fanny Kemble performing the part of Belvedere in Otway's Tragedy of Venice Preserved. Betsy Morris never having been at either of the Theatres and expressing how delighted she should be to make one, I went to Hampstead in the stage at 12 and returned with her, reaching Brick Lane in excellent time for her to dress before dinner. We went in good time after dinner in two glass coaches. The party all enjoyed Miss Kemble's acting. I returned with my wife as soon as the tragedy was over. The rest of the party stayed to see the after-piece.'

He refers to 'either theatre' because, until the Theatres Act 1843, the Haymarket and Drury Lane had a monopoly of legitimate drama (i.e. plays without introduction of music) and Covent Garden was usually (but not always) given up to opera.

108

Although not musical he was a frequent attendant at the opera.

May 22, 1827

'Having engaged a box at the Opera a week ago we went there this evening to see Medea in which Madame Pasta is astonishingly great. All our party were highly delighted. The house was extremely full. Our box was No.XX on the first or Pit Tier, an excellent situation for seeing and hearing. But I think one tier higher preferable on account of the conversation of those who stand up in the pit being occasionally an interruption.'

Those who 'stood up' in the pit were a mixture of the riff-raff of the town and young bloods. They were apt to be rowdy and were one of the reasons for the disrepute in which the theatre stood.

A year later 14 May, 1828, he records a milestone in the development of the theatre.

'Engaged seats in the third row at the Opera provisionally, that is, in case Mlle. Sontag performed on Saturday next, the first three rows in the Pit being by a new arrangement converted into locked up seats or stalls, at an additional price viz. 12/6 each, in consequence of the great number of people wishing to hear Mlle. Sontag sing who is all the rage now.'

May 17, 1828

'Engaged in the west end of the town in the morning. Returned to Brick Lane to dine and dressed to accompany the ladies to the Opera.

The seats were excellent and reserved for us. The House extremely crowded. We were all highly delighted with Mlle. Sontag who sang in her best manner and was most rapturously applauded. She is very good-looking, very animated when she is singing, and altho' not perfectly beautiful you cannot but be prepossessed in her favour. Her looks are very sweet and her physiognomy bespeaks great good nature. Light blue eyes, fair complexion, with a beautiful hand, arm and foot. We all left much pleased with her performance.'

It was not music which took John Izzard to the opera.

He also occasionally patronised the ballet.

February 6, 1834

'We went in the evening to Covent Garden Theatre, having

previously engaged four stalls Nos. 1 to 4 in the Dress Circle. It was the second night of the performance of a grand new spectacle or Ballet called *The Revolt of the Harem.*

The scenery was extremely beautiful and the dancing very good indeed, the latter not quite to the taste of the ladies. The military performances of the female army were astonishing. The house was very full and the piece was rapturously applauded.'

As he grew older John Izzard's interest in theatre and opera waned. But he did go to hear the celebrated Jenny Lind.

August 2, 1847 (in London)

'Went in a cab to the Four Swans. Left my carpet bag there and proceeded to the West End, paying some bills on the way. Finding the celebrated Jenny Lind was to perform at the Queen's Theatre in the Haymarket tomorrow I called at Evers Library and was fortunate enough to engage a stall in a good situation in the fourth row from the orchestra for which I paid £2—12—6. They have made as much as £5—5—0 in the season.'

August 3, 1847

'Dressed for the opera and was there quarter before 8. Made my way to the stall I had engaged and bought a book of the Sonambula, the piece to be performed which began soon after 8. The house was crowded to excess, stalls, pit, boxes and galleries all being full. I was highly delighted with Jenny Lind, the great attraction of the season. Her singing is the sweetest I ever heard, her acting good. She was not looking her best but exerted herself to the utmost, this being nearly the last of her performances. The ballet was also good, Taglione and Cerito performing.'

Only on one occasion did John Izzard visit the Drury Lane theatre.

January 29, 1830

'Took a mutton stake *(sic)* at half past 4 and went to Drury Lane. Keen was to perform as Othello and Young as Iago. I thought Young was the superior actor, the villain Iago being portrayed in a striking manner by him. Miss Phillips as Desdemona had not much to do.'

In place of the cinema Early Victorian London had the diorama or panorama. From John Izzard's point of view these were chiefly useful as a form of diversion for little Fred when he stayed in

London on his way back to Twyford or Winchester. In 1831 Fred's failing morale was powerfully supported by a visit to the panoramas of Calcutta and Quebec in Leicester Square. But occasionally John Izzard himself would patronise this form of entertainment. In 1848 while waiting for the Botanic Gardens in Regent's Park to open he visited the Colosseum in order to take a view of Paris by Moonlight. The Colosseum which stood on the site of Cambridge Terraces was Decimus Burton's greatest work. It was built purely for the exhibition of Dioramas and was on a huge scale, the dome being slightly larger than that of St. Paul's. Samuel Rogers said it was finer than anything in Italy. It failed, however, to impress John Izzard, who hurried back to admire the roses directly the gardens opened.

Exeter Change in the Strand was another favourite of Fred. He was 'much pleased with the collection of wild beasts and foreign birds.' The roars of the lions and tigers, however, frightened horses in the Strand, and there was general relief when this Zoo, after a short sojourn in the Royal Mews where the National Gallery now stands, was banished to the suburbs. Fred transferred his affections to the Zoological Gardens in Regent's Park in 1830. In August 1837, at the end of the Bartlemy holidays, he visited Astley's, a combination of theatre and circus wherein were enacted Macbeth, the battle of Waterloo, or the Burning of Moscow, done as equestrian tragedy, the maxim being 'to cut the cackle and come to the "Osses".' It brought him good luck. Awaiting John Izzard at Brick Lane was a letter from Dr. Moberley giving notice 'of a week's longer holiday at the desire of the Queen'. (It was Coronation Year.)

Mrs. Pryor and Emma, and Juliana until her marriage, usually accompanied John Izzard to London when he went there in the early summer. Besides shopping and drawing dividends, they were energetic sightseers.

May 26, 1830
'Set off for the Regent's Park to see the beasts, birds etc. at the gardens belonging to the Zoological Society. A heavy storm of rain prevented us seeing the whole of them. From there we went to Crockford's in St. James Street which is shown to those who have an order from a member of the Establishment which my brother Robert had. We were much gratified with the grandeur and tout

ensemble of the principal suite of rooms fitted up in the most superb and expensive manner. The outlay for the buildings, fittings up and furniture the person who attended us said cost £140,000.

We then went to hear the Prague Minstrels at the Egyptian Hall, and at 10 o'clock went by appointment of Mr. Will Lee to the Athenaeum, which is now lighted up twice a week for company to see and promenade about that are introduced by the members. We passed an hour very pleasantly there.'

Crockford's was a gambling establishment to which only the smartest and wealthiest resorted. The Egyptian Hall was renowned for conjuring shows.

Whatever else they did, the Pryors rarely failed to attend 'The Exhibition' as they called it. (By this was meant the summer show at the Royal Academy.) And they were equally zealous in their attendance at the Horticultural Society's Principal Days at the Gardens at Chiswick.

May 21, 1830

'Accompanied my wife and daughters and son Morris to the Exhibition at Somerset House. Stopped there nearly two hours. The paintings not so good as last year.' After handing the ladies into a glass coach (as they had several shops to visit), he went off in his unselfconscious manner to collect a bill for beer from a resident of Harley Street and having got a cheque for £36, 'rejoined the ladies at the Water Colour Exhibition, and from there went to see the solar microscope in Regent Street with which we were much pleased.'

'With an annual pilgrimage to the Academy . . . the Englishman of the first half of the nineteenth century had done his duty by art,' remarks Paul Oppe in *Early Victorian England*. This was true enough of John Izzard, but to do him justice, with the Academy must be included one of the two Water Colour Societies. 'Their Exhibitions were held at the same time as the Academy's and with similar pomp . . . Thackeray notes the invariable presence of bishops and pretty girls.' (Paul Oppe.)

Having attended these two functions, and noted in his diary that 'the pictures are not so good as usual' John Izzard bothered his head no more with art. He never mentions buying a picture, other than portraits of himself, his wife and his hunter.

But if he looked at pictures as a duty, he attended flower shows for pleasure. The Horticultural Society then held its shows at Chiswick (hardly a convenient site one would think: it took over an hour to drive there). But he rarely omitted to attend, and when he could not do so he would often mention the date, showing that it was not out of mind.

The first show he described was on—

June 27, 1829

'Soon after 12 Mrs. Vickris, Mr. Aveling, Bro' Robert and myself set off in Mrs. V. P.'s carriage to the Horticultural Gardens at Chiswick, this being the day of the fete. No expense had been spared to accommodate and entertain the public, and about 4,000 tickets had been issued at a guinea each. We arrived at half past 1 and promenaded the gardens which were in beautiful order. Marquees and tents set out in different parts of the lawn; two very fine bands playing and platforms prepared for those who chose to dance. We then viewed the show of fruit which was all arranged in a long covered way exhibiting the most beautiful description of Pines, Grapes of all the finest descriptions, Peaches, Nectarines, Melons, Strawberries and Cherries, two bunches of grapes grown by Hartopp Esq. of Four Oak Hall exceeded any I had ever seen. Refreshments were laid out on long tables under cover to which the company resorted until 3 when the rain descended in torrents, almost flooded the gardens and spoilt the whole thing. The ladies being beautifully dressed had many of their bonnets and dresses completely spoiled and were obliged to walk to their carriages all in the wet. Nothing could be done. The bands could not play and the gentlemen got wet through and through waiting upon the ladies.'

Twelve years later, the scene was not very different.

June 12, 1841

'We set off at 2 o'clock in a glass coach, and arrived there at half past 3, the latter part of the way not being able to move faster than a foot's pace owing to the immense number of carriages. It was bitter cold altho' fortunately without rain. The number of well dressed persons, male and female, particularly the latter, was very great, above 8,000 it was said. I took care of Emma and Alfred took my wife and Juliana under his care.

The Show of roses and geraniums was magnificent, and all the choice flowers and orchidaceous plants in the greatest perfection.'

His last visit was paid in 1854 when he was 80. On that occasion he travelled by omnibus from Trafalgar Square, and got there in an hour. It was a memorable day since Arthur Pryor, his nephew, won a gold medal for fruit.

Three days later he attended a rival Show in the Botanic Gardens in Regent's Park. It started to rain, and it took them 1½ hours to get to their clarence, so ill organised was the traffic. When he expressed a wish to attend next year, 'it was judged not prudent.'

The London of John Izzard's latter years is one which still lingers in human memory. He used to stay at the King's Cross Hotel and make his way about by cab and omnibus. When he first began his diary, if he did not walk, he engaged a glass coach. This Surtees describes in *Ask Mamma* as 'a better sort of hackney coach with a less filthy driver'. But the standards of cleanliness of even the glass coach varied.

May 19, 1833

'The glass coach we hired was so bad and so dirty that my bro' Robert sent to Croft's in Whitechapel to know if we could have a good one from them. They sent word we should have a very nice one which accordingly came. The ladies were much pleased with it.'

The diaries in which John Izzard recorded his entries contain, as their successors do nowadays on a more modest scale, information of general interest, including London coach and watermen's fares. The principle which governed fares was the further the distance travelled, the greater the charge per mile. A mile cost 1/-; three miles 3/6d. The same principle applied when the vehicle was hired by the hour.

John Izzard only once engaged 'oars' in order to go to the Red House, Battersea, on an occasion which will be described later The days of the waterman were already numbered. In 1836 the table of watermen's fares disappears from the diary preface. The improvement of street surfaces, and the growing pollution of the river are often said to have put the waterman out of business. But, in fact, he succumbed to mechanisation. His place was taken by the fleet of little iron steamers which plied up and down the river between Richmond and Greenwich, covering their crowded

passengers with smuts, stranding them on mud banks, appearing to
be on the verge of explosion, and otherwise comporting themselves
so as to provide material for the pages of *Punch* in the forties and
fifties of the century.

But except for trips to Greenwich, John Izzard does not seem to
have used the steamers. They were probably popular with men
less well endowed.

July 17, 1838

'Proceeded with my two bro's above bridge and got into a
Greenwich steamer, about ten of our party meeting them at the
same time. Started at quarter past 5 and reached the Crown and
Sceptre at 6 and sat down to an excellent dinner. The fish was
excellent, particularly the whitebait. The venison not so good,
being a little too high. The champagne and port very good. The
whole party consisting of 16 enjoyed the day much. It was a very
fine afternoon and the river was crowded with vessels.'

He first mentions a hansom on—

September 8, 1851

'The train did not arrive in London until 11.30 and I was afraid
I should be too late for the train which leaves London Bridge at
12. I got into a Handsome and told the driver to make all the haste
he could. By dint of galloping we just got in one minute before
12—a very nice point indeed.'

When in London he himself often made use of the omnibus, but
the Pryor ladies never did so.

In early days he used to stay at the 'Three Cups' at Aldersgate or
the 'Four Swans' at Aldersgate. In 1838 the family stayed, for the
first time, at a hotel—Woods in Furnival's Inn, and 'passed a comfortable night in nice clean beds.' After that, for some years he
patronised the Berners Hotel.

In 1845, his wife's depression being then at its worst, he took
lodgings in London for her and for Emma, hoping that the bustle
of the summer season would divert her.

May 21, 1845

'First called on Mr. Mitchell and his wife at their lodgings No. 6
Sackville Street. They had just finished breakfast. He accompanied me in looking out for lodgings. We made the tour of many
streets and looked at several but none that I quite liked until on

my return into Regent Street where Mr. Mitchell said some friends of theirs had lodgings last year at a Miss Denham's No. 189 Regent Street, in the best part of Regent Street which they spoke highly of. We accordingly called there and saw Miss Denham. She said her lodgings were occupied for the present but she expected they would be at liberty in a week or ten days. The family were at present within but I agreed to call again in two hours. I did, but could only see the sitting room and dining room as the ladies were in the bedrooms. I agreed to take the lodgings at 7 gns. a week.'

June 11, 1845

'My wife, daughter Emma, and myself set off from Shoreditch station with our luggage and the three servants we took with us in three clarence cabs. We found everything ready for us and our lodgings very good.'

June 12, 1845

'A very hot morning. Ascot Races! This is the principal day. The Queen and the Duke and Duchess of Nemours who are in England are to be there, and people without end pouring down by rail to Slough. I expect sons Morris, Alfred and Fred will be there.

Soon after our arrival Mrs. Bliss and Mrs. Mitchell called. My wife, not having been well before, after the heat and fatigue of the journey, found herself much depressed. I am afraid she will have no pleasure in going about London, seeing her friends, the sights etc. This morning, my wife being sadly out of spirits, I got into a cab and drove to Hampstead to consult with my sister Mrs. Thomas Pryor who has had great experience in nervous cases. She strongly recommended Dr. Watson. On my return I prevailed upon my wife to write a line or two to Dr. Watson, soliciting an interview.'

June 13, 1845

'Brilliant sunny morning, after a very hot night. My wife passed a sad night, having been able to obtain but little sleep. I walked out after breakfast to order a clarence and horses to take us a drive out towards evening into Kensington Gardens. It was at Mallalue's Livery Stables in Wigmore Street. A single horse clarence they let go on the stones, but for drives in the Parks and country a pair of horses they say is requisite and customary.' (The expression 'On the Stones' was current at this time to denote The City, West End, and the urban parishes adjoining which enjoyed the benefit of Paving Commissioners.)

'Dr. Watson came according to his appointment, and after hearing my wife's symptoms he prescribed for her. He was struck with the thick coat upon her tongue.

At half past 4 a pair horse clarence took us a drive for a couple of hours in Kensington Gardens. After taking a turn or two, the carriage drew up as near as they could get to where the band plays. Emma remained with Mrs. Pryor and I got out and walked with the gay throng. The ladies were all beautifully dressed and the crowd prodigious. Rejoined my wife in the carriage and returned by 7 o'clock for dinner.'

June 14, 1845

'Very fine and very hot, a circumstance some people attribute to a bright comet which has unexpectedly made its appearance.

After luncheon my wife and daughter Emma drove out in a single horse clarence to do some shopping. My wife passed a better night last night but feels her spirits still sadly depressed.'

Poor John Izzard! The plan was a total failure. Within a few years it was possible to go to London for the day.

May 10, 1851

'Reached London at 11.15 and proceeded to the Crystal Palace leaving my portmanteau at my tailors in Bond Street. I arrived there about noon, paid my five shillings and was almost over-powered by the gorgeous spectacle which presented itself to my view. The day was beautifully fine and showed off everything to the greatest advantage. It was a complete fairy scene. Scores of well dressed ladies and gentlemen swarmed in like bees to a hive. I saw the Duke of Wellington, the Duchess of Gloucester, and the young Prince of Wales. The chrystal fountain playing in a lovely manner refreshed the air circulating among thousands of visitors. I spent about four hours there examining the costly treasures of all countries until I was quite tired. The statuary from Milan was quite exquisite, particularly a veiled vestal and a slave in chains, also veiled. Left at 4 and reached home soon after 7.'

A few days later he paid it another visit.

'Set off from 36 Conduit Street with Mr. and Mrs. Mitchell in the carriage which they hire during their stay in London (very clean and nice with coachman and one horse for £1 per diem) to the Chrystal Palace in Hyde Park. There were a great many people there, the price of admission being now only one shilling for the first four days of the week, the fifth day being 2/6, the sixth, Saturday, 5/-.'

The Great Exhibition of which John Izzard was so enthusiastic an admirer did something for the people, as the following entry shows.

July 28, 1851

'My coachman Beckwith with my bailiff John Pike and man Gundall set off early this morning in the spring cart to Hertford to proceed by an excursion train to London to see the Chrystal Palace. They are to return tonight.'

John Izzard's admiration was not by any means universal. The City did not share it. The writer of the essay on commerce in Letts' Diary for 1852 does not concede that it made much contribution to business prosperity. He does admit, however, that 'it will be considered a marvel by future generations.'

Two years later, having in the meantime been incapacitated by a broken leg, and again by a carriage accident, the indomitable old man went to see the 'Chrystal Palace' at its new home.

June 22, 1853

'Having some bills to pay and exhibitions of painting to see, I made up my mind to go to London, intending, should it prove fine, to see the Chrystal Palace, now making rapid progress at Sydenham. The day proving fine, tho' rather cloudy, I took cab to the Brighton station at London Bridge. I took my day ticket for 1/6, reached Sydenham in a ¼ of an hour, took a cab to the palace, distant about 1 mile. I also bought at the station a ticket of admission to the Palace price 5/- which gave me admission all over the Palace and Park.

I was very much amazed with the structure, it far surpassing anything I had any idea of. I made my way over a great part of it, a rather difficult thing to accomplish as you get bewildered and lost on traversing the different galleries. The day became hazy which prevented my seeing the distant prospect which it commands but I could see the works going on over the gardens, the ground work preparing for three large fountains, the centre one of wonderful power.'

A more permanent addition to London made during John Izzard's days is to be found in the squares and terraces which lie

The Brewery House, Baldock, (now sadly decayed), seen from the garden

(facing page 118)

The residence of Vickris Pryor, Hitchin Street, Baldock

(*facing page 119*)

between the Edgware and the Bayswater Roads. Here his nephews Marlborough, a City merchant, and Robert, a barrister, took up residence.

While staying with Marlborough John Izzard wrote:

December 3, 1846

'I sallied out with Marlboro' and looked over several houses nearly finished and ready for being inhabited in Westbourne Terrace, none of which we liked better than his.'

December 5, 1846

'We looked over several large sized houses as well as small ones in Westbourne Terrace and Sussex and Gloucester Squares. The same style and arrangements seem to prevail in most of them.

There is a passage thro' in front with a dining room of a good size and a breakfast room at the back. On the next storey a spacious and elegant drawing room, taking the whole of the front, with folding doors to shut or remain open, over the breakfast room. Best bedrooms next storey and attics above them. Offices all below with area entrances and the kitchen behind in an area lighted by a sky light. A conservatory above half of the area opening on the landing level with the drawing room.'

Nearly two years later there is this entry—

October 17, 1848

'Received a letter this mornings post from my nephew Robt. Pryor, 109 Gloucester Place, London, announcing the birth of a son and heir, his wife and baby doing well, which we, one and all, were delighted to hear.'

The baby, Marlborough Robert Pryor (1848—1920), afterwards Chairman of the Sun Assurance Company, must have been one of the first to arrive in this delectable quarter.

These entries prompt a comparison between the Pryors and Galsworthy's Forsytes. Galsworthy wrote of the latter as they were two generations after John Izzard's day. Like the Pryors the Forsytes were countrymen by origin. But when Galsworthy describes them, they had become urban folk, and when prosperity enabled them to return to the country, they did so as townsmen. The Pryors' roots in the country were never severed. There was no Pryor equivalent to Timothy's in the Bayswater Road.

Marlboro' built himself, what he insisted on calling a 'Cottage ornée', at Weston near Walkern, and retired to it in 1848 when disaster seemed to have (actually it had not) overwhelmed his firm, Cotesworth, Powel & Pryor.

Robert moved to the family house at Hampstead in 1850 and thence, in 1869 to what was then the rural seclusion of Watford in his native Hertfordshire.

Both families shared the prosperity of Victorian England. But the Briton is at heart a countryman. The Forsytes would have been more typical of their class had they been drawn with some love for country pursuits.

XIV

IN JOURNEYINGS OFTEN

S urtees remarks in his novel *Plain or Ringlets* that previous to
the introduction of railways the country gentlemen were a
'landlocked legtied tribe.'

But this does not, in fact, seem to have been the case. During
the last decades of the threescore years and ten during which the
stage coach and post chaise flourished, the gentry and the better-
endowed clergy became accustomed to taking a yearly holiday
away from their homes. In response to their requirements sea-side
towns were springing into existence. Nearly every sea-side resort
of note today assumed its present style and pretensions at least
ten years before the first railway engine steamed into its station.
Before the end of the coaching era the Pryors had visited all of
these 'sauntering, simpering, watering places.' Scarborough might
boast 'her pay bridge and newly built dovecote, Hastings her
castle, St. Leonards her silence, Weymouth her sands, Dover her
castle, Margate her merriment, and Broadstairs her lugubrious
solemnity.' The Pryors knew them all and more besides. The
gentry, in spite of all the discomforts Surtees emphasises, were
travelling far afield long before there were railways.

But if we cannot agree with one remark of Surtees, we may do so
with another. He hailed the introduction of railways as a 'down-
right prolongation of life'. It will not need deep study of Pryor
journeys to agree with him.

In 1827 he took Emma and Julia to stay with a school friend at
Ripon. This is his account of the journey as far as Leeds.

August 23, 1827

'Reached Leeds at 9 o'clock this morning after travelling 20
hours. We started from Baldock yesterday at 1 o'clock, stopped
20 minutes for dinner at Eaton [Socon, Bedfordshire], and ¼ hour
for tea at Stamford. We breakfasted at the White Horse at Leeds
after a good washing to refresh us after the fatigues of travelling

all night. We bore it well considering we could not sleep. We found the inn very dirty but as the Ripon coach goes from the same inn we made the best of it.'

Leaving his daughters at Ripon, he went on to Scarborough, and admired 'the new Iron Cliff Bridge, very ornamental as well as useful and lately erected over a deep valley between the town and the spa. It forms the general promenade morning and evening.'

On his return journey, he encountered yet another inferior Yorkshire hostelry. This gave itself airs as *The York Hotel,* 'but I found it a very bad place. My dinner which I bespoke on my arrival to be ready at 3 o'clock was so bad I could scarcely eat it, the fish not being sweet, and the fowl quite passée. Very different from the George where I was exceedingly well used.

At half past 4 I mounted the Highflyer which had arrived from Edinburgh at 4 when the passengers dined. I rode outside as far as Doncaster.

I forgot to mention that I visited the (York) Minster in the interval between my arrival and dinner and was highly gratified in taking a minute survey of the interior of that preeminent structure, altho' not without some faults. The sculpture is inimitable and the tout ensemble strikes you with astonishment and admiration.'

August 31, 1827

'After leaving Doncaster night closed in and I could discern nothing. But as we passed thro' the different towns where the lamps burning bright showed the different houses and buildings very plain, I could sleep very little and was not sorry when breakfast was announced at the George at Stamford, an excellent inn. I made as good a meal as the short time allowed for that purpose would permit. A lady and two gentlemen were my companions who were very conversable and agreeable. Our next stoppage was at Biggleswade where a luncheon is provided at the Royal Oak of which I did not partake as I was so near home. At 1 o'clock I was set down at my own door, being exactly 20 hours and a half travelling from York to Baldock. The coach reaches London at half past 5 o'clock, performing the whole distance of 157 miles in 25 hours, which is good travelling.'

There was little enough to be said for travelling inside a coach at any time. But in spite of the discomforts—the roastings, the soakings, the freezings, the smotherings with dust—there were moments of exhilaration for those on the coach roof, as they travelled, sometimes at a brisk trot, sometimes at a gallop, through the lovely English countryside. On occasion the description of it quickens even John Izzard's pedestrian pen. His contemporary and neighbour William Lucas[1] of Hitchin, a man of progressive mentality, recording a journey from Brighton to London in the Splendid Age coach on 19 May 1840, muses, 'It is melancholy to reflect that this fine and English style of travelling must soon yield to the rising power of steam.' The glamour of the coach was not invented by a generation who had no practical experience of it; it was contemporaneous. The coach had a panache which was possessed by only the finest long-distance express in the days before nationalisation stole the romance from the railways.

On 19 September 1842 John Izzard performed one of his last long journeys by coach, from Dover to London.

'The morning was beautiful. Not a cloud to be seen. I left for London at ½ past 8 when the Eclipse Steamer was just leaving the harbour immediately the tide would allow of it, to have the advantage of it to London.

The Mail was remarkably well horsed, and driven by a superior coachman. We travelled beautifully. The inside was full of a party who had engaged the whole of the places. We changed about every ten miles and went away famously. High rocky clouds began to show themselves before we got to Canterbury and the road we soon found very wet in places where the shower had passed over. A gentleman next me who was conversant with Kent pointed out to me most of the gentlemen's seats as we passed on. The sun shining out bright most of the time, the distant view of the Thames and Medway, covered almost in different places with vessels and steamers also, was delightful. At Chatham, Rochester and Strood, all was bustle, and the number of vans, omnibuses and carriages of all descriptions passing along was quite astonishing. A powder mill had blown up at Dartford this morning, but no lives were lost. Just before we arrived at Blackheath a heavy storm came on. Notwithstanding my great coat and umbrella I got very wet. It lasted until we got close to London which we reached at half past 4. I had just time to get a lunch of bread and cheese and a glass

[1] Bryant, *A Quaker Journal*

of ale before getting to the station at Shoreditch at half past 5 for
Broxbourne.'

(Shoreditch Station was the original terminus of the Eastern
Counties Railway; Liverpool Street Station was not opened until
1874.)

September 20, 1842
'Fine morning. Symptoms of a cold coming on. Settled my
journey accounts. I was very economical as the times require it,
the whole of my expenditure for the six days being £9, having
been 200 miles.'

There seems to have been no standard coach fare. An account
book belonging to Morris Pryor has survived. In 1823 from
Baldock to London, the 'outside' fare was 8/- or $2\frac{2}{3}$ d. a mile.
From London to Oxford 2½d; from Oxford to Bath 4d; from
Bath to Weymouth $3\frac{2}{3}$ d. per mile. 'Insides' paid more. These
were stage-coach rates. When Morris travelled by the Dover Mail
it cost him 5d a mile. In addition it was customary to tip the
coachman invariably, and the guard sometimes. On returning
from Dover Morris tipped the coachman 3/- and the guard 2/-. The
tip for a short journey such as London to Baldock was 1/-, and
this at a time when farm workers were earning from 8/- to 9/- a
week. The railways at least delivered the Early Victorian gentry
from the extortion of coachman and guard. But they also made
travel possible for the masses. Reference has already been made to
the excursion train to the Chrystal Palace. In 1855 they enabled
the Clay Hall butler to seek from the sea breezes, health and
refreshment not to be found in the pantry.

August 16, 1855
'H. Young, my butler went to London this morning for a little
change, intending to go to Brighton, as I gave him leave of absence
for a week or ten days.'

When the Pryor family travelled on holiday they usually either
hired a conveyance or took their own. Coaches had limited accommodation, and a family of five or six could not be certain of all
getting on to the same coach.

In 1828 on July 8, they 'left in a barouche landau hired for the
journey, taking the four ladies, myself, and Fred inside, John
Wilson and Mary on the box, the luggage occupying the seat

behind, sons John and Alfred stopping all night in London and
going to Margate by the steam packet.'

Margate they did not find much to their taste.

July 10, 1828

'Rambled Margate and its environs. We were much amused seeing
the steam packets land their numerous passengers from London
in the afternoons. Two arrive every afternoon, one about 5 o'clock
and the other about half past.

The bathing especially when the sea is rather rough is not good.
The warm baths are good. There are promenades and music every
night at several of the hot baths, besides the Library at Bettison's.
The former were crowded with 2nd and 3rd rate and perhaps lower
company every evening. But at Betterson's frequented by the more
genteel part of the company there was a very thin attendance when
we were there.'

After a few days at Margate they moved on to Ramsgate. There
they found 'the company very genteel and the place remarkable
quiet.'

July 17, 1828

'Bathed every alternate morning before breakfast. After that
looked in at Saket's Library, read the papers, and then promenaded either the piers or sands with the ladies.'

The standard equipment of a watering place was copied from
Bath: an assembly room, a parade, a band, a circulating library, a
theatre, and a place of worship. The Pryors made good use of
them all.

In October 1833 they drove to Brighton in their own carriage,
the servants following by coach. They took No. 80 King's
Road—'a private house very nicely furnished and clean' for
five weeks at 12 gns. a week. 'The situation is very pleasant
and lively, it being the drive for all the fashionable company, and
the Esplanade in front being thronged with all the best company
on foot.'

It was here that that ill-starred clergyman Mr. Bailey asked,
and was refused, John Izzard's permission to pay his addresses
to Julia. But except for this episode, the visit seems to have
been enjoyable. The time passed pleasantly with visits to the
Chain Pier, one of the wonders of the South Coast. John Izzard
notes—

October 15, 1833
'About 7 o'clock the storm of wind was so tremendous as to destroy a great part of the Chain Pier at Brighton.'

October 16, 1833
'A great number of people went early this morning to look at the Chain Pier which is quite a wreck.'

But, in fact, it survived to perish later in mountainous seas on December 5 1896, and nine years afterwards, John Izzard saw it 'wrecked', as was described in *Punch* as follows.

'This structure stretches "in linked sweetness" far into the sea, and offers ample accommodation for a band of music . . ., for a cutter out of black profiles, a dealer in ladies' shoes, and for a toy seller, each of whose depositories are situated in the iron towers which support the chains. It is also a rendezvous for the inmates of boarding houses, who having just separated from the dinner table, encounter each other with many expressions of happiness at again meeting. Twice a week for about 5 minutes each time, the pier is really used for its intended purpose—a steam boat embarks or lands passengers for Dieppe.'

There were races to go to, the downs to ride upon, the beautiful suspension bridge at Shoreham 'to be much gratified with', and fashionable preachers to sit under. There was the preacher at St. James, 'a handsome new building, built in a correct and chaste stile', who preached 'mostly extempore in a most energetic manner in what is generally denominated the Evangelical style' and 'condemned those kind of sermons that please the congregation at Brighton generally, saying they wanted awakening and frightening.' His discourse 'was certainly rather of a terrific nature. The ladies disliked it very much.' Then there was the Rev. Jas. Anderson, 'a first-rate preacher, and is now chaplain to the Queen, and on the road to preferment. But as it was a charity sermon for the benefit of a church being built for the poor to be free for them, we could not judge so well of his abilities as in a sermon not confined to one object.'

Nephew Henry who had been subject to uncommonly severe fits of cramp and came to try what effects warm bathing and shampooing would have upon him, helped to distract the young ladies. He stayed a fortnight and left, 'having derived considerable benefit from Mahomet's Vapour Baths and shampooing.'

This enterprising oriental, by name Sheikh Din Mahommed, was the body servant of a John Company's military officer, and had been with his master at several battles. He accompanied him to Europe, and set up a Turkish bathing establishment at Brighton. He was appointed Shampooing Surgeon to George IV and William IV, and his official court dress is preserved at the Pavilion.

Undoubtedly John Izzard's most notable holiday was his trip to France in company of brothers Robert and Vickris and nephew Henry.

June 1, 1838

'On my arrival in London I went to No. 6 Poland Street to procure my passport which had been bespoke but which you must procure yourself in consequence of a description being taken of your person, age etc.'

This passport, which has survived, was issued by the French Consular Authorities.

June 2, 1838

'Our party rose at 4 in the morning, breakfasted at 5, got on board the Magnet steamer at the London Bridge wharf by 6, and set off directly afterwards, the morning being propitious. After a pleasant voyage, we landed at Boulogne at 5 o'clock in the afternoon, making the passage in eleven hours. The day continued fine with only a gentle ripple upon the water until we arrived at the North Foreland where we experienced for half an hour more of a sea. None of our party were at all affected by sea sickness.'

June 3, 1838

'Breakfasted at 8 and started at 9, RP, VP and self in the coupes and HP in the blanquet above. All of us much amused with the style of driving, setting off with five bony mares of the Flanders breed, the driver in a small seat high enough above the windows of the coupee so as not to obstruct our view. The coupee is by far the most preferable place in the Diligence which carries altogether 17 persons viz. 3 in the coupee, 6 in the middle, 4 in the rear. Monsieur le Conducteur and 3 others in the blanquet. There is also the driver making 18.

The latter with very bad reins manages to drive the 5 horses, viz. 2 next the wheels and 3 before, with wretched harness, part rope and part leather. Some of the stages we had 6 horses, driven 3 abreast, and for a short distance out of Poix we had 8, the postillion riding with both legs on one side. Two of the stages the driver rode the near wheel horse. They manage their horses more by the voice of which they make incessant use and the smacking of their whips than by the reins which would certainly break if pulled hard.

The horses after the 2 first stages were nearly all stallions of the strong, active, Flemish make and shape, and nearly all of a grey color, making a great noise while they are standing at the various posts waiting to be put to. They gallop along at a great rate, particularly down hill, the Conducteur making use of a retardateur which he winds close to the wheels by a handle at his side—an excellent contrivance well worth adopting in England. Immediately they reach the bottom of a hill he releases it without moving from his seat.'

June 4, 1838

'After changing horses about 16 times, and only stopping to dine at Abbeville, we arrived after travelling for 23 hours, day and night, at 8 in the morning at Paris, being set down at the Messageries Royales. Proceeded by fiacre to the Hotel Meurice, Rue de Rivoli, which being extremely full we had some difficulty in getting in. We were obliged to put up with bedchambers sky high for a night or two.

After shaving, washing and dressing we sat down to a very good breakfast to which we did ample justice, not having taken anything since dining at Abbeville.

We then engaged a valet de place and a carriage and set off to see some of the public buildings, beginning with the Chamber of Deputies which answers to our House of Commons in England, a very fine and noble building and fitted up in a most elegant manner. Thence to the Hotel des Invalides, a noble establishment and kept in the best order, being a retreat for life for wounded officers and privates in the army, and in some measure answering to our Greenwich Hospital for the Sea Service. They were relieving guard as we entered. We saw the dining tables prepared for the officers and privates and the bedrooms, all very clean and nice. Afterwards to the Madeleine, not yet completed, an extraordinary fine building, lighted only at the top by three cupolas, the ceiling, panels etc. highly gilt and ornamented, the whole superb.

Returned to our hotel and sat down at the table d'hote at half

past 5, about 50 dining, chiefly English.   Took our coffee at 9.
Retired to our beds at 10, sleeping very soundly.'

June 7, 1838

'Dined at the Caffee de Paris in the Boulevard des Italiens, ordering our dinner at 10 francs a head inclusive of wine. They gave us
a very good dinner in the French style—Champagne beautifully
iced and the claret very good.'

June 9, 1838

'Dined a second time at the Caffee de Paris and had an excellent
dinner, and amongst other dishes fricassied frogs which we all
partook of and really liked.'

June 10, 1838

'A grand review of troops in the Tuileries and Champs Elysées by
the King Louis Philippe. We were much gratified by seeing the
King and his cortege ride through the gate of the Tuileries into the
Champs Elysées near which we were stationed. The King had a
number of general officers with him. The Queen and three other
ladies in an open carriage, and two other carriages with laides
followed.

The King had previously rode along the lines, and after coming
into the Champs Elysées took his station by the column, the Duke
d'Orleans and the Duke de Nemours with a large assemblage of
distinguished officers being close by him.

The National Guard first passed in review before him in legions,
almost interminable, being about 50,000 altogether. Next followed
the troops of the line who marched with the greatest regularity,
each division of about 300 preceded by their band, playing martial
airs. A train of artillery next passed, and last of all a great many
troops of cavalry.

The scene was very imposing. We were nearly opposite the King.
He bowed to all the officers as they passed in front of their different companies, and also to the lines of privates as they passed, and
was extremely well received. It did not end until half past 4. The
day being extremely fine made the whole affair gratifying. I never
expect to see such a sight again.'

On June 12 they left Paris in a large omnibus which took them
12 miles to Maison-sur-Seine where they embarked on the packet
at half past 8 for the 150 miles of 'delightful passage' to Rouen.
The scenery was beautiful.

'We passed under many bridges and shot through with great credit to the steersman, lowering of course, our chimney as we passed. There are also a great many islands in the river.

We arrived at Rouen about half past 6 in the evening and proceeded to the Royal Hotel situated on the Quay where we had a late but very comfortable dinner and most excellent claret (vin ordinaire) we preferred to the higher priced claret. We had also good sleeping rooms and clean beds.'

After a day at Rouen they hired a phaeton and drove to Dieppe where they embarked for Brighton.

'We did not make way nearly so fast as when we crossed from London. It was near 12 when we reached within a short distance of Brighton. We hung out lights and signals were made but we could not be landed for another hour, the tide at the pier not being high enough. We therefore laid by for another hour which seemed very long, and then effected our landing and got beds at the Albion soon after 1 o'clock.'

It was characteristic of John Izzard that he should have been able to record that next morning he awoke refreshed and in excellent spirits, and that, after a capital breakfast, he set out to call on his daughter Eliza Lafont, who was spending a summer holiday at Brighton with her husband and children.

He had already experienced his first railway journey.

May 17, 1838

'Set off this morning for Oxford. At quarter before 12, having paid my fare of £1−0−0 at the Spread Eagle, Gracechurch Street, to be conveyed to Oxford by the rail road as far as Tring and thence by coach as inside passenger to Oxford, I left in the railway omnibus for Euston Square station where we arrived at quarter to 1. Precisely at 1, the bell ringing, I took my place inside one of the first class carriages on the train, and arrived after a very pleasant ride at the Tring station in an hour and a half, the distance being about 30 miles. A coach was in attendance to take the Oxford passengers on, and in the course of quarter of an hour we again started and arrived at Oxford at quarter past 6, making the journey in 5 hours and quarter.'

The journey all the way by coach used to take a little less than 6 hours.

In July 1841 the Pryors went to stay with the Colstons (Mrs.

Morris Pryor had been born a Colston) at Roundway Park in Wiltshire.

'We took our own horses as far as Hatfield and proceeded with post horses to Barnet and London. We reached the Bank by about half past 12, calculating it would take an hour to go thence to the station at Paddington, going round that way in consequence of wishing to receive Dr. Colston's half year's dividend and pay the same in at his Bankers, Messrs. Hoares in Fleet Street; also stopping at Messrs. Carbonell to pay their bill for wine.

Drove to the Great Western Station at Paddington, took our places for Chippenham and had the briskza placed on the truck. Henry and Cross met us there with the remainder of the luggage in a hackney coach and saw it safely deposited. Henry and Cross rode in the briskza and we in a first class carriage. Started at 2, arrived at Chippenham at half past 5, dined there and proceeded to Roundway Park and arrived there at 8. We found our friends were all well. They gave us a hearty welcome. The dessert was still on the table of which we partook.'

On their return journey, they had the carriage put on a truck at Shoreditch station and travelled by train to Broxbourne for the first time.

In September 1845 the Pryors and Blisses spent a holiday at Brighton.

'Dr. Bliss had previously engaged a sitting room and two best bedrooms besides servants' apartments at Mrs. Wells' Boarding house in German Place and we found everything ready on our arrival. The dinner hour at the public table we found was half past 5. We had therefore ample time to unpack and dress for dinner. The long table was occupied from the top to the bottom by the company in the house some of whom were expected to leave next day, when we should take our seat at the bottom of the long table, the usual custom being for the last visitors to take their seats there. There were 30 ladies and gentlemen at the long table and they appeared genteel and agreeable.'

September 17, 1845
'The wind blew a hurricane during the night accompanied with heavy rain and the storm continued all through the day. The waves and spray of the sea presented a most magnificent and grand scene. The company on the chain pier got wet by the

spray beating completely over the end of the pier and also the sides at intervals. The wind blowing so furiously the company were obliged to vacate the pier. The ladies had some difficulty in keeping their clothes around them and the gentlemen their hats on their heads without guards.

I was pleased to think that the high wind would dry the corn and particularly my oats at Clay Hall and prevent them sprouting after the heavy rain which fell yesterday and last night.

We breakfasted, lunched and dined at the long table and drank tea in the drawing room and found everything quite to our hearts' content. Some of the company played a rubber of whist and other games, and others conversed very pleasantly. Mrs. Wells' rules limit the stakes to a very low sum, viz. 3 points, to prevent gambling. Her establishment is altogether admirably managed. She takes the head of the table at dinner and makes the tea and coffee for the whole of the party in the drawing room at 8 o'clock. Breakfast is at 9, lunch 1, dinner 5.30, tea 8.'

Two years later they paid a visit to Julia and her husband Richard at Spettisbury, the most memorable day of which is described below.

May 25, 1847

'This was a festive day at Spettisbury. An old-established club of nearly 200 members meet annually on Whit Tuesday and attend church at 12 noon after parading before the Rectory with a band of music. A sermon appropriate to the occasion is preached by the rector who with the curate preceded them to church. We made a part of the congregation. Preparations were made for dining the whole under cover in a field in the middle of the village. We went to see them. After Grace they set to work with a good appetite, being also very orderly and happy, the rector heading the table and the curate at the bottom. About 6, the young women of the parish assembled and dancing commences, the band playing from a temporary orchestra. There were marquees and booths for refreshments. They danced merrily and it was a pretty sight. Two members of the club admit visitors at the entrance gate. All is over by 10 o'clock and the company separate peaceably without a single policeman being required.'

The summer holiday of 1848 was spent at Dover whence, one afternoon, they drove to Walmer.

'We drove up to the Castle and Dr. Bliss alighted to ascertain whether the Duke of Wellington was in residence, as the gardens only, and not the house, are shown when he is there. But in consequence of Dr. Bliss being well known to the Duke we were allowed to see both. The gardens partake more of the appearance of an arboretum than a flower garden. They are well sheltered from the sea breezes by a belt of trees. There are two laurustinas, the largest I ever saw. The housekeeper showed us the different apartments of the house. All the beds, curtains, chairs etc. are of yellow moreen except the drawing room which is of yellow damask, the Duke's favourite colour. From one of the windows we saw the Duke walking on the ramparts.'

It was returning from his holiday at Brighton in 1851 that John Izzard broke his leg.

September 29, 1851

'Left Brighton by the 12 o'clock train for London, intending to return home. But after leaving London Bridge Station and walking towards the Great Northern at King's Cross, I met with a dreadful accident—no less than a broken leg. Having just crossed the road in King William Street and close by the foot pavement I fell and found myself surrounded by a crowd of people. (But what caused my fall I had no idea of and have never been able to account for it.) On being helped up I found my leg was broke. The persons gathered round me proposed taking me to a hospital. But I made up my mind to be taken to the Berners Hotel where I was known. I was helped into a handsome cab where I had room to lay my leg out straight and arrived there as well as could be expected. The head surgeon of the Middlesex Hospital which is near by was recommended to me and came directly. I was carried into a small room on the ground floor. I wrote a few lines to my wife to inform her just before he set my leg. The fracture is a compound one but the bone is not much shattered.'

September 30, 1851

'My wife came up by an early train from Brighton which was a great alleviation to my forlorn state. But she was badly distressed on seeing me; but thank God it was no worse.

The surgeon pronounced favourably on my fracture and hoped the best from my constitution being good and my mode of living regular, although at the age of 77 the bones take more to unite.

My wife occupied the room adjoining mine and I had one of the Hospital nurses to sit up the night and attend me in my room.'

Something will be said of his illness and recovery later. A year afterwards the redoubtable old gentleman was holidaying at Brighton—not this time at Mrs. Wells' admirable premises.

September 16, 1852
'Left by the quick train for Brighton which goes thro' without stopping in an hour and half, proceeding thence in two cabs to the Albermarle on the Marine Parade. After seeing our luggage deposited I took a walk on the West Cliff. There was scarcely a breath stirring and the little sailing vessels were obliged to have care to get them on shore. Dined at 6. There were 17 at the table d'hote. A very good dinner was served up and the company agreeable. A short time after dinner the ladies withdrew to the drawing room. The gentlemen followed an hour or two later to take tea and coffee and have a game at whist or round game.'

September 17, 1852
'Dr. and Mrs. Bliss made their appearance at 4 p.m. having travelled from London by the slow train. We all took a walk together but no band played on the pier in consequence of the Duke's death.'

September 23, 1852
'Fine morning, the sea quite calm. Dr. Bliss, my wife and myself and two servants went out in a boat to sea for about an hour and a half, going round the famous American clipper, lying about 1½ mile from the shore. The day was very fine without much sun, and we all enjoyed our trip on the water.'

September 24, 1852
'Brilliant morning at 8 a.m. after fog. Walked out before breakfast. My wife took her shower bath as usual. After breakfast I took a ride in a chair for an hour. Paid Miss Newsom a cheque for £9—11—8 for 1 week's board lodging and wine including our two servants as per bill.'

September 27, 1852
'Bought *Uncle Tom's Cabin* for seven pence, a kind of American

novel, founded in some degree on facts, to show the cruelty and abomination of slavery, by Mrs. Becher Stowe, which has a very great run.'

The repeal of the Navigation Acts had brought the stimulus of American competition to our merchant marine. The first American clipper to land a cargo of tea in England hauled into the West India Docks 3 December 1850. The Blackwall frigates from Mr. Wigram's yard were the best British ships at the time.

This was the last of his seaside holidays.

The development of the railway which he watched with admiration and wonder made it possible for him to spend the day in London and return home at night. On 31 October 1843 he witnessed the passing of the first train from Hertford to London, and thereafter Hertford was his station until

August 5, 1850

'We set off soon after 10 for Stevenage to see the Directors of the Great Northern Rail Road pass at Stevenage on inspection of the line to Peterboro' previous to the opening of the line to the public next Wednesday, 7 August. After being there ¼ hour the engine and train passed at a rapid pace. The train of carriages with the directors and their friends was rather a long one. Just as they passed the fore part parted from the hinder part and went on with the engine which might have caused a serious accident.'

In spite of this somewhat comic beginning, the Railway Company provided a service which can compare with that provided by the nation for a satellited Stevenage.

XV

THE CHURCH

John Izzard recorded his diary for 1835 in Dunn's Daily Remembrancer for that year, the preface of which concludes with the following statistics relating to the Established Church.

Net average annual value of a bishopric	£5,950
Net average annual value of each benefice	£285
Number of curates	£5,282
Average annual stipend of a curate	£80
62 sinecure rectories had an income of	£18,622

It must not be supposed that every Early Victorian gentleman who read this paragraph, there and then resolved to work for the reform of these financial arrangements. Canon Sydney Smith who was not a Tory wrote, 'The great emoluments of the Church are flung open to the lowest ranks of the community. Butchers, bakers, publicans, schoolmasters, are perpetually seeing their children elevated to the mitre.' The whole income of the Church, he pointed out, if equally divided, would be about £250 for each minister. Who would go into the Church and spend £1,200 upon his education, if such were the highest remuneration he could ever look to? This would result in a lower stamp of man taking orders, and the clergyman would soon be seen in the kitchen of the squire; 'and all this would take place in a country where poverty is infamous' (Rev. Sydney Smith, *Wit and Wisdom,* 1865).

Something has been said of the contribution which the country clergy made to the administration of the country. It will, perhaps, not be irrelevant to glance at an Early Victorian bishop.

Charles Blomfield was a son of the headmaster of what would now be called an independent school, at Bury St. Edmunds. Here it was that Alfred and his elder brothers had their schooling. The bishop's brother George was rector of Stevenage near Walkern. It was natural, therefore, that the Pryors should take an interest in him.

136

Blomfield first won fame by an excellent edition of Aeschylus, and secured the wealthy living of Bishopsgate. This, he wrote, 'after curates, poor rates, and other rates have been paid will be worth £1,600 p.a.' His abilities were soon displayed in the administration of this urban parish, and he was promoted to the Bench as Bishop of Chester. The see was only worth £1,400 p.a. and he was allowed to retain the living of Bishopsgate. When in London of a Sunday the Pryors, until the bishop's translation to the see of London, used to attend St. Botolph's 'to hear the Bishop of Chester preach.' It does not seem, however, that they were personally acquainted. Both families were staying in the Isle of Wight in the late summer of 1839.

September 30, 1839
'Walked on the pier with my family a great part of the morning. Saw the Bishop of London and his family take boat and proceed to a fine yacht The Stag, in which they had a sail most of the day.'

October 2, 1839
'Embarked on board the Portsmouth steamer at 9 precisely. The morning was fine and the sea calm. There were about 20 passengers on board including the Bishop of London and his family—a boat attached to the steamer had his carriage on board.'

It does not appear that John Izzard made himself known to the bishop. But, then, Blomfield was a formidable personality. Sydney Smith, when told that the bishop had been bitten by a dog, remarked that he would reserve judgment until he had heard the dog's version of the incident.

Blomfield's services to Church and State were manifold.

He had a hand in the passing of the Commutation Act, which settled the vexatious question of Tithe; he was the moving spirit behind the regulation of pluralities, and the levelling of incomes in the Church (although he retained his own unimpaired); he procured the building of 200 churches to serve the needs of the rapidly expanding population of his diocese; and he was virtually the founder of a number of colonial bishoprics.

He voted for the Reform Bill of 1832; was a member of the Commission which enquired into the Poor Law and prompted the Act of 1834; and was the originator of the Sanitary Enquiry of 1839.

The bishop's see was worth between £15,000 and £16,000 a year. Of this £5,000 was set aside for charity, and the remainder was not more than adequate for the upkeep of London House and Fulham Palace and the endowment of eleven children by means of the purchase of life insurances. When he resigned in 1856 he was secured by Act of Parliament a pension of £6,000 and the use of the Fulham estate for life. (A. Blomfield, *Memoir of Bishop Blomfield,* 1864.)

Of Blomfield, it may be said, as of many of the clergy of his day, that his practical was more important than his spiritual contribution. But as time went on and less was required of the clergy in the way of secular administration, they grew more spiritually minded. Something of this may be seen in the four clergymen of whom John Izzard speaks most—Lafont of Hinxworth, Wright and Harding of Walkern, and Malet of Ardeley.

John Izzard's son-in-law John Lafont was rector of Hinxworth, a very small village near Baldock, and vicar of Sutton Bonington, Notts. He lived at Hinxworth in the ample rectory adjoining the little church, and visited Sutton Bonington at Michaelmas in order to collect his tithe. He was an active magistrate and a good shot. The diary shows that he was most conscientious in making arrangements for the services to be held at Hinxworth when he was absent, and he inaugurated the Sunday School there. He owned the advowson of the living, and regarded Hinxworth as private property and the rectory as his family house. Soon after his death in 1844 there is the following entry in the diary.

November 7, 1844

'I set off in my gig to Baldock and had a conference with my sons John and Morris respecting my daughter Lafont's affairs, but more particularly respecting the living of Hinxworth, which must be held by some honourable person for her son Ogle until he becomes of the proper age to hold it, which will be in seven years time. It being an advowson my daughter must nominate and the acting executor present. Dr. Bliss is the person we all think the best and correspondence has passed respecting it.'

A few days later he wrote, 'Dr. Bliss in his letter declined holding the living of Hinxworth in consequence of his health being indifferent and onerous duties to attend to besides. Morris took the letter with him to show my daughter Eliza, which depressed her very much as she was quite in hopes he would have held it for Ogle. Someone else must now be thought of who will be eligible and agreeable to her.'

Dr. Bliss who was hoping to rise in the hierarchy of the University could not afford to expose himself to a charge of simony, and must have shuddered at the suggestion. Eventually the Rev. John Donne, a relation of son John's wife, and vicar of Weston agreed to fill the gap. He put in a curate the Rev. H. Heatley, 'a gentleman' John Izzard notes, to act for him. Heatley married Marian Lafont in 1849.

John Izzard had no grandfatherly feelings towards Ogle.

April 23, 1844

'Received a letter from my daughter Lafont announcing the gratifying intelligence of her son Ogle having obtained the first prize in the 5th Class of the Charter House and of his advancement to the Sixth Class.'

John Izzard acknowledged the letter and agreed that the news was gratifying. But that was all. Reginald, Alfred's son (later a Jesuit), had a tip of £20 when he won a scholarship at University College, Oxford. Henry, John's son, turned up at Clay Hall in his regimentals before he joined the 60th, and was presented with two sovereigns.

June 22, 1852

'Grandson Ogle Lafont left us this morning for Oxford to take his Master's degree. I sent him in the spring cart to Stevenage. Daughter Emma made him a handsome present of £30 to pay for his taking his Master's degree.'

Ogle became rector of Hinxworth in 1852, and remained so until his death in 1914, but from 1876 he was a lunatic. *Sunt lacrimae rerum et mentem mortalia tangunt.*

The Rev. James Camper Wright was, like the Rev. John Lafont, a pluralist, being both rector of Walkern and Fellow of Eton. He had to reside for long periods at Eton, but he took his duties as rector seriously. He founded the village school.

April 19, 1830

'About noon called upon Mr. Wright, who I found at home. Conferred with him about a school being built upon which subject he had previously written to me, being very desirous it should be accomplished. He calculates the expense at about £80 or at most £90 and gives himself £20 towards it. He superintends the building it himself. The walls are to be in Pisa which he thoroughly understands the construction of. I therefore agreed to give £30 towards it. Walked round his garden with him afterwards.'

At this time the State took no part in the education of the people. They had to rely upon numberless little dame schools, and the schools of the two societies, the National Society for Promoting the Education of the Children of the Poor in the Principles of the Established Church, and the British and Foreign School Society. One of the first acts of the Reformed Parliament was to authorise a grant of £20,000 a year to be divided between the two Societies, provided that an amount at least equal to the grant was raised by private subscription. In 1839 the grant was raised to £30,000 and an Inspectorate established. With that begins the modern history of State education.

All honour to James Camper Wright and his colleagues among the country clergy who laid the foundation of education in the villages!

In another respect this rector was ahead of his time.

September 5, 1830

'We all attended church morning and afternoon. Mr. Wright gave us an excellent sermon addressed to the farmers particularly to impress upon their minds the duty of gratitude for a plentiful and well gotten harvest.'

The good rector may well have puzzled over the fact that the Prayer Book, which appoints Rogation Days on which God's blessings are to be invoked on the growing crops, and which includes a special petition in the Litany—'That it may please Thee to give and preserve to our use the kindly fruits of the earth so that in due time we may enjoy them'—makes no provision for harvest thanksgiving. It does not seem that there existed in medieval times any feast which corresponded with the modern harvest festival; and this in spite of the fact that the ties between the Church and Agriculture were then very strong. Lammas (loaf mass) is sometimes cited as being the medieval harvest festival. But August 12[1] is much too early in the season (at any rate in Britain) to celebrate

[1] Originally of course August 1 until New Style adopted in 1752.

the safe gathering of harvest—even in these days of combines. For this reason it is possible that Lammas never attracted much popularity. The Reformers may have had no festival to take over from the medieval church, and being anxious to keep feasts to a minimum, did not create one. It was thus left to Hawker of Morwenstow and the Victorian country clergy to institute what is now the occasion which draws more people to attend church (or indeed chapel) in the country than any other, Christmas included.

Except on 17 October 1847, when a prayer was said in thanks for a harvest, the bounty of which appeared excessive to the City (p. 171), there was no harvest thanksgiving at Walkern in John Izzard's lifetime. It seems to have become popular in Anglican churches in the sixties and seventies of the century. Some verses in *Punch* for 17 October 1868 indicate that it was not yet generally accepted.

(A footman is speaking)

> And all them gorgeous vestments and them crucifers and copes.
> They ain't for English parsons but for Papishers and Popes.
> While as for Arvest Festivals which now is all the go,
> To me a church it aint the place to hold a Flower Show.

With the following paragraph from the diary for Christmas Day 1836 we may take leave of this worthy Early Victorian clergyman.

'Mr. Wright gave us an excellent sermon very appropriate to the season, and after morning service administered the sacrament in a most impressive manner. Mrs. Wright was very much affected which caused Mr. Wright considerable exertion to suppress his feelings whilst administering the sacrament to her.'

He was succeeded on his death in 1838 by the Rev. John Harding, who during his term of office transformed worship at Walkern.

May 5, 1839

'Went to church morning and evening, Mr. Harding our rector beginning to give a sermon both morning and evening.'

October 9, 1841

'Rode down to the rectory, returning Mr. Harding the subscription paper for the organ for Walkern church. Mr. Harding had put his name down for £10, and Mrs. Harding for £5. I put down my name for £10, Mrs. Pryor £5, Emma £5, Juliana £5 and Fred £1. The servants also raised 7/6 amongst them.'

August 7, 1842

'The organ put up in the gallery of the church a fortnight ago was heard for the first time this day. It appears a good one of the kind, being what is termed a grinder. It was played very well by young Bray the wheelwright's boy.'

The introduction of an organ made it necessary to change the mode of singing the service.

March 28, 1842

'Attended a meeting in the school where a lecture was given on a new mode of teaching singing—particularly for psalm singing in church. My daughter Emma wished to attend. I therefore accompanied her.'

Two years later, he urged upon his flock the proper observance of Holy Week.

March 31 (Palm Sunday) 1844

'Lovely day. Brilliant sun all the day with a cold wind pretty full east. Rode in the omnibus with my wife to church in the morning and walked together there and back in the afternoon, the ground getting quite dry.

This is my wife's birthday. We dined together alone, a circumstance which has not occurred for many years.

Mr. Harding gave a long sermon, both in the morning and afternoon, adapted to Passion Week but more particularly relating to the observance of Good Friday when there are to be two services, one at 11 in the morning, the other at 6 in the evening. There are also to be prayers every evening during the week until Saturday.'

April 5 (Good Friday) 1844

'I breakfasted at 8 a.m. at Baldock and rode up to Walkern to attend the morning service at 11 o'clock, having had no horses at work and setting my men all at liberty to attend church the same as on a Sunday. I therefore rode up wishing to see what sort of attendance there was. I was glad to see a good congregation assembled. Mr. Harding gave a good sermon in addition to the prayers for the day; and does the same at 6 o'clock in the evening.'

At Christmas 1849 comes the first mention of the church being decorated 'with holly'. At Christmas 1852 John Izzard notes that 'the church was beautifully decorated with holly and laurel under the direction and assistance of Mrs. Harding.'

Stow in his *Survey of London* states that it was the custom for every man's house to be decked with 'holm, ivy, bays, and whatsoever the season of the year affordeth to be green.' According to the old English mode, sprigs of holly and yew stuck into holes in the high pews used to make the churches into miniature forests. This custom which George Herbert describes, lapsed in the eighteenth century. It was now revived as a result of the influence of the Oxford Movement.

At Ardeley, the church of that ardent Puseyite William Malet, it was already the custom to decorate the altar with flowers.

In his Charge to his clergy in 1842 (the Charge which had so shocked the more Protestant by advocating a regular Sunday collection) Bishop Blomfield wrote, 'I strongly disapprove the practice which, as I am informed, has been adopted by a few of the clergy, of decorating the Communion Table with flowers, especially when that decoration is varied from day to day.'

Some years were to pass before there were flowers on the altar at Walkern. The next development after Christmas decorations was the adornment of the church at Easter with flowers. From there to floral decoration of the altar was a short step.

During Harding's incumbency great changes were made to the interior of the church. John Izzard seems to have been the first to become 'pew-conscious'.

September 27, 1844

'The churchwardens and rector examined my pew and I got permission to alter it by lowering the front 18 inches. I am about to alter the arrangements of the interior and to have the seats all made so as the persons frequenting them may all face the clergyman and have bookshelves in front and room to kneel, viz. five in front, two in the middle and four in the back seat. At present the seats are all round the pew. It will make the pew more airy and will allow all to see the clergyman and congregation whereas before none could see without standing up, and those in front sit with their backs to the front.'

The squire's pew at Walkern was built above the floor level of the church. He altered the seating but not the level of the pew. In 1851 he had broken his leg.

April 15, 1852

'I went to church and as I could not manage the winding stair

into our own pew I sent the two ladies' maids there and sat with
my wife in the foremost servants' pew in the north aisle below,
which we found very comfortable. My daughter Emma sat in the
front seat in our pew above as usual.'

In 1846, perhaps impressed with the squire's new pew, the
Vestry decided to repew the church.

July 26, 1846

'Mr. Harding gave notice there would be no service in the church
until the repewing which is to be begun tomorrow is completed. It
will probably be six weeks. Mr. and Mrs. Harding take advantage
of its being closed to visit their friends in Yorkshire.'

July 27, 1846

'Mr. Andrews of Hertford who has contracted for the repewing
of our church came over with his men. The lath and plaster
boarded blockade above the screen, dividing the church from the
chancel was all taken down which is a great improvement. The
Ten Commandments which were painted upon it, all came away
with it. Two tablets of slate, one on each side of the altar table,
are to be placed against the wall there in lieu.'

August 7, 1846

'Attended at Walkern church to meet the churchwardens and Mr.
Hollingsworth the architect and Mr. Andrews the contractor. The
foundations of a pillar that were found in a bad state were agreed
to be made secure. But Mr. Stacy and Mr. Rayment were so dis-
satisfied with their projected new pews or sittings they said they
should write to Mr. Boodle (Lord Essex's steward). Both the
architect and contractor said they had no power to vary the plan,
but they would proceed with the other parts of the repewing until
something was settled. I therefore wrote to Mr. Harding who is in
Yorkshire.'

Mr. Boodle was far too wily a man to involve his master in
quarrels of such a kind, and Messrs. Rayment and Stacey had to
accept their pews.

It was a pity that the Vestry did not at this time undertake the
repair of the church. When Harding died in 1873, it was found,
despite his improvements, to be 'in a sadly dilapidated condition.'

The Hardings had no children. There are numerous entries in
the diary which describe entertainments given by the rector and
his lady to the village children. One such reads as follows.

August 14, 1845

'Mr. and Mrs. Harding gave a Picnic party in their grounds and house this day, and the boys and girls of the National School were regaled with cakes and tea, and had each of them presented to them a Prayer Book by Mr. B. Heath of London. They had their gambols afterwards and finished with singing God Save the Queen. There was a very good assemblage of the neighbouring gentry.'

John Izzard rarely criticised the rector. But on 30 January 1853, he wrote—

'Our rector gave us the whole of the service appointed for the 30th January in commemoration of the martyrdom of King Charles 1st altho' the rubric specifies that when the day falls on a Sunday it is not to be performed until the next day.' The fact of the matter was, although John Izzard would not have acknowledged it, that the office for the Royal Martyr, together with those of May 29 (the Restoration of Charles II) and of November 5 (Gunpowder Treason) were no longer acceptable to contemporary taste. They had been put into the Revised Prayer Book of 1662 by Order of Crown and Convocation. They were removed on 17 January 1859 by Royal Warrant issued upon an address of both Houses of Parliament.

John Harding was a man of moderate views. He was neither an Evangelical nor a follower of the Oxford Movement. But it is clear that he took the spiritual duties of his office seriously. The only shortcoming which the diary exposes is his occasional absence from Walkern without making provision for services in his church. He was rector for 35 years, until his death. In Early Victorian times the country clergy were contented with their lot, and livings were held for long periods. Many a village up and down the country benefited, as did Walkern, by the presence in its midst of a pious and learned gentleman, a beacon not only of Christianity but of civilisation.

Something has already been said of William Malet the parson of Ardeley. He was a man of more ardent temperament than Harding. He had a greater idea of his priestly office. Having served in the Civil Service in India, he had seen something of the world and was able to view the Anglican Church against a wide background and to claim for it the standing of a branch of the Catholic Church.

In 1867 he undertook a pilgrimage to Rome and the Holy Land in the cause of Christian Reunion. His book *The Olive Leaf* tells the story of his travels.

He travelled dressed in a dark brown habit as Brother Michael of the Society of St. Joseph which had been founded in 1864 with the laudable, but somewhat disparate, aims of raising the fallen, preventing infanticide, and restoring collegiate life to the Church of England. He was accompanied by Brother Cyprian (the Rev. C. A. W. Dundas who is described as Prior and Founder of St. Augustine's College, Bristol).

Their farewells were made at a Conversazione of the Society of St. Joseph held at the Schoolroom of the Street Crossing-Sweepers Brigade, 25 East Castle Street, London. On this occasion the brethren Michael and Cyprian washed the feet of sundry crossing-sweeper boys whose services—they being Roman Catholics—had obligingly been lent by a complaisant Roman priest.

They set out armed with credentials which included a letter in Latin from the Rector of the Society, another from the Secretary of the Association for Christian Reunion, and a delightfully non-committal document from Lambeth which the late Archbishop Davidson, at the top of his form, could scarcely have bettered. His Grace wrote that he commended the Rev. W. W. Malet to the care of all Christians 'as one well worthy of such attention as they may please to bestow upon him.' Had it been known that Malet also carried a letter of introduction from Archbishop Manning to Monsignor Talbot, even this moderately phrased encomium must have been withheld.

At Rome the Brethren were received in audience by the Pope, and were given his blessing. They then embarked at Brindisi for Alexandria on an Austrian Lloyd steamer built and equipped in Britain and manned by British engineers. They crossed the Mediterranean for 200 francs, 2nd class. Another 59 francs took them on the Messagerie Imperiale steamer to Jaffa. Here they hired horses at 10/- each, and paid a guide 5/- to lead them over the sands and up the rocky track to Jerusalem. On the following day, Ascension Day 1867, they rode into the Holy City.

Mounted on a black donkey Malet visited all the Holy Places. He also conferred with the Patriarch of Jerusalem. By June 20 he was back at Jaffa, and had in the meantime made, for a pilgrim, the unusual acquisition of an Armenian man servant. Accompanied by him, but not by Brother Cyprian, he sailed to Constantinople where his brother Edward was Secretary at the British Embassy. He carried a letter of introduction from the Patriarch of Jerusalem to the Patriarch of Constantinople. 'Among other things', wrote the former, 'His Reverence asked if it might be permitted him to communicate in the Holy Church of the Resurrection: but with respect to this request His Reverence received the necessary answer from us'.

Malet called on the Patriarch and got very much out of his depth in a discussion on the Filioque clause. He had, however, the satisfaction of ascertaining that the Greek Church admitted the validity of Anglican Orders.

Accompanied by his servant, Malet returned by way of the Danube and Vienna, travelling thence by Cologne and Brussels. Tickets from Constantinople to Brussels for himself and servant 2nd class amounted to £22 odd.

Returning to his living Malet threw himself into the task of raising £900 for the restoration of his church. The restoration was undertaken in 1871 and was excellently done.

The contrast between John Lafont and William Malet is striking, but it is probably representative of the difference between the Early and the Mid-Victorian Church.

It would be wrong to leave the Early Victorian Church without mention of sermon and preachers. The latter occupied in the public mind a position equivalent to radio and television stars of today. John Izzard fancied himself as a judge of sermons, and heard some of the better preachers of the day.

The following entry relates not only to sermonising, but also to another feature of the times, the proprietary chapel, managed on commercial lines. Readers of Thackeray will recall Lady Whittlesea's Chapel, and its eloquent incumbent, the Rev. Charles Honeyman.

September 15, 1839

'Attended morning service at a new chapel belonging to the Rev. Mr. Sibthorpe who is considered a very eminent preacher. He gave us a good sermon but we did not like his manner. He evidently studies effect too much, but has his chapel well filled especially by ladies. The organ is a good one and is played in first rate style and two sets of choristers sing beautifully.'

Mrs. Pryor belonged to the High and Dry school of Oxford theology. It seems that to their way of thinking sermons must be read, or perhaps, delivered as if written.

October 10, 1830 (Southampton)

'This morning we went to attend service at Holy Rood which was crowded. The living is in the gift of Queens College Oxford and the present clergyman named Williams is a very clever and learned man, I should say from his discourse. But as he preached ex tempore my wife (not approving of that system) did not feel edified. His doctrine was orthodox and well received by his audience in general.'

A celebrated preacher under whom John Izzard frequently sat was the Rev. Henry Melvill, Principal of the East India Company's College at Haileybury near Hertford. On the closure of the College he was made a Canon of St. Paul's.

October 3, 1844

'Left Clay Hall at 9 a.m. in the brisktza with my wife and daughter Emma and were set down at All Saints' church, Hertford at 11 just as the service began, the Rev. H. Melville, the Professor of Haileybury College, preaching the sermon for the benefit of the Societies of Christian Knowledge and Propagating the Gospel abroad. It was one of the most impressive and eloquent I ever heard. A collection was made at the church door amounting to nearly £50.'

According to the *Dictionary of National Biography* 'his sermons generally occupied ¾ hour, but such was the rapidity of his utterances that he spoke as much in that time as an ordinary preacher would have done in an hour. His delivery was earnest and animated without distinctive gesticulation; his voice was clear and flexible; while his emphatic pronunciation and his hurried manner of speaking impressed his hearers with a conviction of sincerity.' But his sermons lacked simplicity and appealed more directly to the literary than to the spiritual sense.

While staying with Dr. Bliss at Oxford in 1848 John Izzard heard a sermon from Dr. Pusey.

November 26, 1848

'The celebrated Dr. Pusey, Professor of Hebrew and one of the Canons of Christ Church, being appointed according to rotation to preach the University Sermon at Christ Church this morning at half past 10, and from the noise he has made in Oxford, and indeed in England, from some of his writings having a Romanising tendency, the church was expected to be extremely crowded. We were admitted by one of the students into a good place before the regular doors were opened. The church was soon filled and half the congregation obliged to stand. Dr. Pusey on entering his pulpit was long engaged unseen in private prayer, the organ playing. He then rose and preached what I should call a most excellent charity sermon, thereby avoiding all doctrinal points and I have no doubt disappointing many.'

But the greatest preacher of them all was no Anglican, but a Nonconformist divine, the Rev. Joseph Sortain (1809–60).

October 5, 1845, Sunday (at Brighton)

'Having heard that there was a celebrated preacher at the Chapel in North Street (Lady Huntingdon's), Dr. Bliss and I concluded to go and hear him. On arriving there before the service began we could only get standing room for a long time, but the pew opener brought us some chairs until she could do better for us. The prayers were read by a clergyman with a fine voice and excellent pronunciation. When Mr. Sortain who is the celebrated preacher and is a bachelor of Arts of the University of Dublin ascended the pulpit you might almost have heard a pin drop, such was the silence. His prayer and exordium were delivered in a very low tone of voice and his eyes completely closed, but the matter was to the purpose and extremely good. He handled his subject (the vision of St. Luke) in a most energetic and impassioned manner. He might be thought probably by some to make too much use of his hands, but it was so judicious as to cause tears to be shed by some in the congregation. His language was first rate and I think his discourse the most affecting I have ever heard with perhaps the exception of Mr. Melville.

Addenda to Mr. Sortain's sermon.

The vision seen by St. Luke of the heavens being opened and the Son of Man being seen by him standing at the right hand of God, he explained to be such an important circumstance, showing that He was still most anxiously concerned for the welfare of mankind; whereas had He been sitting it might have given rise to the opinion everything had been that could be done whilst on earth and was

resting from taking further interest in ungrateful man. His knowledge of inmost thoughts and actions he dilated upon in a very
affecting manner.'

In no other case did John Izzard summarise a sermon. It must,
therefore, have been singularly impressive. *The Times,* writing
about Sortain after his death, paid tribute to the originality of his
sermons, which were attended by vast congregations among whom
were often the leading men of literature and science of the day.

In admiring this dissenting minister John Izzard was in good
company.

XVI

JOHN IZZARD AND THE CROWN

On 26 June 1830 John Izzard wrote, 'His Majesty King George the Fourth died this morning at a quarter past 3 o'clock after a lingering illness.

Lafont and Alfred rose at 4 o'clock to fish for trout in the river, thinking after the close night accompanied with a good deal of lightning the fish would rise. They were successful, catching six brace of trout of about ½lb weight each.'

The death of the monarch did not long detain John Izzard. He was more interested in the perspicacity and good fortune of the anglers.

July 15, 1830

'Dined alone my family being out. The late King George the Fourth was buried at Windsor this evening. I heard the cannon firing very plain at Clay Hall.'

The death of William IV was also recorded without any expression of regret.

June 20, 1837

'In the evening the reports of the King's decease were confirmed by some of the morning papers. He died at 12 minutes past 2 o'clock this morning.'

July 8, 1837

'This day was observed in London and many great towns with great solemnity and abstinence from business in great measure in consequence of the funeral of the late king William the 4th which took place at Windsor at about 11 o'clock at night.'

This was the last royal funeral to take place at night.

John Izzard had made not the slightest attempt to see the coronation of William IV. He was in London, however, for the coronation of Queen Victoria. He was staying with brother Robert at Brick Lane, and Mrs. Pryor, Emma and Juliana, and grandson Ogle Lafont were with him. However, no effort was

151

made to procure seats for the ladies and little Ogle. They were left at Brick Lane.

June 28, 1837

'Coronation of Queen Victoria. Everybody on the move early in the morning, particularly those who had tickets for the ceremony at Westminster Abbey. The morning looked rather doubtful but fortunately it cleared and became a fine day, but without much sunshine. The ladies who wished to secure good places at the Abbey were setting off as early as half past 3, and by 4 I understood there was a complete blockade of carriages.

I had fixed with my son John to accompany him to Green & Wards in Cockspur Street where he had been offered two seats; and to breakfast with him at the Berners Hotel at 7. I therefore rose at 5, and set off at 6. Not being able to find any sort of vehicle to ride in before I nearly reached Berners Street, it was just 7 before I reached there. Taking a hasty breakfast we proceeded to Green & Wards arriving there at half past 8. My bro' Robert was to have a seat at the Phoenix Fire Office West End station, opposite the centre of Trafalgar Square but a short distance from us, both excellent places for seeing the procession. It began to pass about half past 10 and was the most splendid and gorgeous spectacle I ever saw in my life. It had all passed by by 12 o'clock; and the millions of people collected began to move, some towards the Abbey, and some to the Parks where a fair was held and grand fireworks were to be exhibited at night.

It struck me that I could get my wife and daughters up to our places in time for the return of the cavalcade. By dint of shoving and pushing I got through the crowd. I was lucky enough after going some distance to get a place in an omnibus as far as the Bank, and in Bishopsgate Street I hired a hackney coach for a sovereign for the afternoon. Drove to Brick Lane and very soon set off again with my wife, daughters and grandson Ogle Lafont. Near the Haymarket, not being able to get any nearer, we alighted and walked to Cockspur Street and found the way not so much crowded as when I left, the populace not having returned. My wife, daughter Emma and grandson Ogle took our seats at Green & Wards. My bro' Robert who I met there, said he could take Juliana and myself to the Phoenix Office. The procession returned as it went and all were most highly gratified.

After waiting some time after the procession passed, we made our way to our coach and dined at Brick Lane. Most brilliant illuminations and fireworks.'

When the Queen came to marry, proper notice of the event was taken at Clay Hall.

February 10, 1840

'The wedding day of our Queen Victoria who married Prince Albert of Saxe-Gotha. The ceremony was performed in the chapel at St. James' Palace. An amazing concourse of people assembled on the occasion, and both Queen and Prince received the hearty good wishes of one and all. Splendid illuminations took place in London but they were by no means general in the country.

I planted this day a fine oak in the centre of the new made ring in Bennington pastures, and the outermost circle of spruce firs to commemorate the occasion.

Soon after 5 p.m. I had all my farming men, gardeners etc. marshalled in front of the Farm House, and gave each of them, boys and all, 1 pint of strong beer to drink the good health of the Queen and Prince; and to every married man 1 quartern loaf, ½ lb. cheese, and 1 quart of beer, and to every boy ½ quartern loaf and a pint of beer.'

The match was not popular, and rejoicings were by no means general, as John Izzard remarks. At Hitchin William Lucas the diarist (G. B. Bryant, *A Quaker Journal*) wrote, 'There were no signs of loyalty beyond ringing of bells and a few squibs and crackers.'

There must have been many a Walkern villager who remembered to his dying day the christening of the future King Edward VII.

January 25, 1842

'The christening of the young Prince of Wales at Windsor this day.

On awakening this morning I found the ground covered nearly a foot thick with snow. I gave a dinner of roast beef and plum pudding for the boys and girls of the Sunday School. About 75; 5 attendants made the party 80. It took place at 2 o'clock in Mr. Harding's Long Room which just held them. Mrs. Harding, myself and J. Wilson my butler carved for them. I never saw such a quantity of eatables disposed of in so short a time. All were helped twice to meat and pudding. The young Prince of Wales' health was drunk with juvenile enthusiasm as I had ordered half a pint of strong beer for each of them. I also had bread and beer distributed to every poor family in proportion to their numbers for them to celebrate the day, for which they were thankful.'

Perhaps the greatest day in John Izzard's life occurred in 1846 when the Queen came to stay at Hatfield House.

October 22, 1846

'Having been engaged to go to my son Alfred, by luncheon time this morning, to see the Queen's entry into Hatfield, we left about quarter past 11 with the carriage open, the day being fine, my wife, Miss West (Fred's betrothed), daughter Emma and myself inside, Fred and Wenham (the lady's maid) behind, and Cooper and the luggage on the box. We arrived about half past 1, passing under one triumphal arch before we entered the town. We took luncheon and afterwards walked up the hill to see the display of triumphal arches of which there were several and flags floating from most of the houses on each side, quite to the entrance of Hatfield House. Lamps were placed ready for an illumination at night. Alfred had a platform raised high enough to command a capital view. A little before 4 the Queen came in, preceded by the Noble Marquis and the Duke of Wellington with a large escort of the South Herts Yeomanry at a quick pace, and was received with great and enthusiastic cheering.

An ox was prepared to be roasted whole in the Park for a dinner tomorrow to the labourers employed by the Marquess. The roasting was to begin at 8 this evening and it was expected to require 18 hours roasting time.

Mr. Branton who had been on duty escorting the Queen from St. Albans dined with us. After tea the gentlemen walked out to see the illuminations in the Park. In going we met with a curious adventure. To avoid the crowd which went by the footpath to the roasting place we went thro' the Great Gates which lead to Hatfield House. When on the inside an officer with several attendants demanded the Pass Word which we knew nothing of. They said they had strict orders not to let anyone pass without the word, and that we might be detained in the Guard Room. We enquired for the Captain a fellow officer with Mr. Branton but he was gone to Hatfield House. We desired to be escorted to see him. After a long detention we went. On the circumstances being mentioned to the officer he laughed heartily, and gave us the Pass Word, which was 'The Queen', whereupon we left to pursue our way to the ox where we found a large concourse of all sorts.

Our party, except myself, had wide-awake hats and dreadnought rough coats which, until we gave our names, made the guard think we were not gentlemen.'

October 23, 1846

'Fortunately the morning proved very fine altho' there had been rain again in the night. People from all the country round about kept pouring in, and by 12 o'clock there were thousands spread about the Park in all directions. Prince Albert and the Marquess and the guests shot in the preserves in the Park until luncheon time. They were in sight all the latter part of the time.

Three sides of a quadrangle were prepared for the labourers to partake of the ox. It was ready about 3 o'clock and brought to the table with 2 or 3 barrels of ale. It did not appear to be quite sufficiently roasted, but most of it soon disappeared.

The Queen drove thro' part of the Park to Brocket Hall in the afternoon and was loudly cheered as she went and returned.

Camp brought the letters, mine and Mrs. P.'s invitation to the Ball amongst them. It takes place tonight, the time being fixed for 9 o'clock. Mrs. Vickris Pryor, Richard and Juliana, sons John and Morris and his wife, my wife and myself have all had invitations. We all dined together at Alfred's with Emma, Fred and Miss West who do not go to the ball.

We set off in three carriages soon after 9 and got there in the nick of time, the company pouring in very fast. The Marquess received the company courteously, and after being assembled in the Library a short time, the doors were flung open, and we passed the Queen on a throne in the splendid Long Gallery. We were introduced to the Queen as we passed. When the part of the gallery beyond the Queen was full, the remainder of the company did not pass and so were not introduced to the Queen. We thought ourselves very lucky in being amongst those who passed and had so good an opportunity of seeing the Queen.

The Ball was opened by the Queen dancing with the Marquess of Salisbury and Dukes and Lords with the Marquess's daughters Lady Hope and Lady Blanche Balfour. The Queen danced with great spirit and appeared to enjoy her evening, afterwards dancing with the Duke of Rutland and others. Supper was announced a little before 12. The Queen with the Marquess and her ladies in waiting, the Marquess's daughters and a few others sat at a table by themselves in the Grand Hall where the company took their refreshments standing. Everything choice and recherché in abundance. The white soup particularly good. Iced champagne and excellent sherry was much enjoyed after the heat of the rooms. Two sets of Quadrilles were formed after supper. The Queen did not appear again. The company began to retire about half past 1.'

October 24, 1846

'The Queen left about half past 2, the Marquess accompanying her on horseback part of the way, as well as an escort of the Yeomanry.'

Five years later, the Queen passed through Hertfordshire on her way north to Balmoral. But this time she travelled by railway.

August 27, 1851

'My wife and daughters Emma and Juliana and I set off in the open carriage for Hitchin at 20 minutes past 12 and arrived there at 2. We had to make our way through a great crowd to get to the platform of the Gt. Northern station where, on presenting our ticket, we were admitted to a very good place on a reserved part of the platform. At 10 minutes past 3 the Royal Saloon Carriage containing the Queen, Prince Albert and three of the Royal children stopped exactly opposite us. We had a very good sight of them, Prince Albert drawing the curtain away from the window and the Queen and himself standing up in the carriage, appearing pleased with the decoration of the station and the immense assemblage of the principal inhabitants and also of the population extending a long way on the banks of the cutting of the Railroad. After staying about 8 minutes for a supply of water during which God save the Queen was sung, and loud huzzas saluted the ear of the Queen, a few moments pause took place, and a young lady (Miss Exton), one of the Society of Friends, presented the Queen with a small plateau of beautiful flowers which were most graciously accepted. N.B. Miss Exton the daughter of a Hitchin banker whose firm are the local bankers of the Great Northern Rail.'

Margaret Exton[1] merits another N.B. from the author. In 1857

[1] There are references to her in Reginald L. Hine's *History of Hitchin* (see his index).

she married Gurney Barclay as his second wife, and became the mother of that latter-day Hertfordshire worthy, Edward Barclay, squire of Brent Pelham, for over fifty years the illustrious Master of the Puckeridge Foxhounds.

The Times' correspondent who accompanied the Royal Party describes the scene at Hitchin station much as John Izzard did, and goes on as follows (28 August 1851): 'The train started in a few minutes and was soon dashing along the level but well cultivated land of Hertfordshire. When the carriage came in sight with the royal standard hoisted, people might be seen dotting the fields as they ran along over the swathes of fresh cut corn, or tripped across the hedges in their race for a good glimpse. Occasionally a stout old squire came rattling along on a good hunter with sons and daughters all mounted, and drew up by the line cheering lustily. All the schools for miles round must have been present, and wonderful ingenuity was displayed in combining gaily coloured handkerchiefs so as to pass muster for flags and banners. Gainsborough would have feasted his eyes on many a bit of rustic life. Old gleaners with grotesque bonnets waving a handful of corn ears; children running down some shady lane, or balanced on a gate in the full swing of good spirits and juvenile loyalty, and such groupings of human and animal life as are to be met with rarely out of an agricultural country.'

XVII

FARMING IN TIMES GOOD, BAD
AND INDIFFERENT

John Izzard farmed the Home Farm at Clay Hall from 1828 to
1861. These thirty odd years were a momentous period in the
history of farming in Britain. They saw the virtual completion
of the enclosure of Hertfordshire, and indeed of Eastern England,[1]
the draining of farm land, much of it with the aid of Government
subsidy; the application of chemistry to agriculture; the beginnings of mechanisation; the Repeal of the Corn Laws; and the
first ten of the twenty years of high farming preceding the agricultural depression which lasted, with a few years' interruption at
the time of the 1914—18 War, until Hitler's armies took the field.

The Home Farm was about 300 acres in extent, of boulder clay.
It grew wheat, barley, oats, beans, peas, tares, mustard, turnips,
potatoes, carrots and clover. The most important stock kept was
a flock of sheep, round which the farming system revolved. But
pigs were also fattened there, and it was the custom to buy in
Scots bullocks in the autumn, and to 'yard' them. Stevenage was
one of the halting places of Scots drovers, taking their cattle to
London. Indeed, Trinity church was built on the site of a large
pond in which drovers watered their cattle.

During the long time during which he kept them John Izzard
had little trouble with his sheep. They were a healthy flock,
probably because being folded they were rarely on stale land.
But he was not entirely exempt from the worries which beset the
modern flock-owner as the following entries show.

April 13, 1831
'Story of Box Hall Farm had several more lambs killed by a dog
this morning early. His shepherd with my man John Pike tracked
the dog as far as Porter's bridge Walkern. From the marks they

---

[1] Essex and East Herts. formed the Kingdom of Essex and were never in East Anglia.

158

have very little doubt it was John Pearman's dog, generally kept at the White Lyon. They went with some other farmers and examined him and found his nose and breast bloody and desired that he might be despatched. But his master said he would tie him up, and if there were no more lambs killed he would hang him as that would be plain proof. But everybody is of the opinion That is the Dog. There have been above 30 lambs killed.'

Neither the dog nor his master has changed. The former still delights to chase the sheep; the latter is still slow to give a dog a bad name, and proceed to extremities. There is one difference. Nowadays it would be unthinkable to hang a dog; a century and more ago it was the usual method of destruction.

March 4, 1841

'Having received a summons to attend upon the Grand Jury I set off in the carriage to Hertford. I did not serve and took my seat in the Grand Jury Gallery to hear the trial of several of the prisoners amongst whom was one from Walkern for stealing a sheep out of Mr. Stacy's fold and who was found guilty and sentenced to be transported for 10 years. He once worked for me as cowman and was a very indifferent character.'

It was astonishing that more farm workers did not leave the strait and narrow way. There was little enough inducement to stay on it. Farmers had their ups and downs. They sold a quarter of wheat for 60/6d. in 1828, for 39/4d. in 1835, for 70/8d. in 1839, for 50/10d. in 1845, for 44/3d. in 1849, and for 43/9d. ten years later, having for two of the intervening years, 1854 and 1855 got between 72/- and 75/- for it. They had their good times and their bad. But for the farm worker there were no good times, but only bad times and worse times.

November 1, 1834

'The farmers in the neighbourhood having reduced their labourers' wages for the last few weeks from 9/- to 8/- per week in consequence of the very low price of wheat I gave my men notice last week that I must do the same this week. It is too low a price for the farmer to live. Rents will be badly paid this year, especially when the crops were bad, which was the case on the light and gravelly land from the great drought.'

Wages followed the price of wheat closely. Nothing else was taken into account.

September 3, 1847

'Examined Pike's book of wages to find out when wages were sunk and raised during the last two years and found as follows—

      July 26 1845 sunk from 10s. to 9 per week.

      Oct 25 1845 advanced from   9 to 10 per week.

      May   8 1846 advanced from 10 to 11 per week.

As the price of bread is sunk from 10½d, the price it was at when wages were advanced in May 1846, to 7½d the present price, I propose to reduce wages 1/- per week on Saturday September 11.'

For one month in the year, the farm worker did better than this. It was the rule then (as it is now) to employ farm labour by the week. An exception was made at harvest when men were engaged by the month.

August 4, 1852

'Took our men into their harvest month this morning. They are to have £3—15—0 and their breakfast at the beginning and a supper at the Hokey—which is much more than £4—0—0 given by the other farmers without either breakfast or supper.'

The Hokey was the traditional party of rejoicing at the conclusion of harvest.

Fortunately, not only Hodge himself but his wife and children would be found employment at certain times of year. If additional men could not be found at harvest, women were employed to reap.

August 9, 1830

'Set all hands to work reaping wheat but as this week many men went into their months but few men made their appearance for reaping. Therefore employed 12 to 16 women who reap low and even but do not tie and set up as well as men. Last week there was a great many reapers enquiring for work which they found readily at Baldock but my wheat at Clay Hall was not ready for the sickle.

Took our men into their month this day as the oats are about ready to cut.'

On such wages as were paid, it was impossible to put by a reserve against the rainy day. Incendiarism, which was a symptom of agricultural unrest, finds frequent mention in the diary. It seems that from time to time the patient sighing of the rural poor gave place to an exasperation which found expression in rick burning.

At the March Assizes in 1843 John Izzard wrote: 'It was very, although at times painfully, interesting. I heard Covington's trial for burning the ricks at Nuneham. He was found guilty and sentenced to 15 years transportation.'

It is, perhaps, not entirely a coincidence that *Punch* in 1844 published Leech's drawing of the Rick Burner's Home—he used to hunt with the Puckeridge. In a bare room beside the bed whereon his wife lies dying, on a half wrecked chair, sits a labourer, plunged in thought, a child on his knee, and three at his feet. A leering devil with a torch in his hand dances in the background.

Punch always had a soft spot for the Early Victorian farm workers. He understood what drove men to such acts as these. So, too, did juries, who were often reluctant to convict.

In 1855 a rick was fired on one of Morris's farms. John Izzard comments: 'It is a diabolical affair, the premises near having been destroyed by fire rather more than a twelvemonth ago. The men worked well, and my son Morris who was very much exhausted in body and afflicted in mind.'

A man was charged with the offence at the Assizes soon after, but the jury acquitted him.

A few weeks later: 'Last night some villain set fire to a clover rick belonging to my son Morris'. It was totally destroyed. The comment: 'It is a grievous thing that no person's property is safe and that on trial at the Assizes the petty juries are very apt to acquit the persons strongly suspected and the wicked rascals escape.'

He was fortunate that no stack was ever burnt at Clay Hall; or was there more than mere chance at work?

The diary speaks of enclosure in two parishes, Walkern and Sandon.

At Walkern, when enclosure was mooted in 1848, although there had been at one time nine 'commons', none was in fact common grazing ground. All had been partitioned and were held in severalty by individuals. But their arable land lay in intermixed strips, and the 'commons' were Open Fields. The lord of the manor held grazing rights over any crops grown on such land until the last Thursday in May, according to custom, a practice which would only be tolerable when both crops and flocks had a common owner. Enclosure put an end to such rights, and enabled holdings to be consolidated, and a system of roads to be laid down to serve farming purposes.

The Walkern Enclosure went forward without any serious hitch. In the place of numerous strips, John Izzard was awarded a block of 30 acres of what was formerly Breach Common Field.

At Sandon, however, some 26 acres of common grazing ground still survived when Enclosure was first discussed.

March 12, 1840

'Rode over to Sandon to attend a meeting called expressly for taking the sense of the small proprietors who have claims for common right, to ascertain their sentiments and wishes respecting which of two modes they would prefer for enclosing the parish— whether by an especial Act to be obtained thro' Parliament which would authorise the enclosure of the common, or by the General Inclosure Act which allows of inclosure taking place but the commons not to be meddled with, provided it has the sanction of two-thirds of the proprietors in number and value.

The meeting took place at the Anchor at Roe Green and was very fully attended by small proprietors who after a great deal of discussion and explanation came to the unanimous opinion that they should much prefer the latter.'

The rights-holders at Sandon were sufficiently numerous and cohesive to prevent the enclosure of the commons. Under the Act of 1801 it would have required a special Act of Parliament, albeit passed by means of a simplified and relatively inexpensive procedure, to enclose the Commons. The Open Fields, however, could be enclosed under the Act of 1836 provided two-thirds of the possessors of open-field rights, in number and value, were agreed.

Thus the surviving commons were left outside the scope of the Enclosure. But there was a small patch of common land at a distance from the other commons which John Izzard wanted to absorb, compensating the rights-holders with land more centrally situated.

January 7, 1842

'Rode over to Sandon this morning to take the agreement signed by all the owners of Cow Common Right excepting two, for an exchange of some waste lands adjoining the road betwixt Gannock Farm belonging to Mr. Fordham and my farm occupied by

R. Walby, for other lands more valuable and convenient for them.

The two individuals are Kingsley who keeps our public house the Six Bells at Sandon and Cannon of Walkern. Mr. Fordham wished me to use my influence with Kingsley. But when I applied he was so obstinate as to refuse to sign, I believe at the instigation of his wife. I told him he was under great obligation to me, and if he did not do as the rest of the owners of Cow Common Right had done I thought he was not a proper person to keep a public house, and he must expect a notice to quit should he continue so blind to his own interest. I then left him and his wife who is a most disagreeable creature. I returned the agreement to Mr. T. Veasey from whom I had received it with an account of my not succeeding.'

This 'Village Hampden, that with dauntless breast The little tyrant of his fields withstood' is commemorated by a piece of common land so situated as to be of little use to common-right holders.

The Sandon Enclosure consolidated holdings which, by reason of historical accident had been much dispersed. It enabled holdings to be fenced, and a road system to be constructed.

April 27, 1841

'I rode over to Sandon and examined the quicks (the new hedges) which appear to be shooting very nicely. A great many men were at work forming the principal new road from Gannock Farm, by Bury Barns in the direction of Odsey to the Royston Road. Men also digging gravel, and many women and girls picking stones.'

The Sandon Commons survive to this day. If the historians are correct in believing that rights of common were important in furnishing means by which the labourer could better himself, then the history of Sandon during the last century has been happier than that of less favoured villages. But it has proved impossible to collect any evidence on this point. It might have been expected that, with grazing available on the commons, small holdings such as are characteristic of peasant agriculture, would have flourished at Sandon. But it does not appear that there are more small holdings at Sandon than in other villages. The Sandon pastoralist may, however, still be observed at his age-old task of watching his cattle as they graze the unenclosed heath. When the wind is sharp he will be found in the glassy shelter of the telephone kiosk.

On the evidence before us, we may acquit the Pryors of stealing the common from the goose. An isolated entry in the diary does, however, illustrate how the poor sometimes lost their rights as a result of enclosure.

March 6, 1829

'Brother Robert came down from London by the Express Coach; arrived at half past 11. Took luncheon at our house after which, at his request I rode over to Dunton with him to look over his farm and inspect the Award. He wished to know the particulars respecting a low piece of ground at the extremity of the farm about 19 acres which is wet and rushy—whether there was a right left open to the Poor of the Parish to dig turf for fuel on any part thereof, or whether it was confined to any particular spot. There is a small allotment marked out in the map for the Poor which has never been divided or fenced off from his and over which his tenants' cattle graze. It, however, appears plain by the Award there is permission for the Poor to dig turf under specified restrictions on or over any part of his allotment. He proposes planting a small part of it to try how it answers, as it turns to very little account at present. It appears very little turf is now dug there for fuel.

Returned home to a 6 o'clock dinner at my sister Elizabeth's.'

> Lo! where the heath with withering brake grown o'er
> Lends the light turf which warms the neighbouring poor

writes Parson Crabbe in *The Village*. It is to be feared that the neighbouring poor cut no more turf on brother Robert's allotment. This word, at the time of the parliamentary enclosures, meant the share allotted to a landowner under an Enclosure Award. Some of the small patches of land, now known as allotments, were, in fact, allotted to the use of the poor when the village was enclosed. But before 1845, not 1 per cent. of the Enclosure Acts made any allotment to the poor by way of compensation for the amenities lost to them by enclosure. Where such an allotment was made, no provision was made to assist the poor to fence it although it was not uncommon for the other landowners to finance the fencing of the parson's glebe.

Most of the Home Farm at Walkern had been long enclosed.

John Izzard started to drain it in 1842. At this time he wrote, 'We dig the drains two feet deep and use strong black and white thorn wood.' White and black thorn at the bottom of the drain were used in lieu of pipes, and worked efficiently. A cylindrical clay pipe for land drainage was not produced on a large scale until 1845. But John Izzard's 'hollow drains', as he called them, the soil replaced in trenches the bottom of which was filled with thorn bushes, functioned very well.

As a consolation to the agricultural community for the repeal of the Corn Laws, Peel passed an Act for the grant of loans of public money to finance drainage of farm land—an Act which Surtees claimed advanced agriculture more than all the previous legislation and inventions put together.

January 19, 1852

'Went out in my garden chair and was drawn over the field lately held by Mr. Stacey, now in hand of the proprietor the Earl of Essex, belonging to Walkern Bury Farm. He is having all the heavy land drained under a late Act of Parliament for advancing money for that purpose. The interest and part of the principal is spread over a number of years. It is drained four feet deep and piped tiles used.'

The Acts (there were two) were widely used, and must have done as much as enclosures to alter the appearance of the countryside. Contemporary novelists certainly regarded them as an important event. Squire Hamley of Mrs. Gaskell's *Wives and Daughters* and Major Yammerton of Surtees' *Ask Mamma* both financed the drainage of their estates by this means.

Drainage was an essential preliminary to the application of chemistry to agriculture. It was no use putting expensive chemicals on land if they were to be leached away by water.

John Izzard was an early believer in the application of chemical manures. As early as 1828 we are told that 'two men are sowing salt petre on the wheat, ¼ cwt. per acre mixed with 6 bushels of cinder dust.' He also used to spread soot on his young cereals.

The first mention of chemical manure as known at present is on 28 April 1841.

'Sowing the nitrate of soda on the oats in Pear Tree Close and Cross Path Field, leaving a land unsown near the middle of each.'

On 14 September we are told that the oats were 'but a poor

crop altho' they looked well early and had a cwt. of nitrate of soda per acre.'

He tried it on an acre of clover also, 'but it did not appear much the better.'

His next experiment was—

December 2, 1843

'I superintended the mixing up a heap of decayed vegetable rakings up of the garden, about 3 cart loads. On this I had the contents of a 36-gallon barrel of ammoniacal gas liquor which I procured from the Gas Works at Baldock. I understood it was a very excellent plan for making a rich compost, to remain 2 or 3 months afterward in the heap.'

The 'ammoniacal gas' odour is most offensive.

July 9, 1844

'I rode over to Sandon. Finding my tenant R. Walby on the field I looked over part of the farm with him. He has a very fine crop of barley on the large field behind the Park Wood. R. Walby is Agent to Mr. Lawes for the sale of super phosphate of lime (a composition of bone dust and sulphuric acid etc. highly spoken of). I bought a bag weighing 2 cwt. by way of trial to drill in on the Shoulder of Mutton Piece.'

July 27, 1844

'Examined the turnips on the Shoulder of Mutton Piece in Brook Field sown to test the different composts, viz. guano, super phosphate of lime, and put in without any—but the whole piece had been dunged before ploughing. The young turnips look the best on the part drilled without either of the composts. The part with phosphate of lime is the next best and the part drilled with guano the worst. I expect the ground has been too dry for any good effect from the composts but how far the drilling in the compost with the turnip seed may have deposited the seed deeper than were the turnips that were drilled without any compost I can hardly judge. Or perhaps the guano destroyed the vitality of the seed.'

Thus, it does not seem that any of John Izzard's experiments with chemical manures was a success. We hear no more of them. But if Walby continued to grow good barley, perhaps John Izzard tried some superphosphate on his. If Walby was a good agent for 'Mr. Lawes' he probably did.

John Bennett Lawes, after an education at Eton and Oxford, studied chemistry at London University, and then applied his knowledge to agriculture on his estate at Rothampstead. He took out a patent for the manufacture of superphosphates in 1842, thus founding an industry, and made a fortune. He left the Rothampstead estate and £100,000 to the nation.

John Izzard was a believer in pedigree seed. As early as 1828 he was buying his grass and clover seed for his leys. He was particular about his wheat seed.

September 18, 1844
'Received a note from my son Morris to say he had bought 12 loads of the seed wheat called Rattling Jack to be ready by the 25th of his tenant Gardiner at Stand Alone Farm, Wilbury.'

This variety had a long life.

July 31, 1852
'Saw a company of men reaping Mr. Rowlatt's large new allotment which is wheat, sadly mildewed during the last week.'

August 3, 1852
'Began reaping wheat this morning in South Field. 10 men and 10 women. It is a good crop, full five loads per acre and of a good colour having escaped the blight of mildew. It is of the sort called Rattling Jack which I sowed for my whole crop and all of which looks well at present.'

John Izzard was interested in agricultural machinery.

August 4, 1849
'Went on my pony to see a threshing machine at work driven by a steam engine. It appeared to do its work remarkably well but looks rather dangerous. But the owner of the engine said there was no danger as the red hot cinders fell into a shallow cystern of water and the steam generated passed by a tube into the chimney which extinguished the sparks from passing out on fire. There were about 30 men employed on passing the sheaves to it, feeding it, taking the straw away in front and the wheat and chaff behind. Extra insurance is paid.'

But it was not until 1856 that this method of threshing was employed at Clay Hall.

September 4, 1851
'I rode my pony over to Great Wymondley to see a Mr.

MacCormick's American Reaping Machine at work. It was exhibited at the Chrystal Palace and was said to reap 12 acres p. diem of wheat, drawn by two horses.

There were a great crowd of agriculturists present. It was set to work in a large field of Rivett wheat, all standing. It did not do its work well at first—the straw being damp from the heavy fog and they stopped proceedings for ½ an hour. It performed better afterwards. It appeared to cut the wheat well except in laid places and in furrows, but on being raked from the machine it lay sprawling in heaps about the size of two of our gavins, requiring readjusting afterwards and having a slovenly appearance. There must be some improvement before any farmer will be induced to have his wheat cut by it. It will not cut in wet weather. I have not a good opinion of it.'

Mechanical side delivery came in 1865, but that triumph of ingenuity, the knotter, did not appear until 1879.

The only machine which John Izzard bought was a 'haymaking machine' which he purchased at a farm sale for £9—10—0. He toyed with the idea of buying a liquid manure spreader, possibly in connection with his scheme for using the house sewage. But he undoubtedly used a drill to sow his crops.

Like most farmers, there was nothing John Izzard enjoyed so much as talking shop.

May 27, 1843

'Left Oxford at half past 9 a.m. by the Mail to Steventon and at 11 got into a first class carriage in the train. A gentleman, who had been in the coach from Oxford and whom I found an agreeable companion being a very scientific agriculturist as well as a sporting man, got into the same carriage. He was on his way to Epsom to see the Derby run. He recognised a gentleman as being a fellow agriculturist and bound likewise for Epsom. They discussed their different modes of farming and their opinion of the different new composts for manuring land and the different modes of feeding stock, much to my amusement. My first companion was named Evans and I found that he had studied chemistry and had made many practical experiments in analysing different soils, but confessed he could get no profit now. The other gentleman said he very seldom ploughed his land, using only the scarifier and harrow. He was extremely particular in managing his dung and making dunghills, and thus he could, even now, make a profit.'

John Izzard was a member of the Royal Agricultural Society and attended the Show at Southampton in 1844. He had difficulty in getting a bed, 'all the beds at the different hotels had been bespoke for weeks'.

On the advice of Mr. Jonas Webb of Babraham, Cambs., the breeder of South Down Sheep (the only farmer who has had the honour of a public statue), he went to the Show at 7 a.m. and 'was much gratified by taking a general survey without any crowding.' When he left at 12, thousands were pouring in.

There was a great dinner at 4 in a large pavilion erected for the occasion, and the speakers included Lord Palmerston. 'But the Duke of Richmond was most applauded.'

Fat Stock Shows—Baker Street was the venue—were popular with the country gentry and with the Pryors. The Prince Consort took an interest in them. Anent one fat beast *Punch* wrote in 1843—

> Some with its symmetry were fired,
> Some praised its growth till they were tired,
> And much the Queen the beast admired
>   Said she ' 'Tis very fat'.
> The Prince into its breed enquired
>   And fodder and all that.

John Izzard was always ready to help anyone design a house, and no doubt would have been glad to do so without the plans sponsored by the R.A.S.E.

March 4, 1850

'Went to the Rectory with Mr. Harding who is about to build a new gardener's house or lodge, taking down the old one. I made a sketch of one I thought he might like to see taken principally from plans of labourers' cottages in the last publication of the Royal Agricultural Society.'

One of the chief events in John Izzard's farming career was the Repeal of the Corn Laws.

September 12, 1845

'Examined my potatoes which partake of the general blight, by some called murrain. It extends over the greater part of the kingdom and also prevails on the continent. I concluded to let mine stand. There appear to be $^1/_3$ of them tolerably sound. Many have not above $^1/_8$ and are taking them up.'

He had no idea that the blight which he saw in his potatoes was to have such momentous consequences. By the end of the month, the Prime Minister, Peel, had realised that half the Irish peasantry would have to be fed on corn in 1846, and that all legal impediments to the import of corn would have to be removed. It was some months before he could make the Tory Party face the grim facts.

Meanwhile John Izzard went off to a rainy holiday at Brighton, unconscious that the future of rural Britain was in jeopardy, and that the spectre of Famine could be seen approaching in Ireland. At Clay Hall in his absence the harvest was got in with loss and difficulty.

A few months later, December 6, while searching for the Puckeridge Hounds whom he had missed, he pondered over 'an extraordinary statement in yesterday's Times proclaiming that the Ministers had decided to repeal the Corn Laws—entirely believed by some, totally disbelieved by others.'

In fact, on 8 December, Peel, meeting with opposition in his Cabinet, had resigned. But Lord John Russell was unable to form a Ministry, and by the end of the month, Peel, 'feeling like a man restored to life after his funeral sermon had been preached', was Prime Minister once more. The Corn Laws were repealed. That summer the blight was even worse.

September 10, 1846

'The potatoes on the farm which looked beautifully green when I left home were all turned quite black and will be good for little I am afraid. The calamity appears to pervade every county in England and Ireland and will be most severely felt in the latter country.'

It was a poor corn crop, and the price of the 4lb. loaf rose from 8½d. in 1846 to 11½d. in 1847. Merchants, rejoicing in the new freedom of trade, combed Europe for grain. By the summer of 1847 the channel was thronged with grain ships, seeking British ports. Wheat was worth 124/- in June; but by September, so efficiently had the corn merchants operated, that the price was down to 49/6d, and they had ruined themselves. In August, seven big London houses failed, including one to which the Governor of the Bank of England belonged. In September twenty more fell; October saw ten joint stock and private banks stop payment.

Firms in the East India Trade began to fail, and a slump of portentous dimensions was launched.

Letts in his Diary for 1848 retailed this gloomy information in a commercial summary in the preface. He does not omit to mention that Cotesworth, Powel & Pryor, a large London mercantile house in the Brazilian trade, was temporarily compelled to pull up.

October 9, 1847

'Sad panic in the City money market. Many failures of large mercantile firms. Great fall in the price of stocks.'

October 17, 1847

'The Thanksgiving Prayer for a bountiful harvest affixed up at all the churches today. A collection was desired to be made for the destitute Irish and Scotch but which as regards the former was not responded to in the agricultural districts.'

City magnates, with money invested in wheat, must have felt as unenthusiastic about this harvest thanksgiving as the farm workers did about the collection.

January 1, 1848

'This morning's post brought me a letter from my nephew Marlborough Pryor containing the sad intelligence of the stoppage of the House of Business in which he is a partner viz. Cotesworth, Powel & Pryor, St. Helen's Place, Bishopsgate Street, London, South American Merchants. Marlborough says he believes they are perfectly solvent but that they consider it more honourable to stop at once than to struggle on and perhaps involve others in these fearful times, so many great mercantile houses having failed.'

January 2, 1848

'My sons had been informed of the sad affair in St. Helen's Place but thought with time the creditors would be paid 20/- in the £, which does not often happen when a concern stops. But it would take the greater part of the property (Landed Estates) to effect that and would fall heavily on Marlboro' who has the largest capital in the concern.'

December 9, 1849

'Received a letter from my nephew Marlboro' Pryor informing me the mercantile house of Cotesworth, Powel & Pryor in which he was a partner when they failed have now paid 20/- in the pound in full of all demands upon them and also 5% interest upon the debts, which redounds very much to their credit. Cotesworth & Powell is the new firm, my nephew Marlboro' retiring.'

Marlboro' retired to his 'Cottage Ornée' at Weston, which soon ceased to have any resemblance to the modest dwelling John Izzard had planned for him. We hear of large-scale entertainment there before long. Evidently things did not go too badly for Marlboro'.

Nor did they for John Izzard. The dreadful things which the Protectionists had foretold for the farming industry if the Corn Laws were repealed, did not immediately happen. The temperature of the times can be judged from the accounts of the Tenants' Rent dinners at Clay Hall.

January 19, 1849

'Rent Day. We sat down 29 to dinner. All appeared very happy and enjoyed their good cheer. Jo. Tranter, my old clerk at the Brewery, was one of the party. Dr. Bliss composed a song which he sung very suitable to the occasion. Ogle also sang a song and Mr. Robt. Walbey several.'

R. Walby, it will be remembered, was agent for 'Mr. Lawes' Manures'; so he probably had something to sing about.

January 18, 1850

'Snowed fast in the afternoon. This being the day for receiving our rents we had tables prepared for 30 guests. They were all very happy, and the greater part of them paid up their year's rent well.

Dr. Bliss sang a good humorous song which pleased them much. Son Fred sang also.'

But wheat slumped after harvest in 1851 to 36/6 a quarter—it was not so low again until 1884—and it seemed as if ruin was at hand. 'My tenants felt grateful for the 10% reduction I allowed them this year in consequence of the depression of all agricultural produce,' he wrote. In 1853, however, things began to look up. However, 'I allowed them 10% on their rents. I hope it will not be necessary to do so next year.' It was not. The Crimean War cut off supplies of Russian corn, and attention was once more turned to the growing of corn at home. Coverts in the Puckeridge country in which as a young man John Izzard had hunted the fox, were, so the historian of the hunt says, grubbed up or curtailed in an endeavour to expand the arable acreage; and the wheat crop in 1854 was over four million acres. (It was two millions in 1951.)

Prosperity having returned to the countryside, thanks to wars in Europe and North America, made more than a fleeting visit. A period of twenty years of high farming ensued during which farm roads were made, ditches dug, fields fenced, land drained, and buildings constructed, and the industry was endowed with the equipment without which it could not have answered the demands made upon it during two World Wars. To this day, many, perhaps a majority of, British farms are dependent upon buildings which owe their existence to this period. John Izzard and his kind loved the land, and for their labours the nation has cause to be eternally grateful.

Providence mercifully suspended the laws of Political Economy for twenty years. But in 1874, the world being again at peace, the cold gales of foreign competition started to blow, and, aided by a succession of inclement seasons, began to bring about all those dreadful things which the opponents of the Repeal of the Corn Laws had foreseen.

But, by this time the remains of John Izzard, and Morris his son, were lying in their appointed catacombs, in the vault below the chancel of Norton church; and the Rev. John Cotton Browne, who had married Morris's daughter, reigned in his stead at Clay Hall.

XVIII

SPORT

John Izzard was fond of his gun without being a particularly good shot. He loved a day on the September stubbles, shooting partridge, quail, and hare above his pointer. He was not greatly impressed with the sport provided by the driven pheasant. He only once attended a pheasant shoot, and that was in 1827. Thirty years elapsed before the first pheasants were preserved at Clay Hall, and this, in spite of the fact that his brothers Robert and Vickris loved what they called the battue—the sport provided by the driven pheasant.

His one and only pheasant shoot took place at Holfield Grange, near Coggeshall, an estate belonging to a brother of Robert Hanbury, partner of Robert Pryor in Truman, Hanbury & Buxton.

January 23, 1827

'Soon after breakfast we sallied forth, but it being very cold and the snow about the hedges very deep, we each took a small glass of gin to fortify ourselves. We proceeded thro' the gardens to the preserve covert called the Vineyard, Mr. Hanbury having arranged the plan of operations with his keeper Old Jacob, a knowing hand.

We were therefore to view the pheasants pass from a small covert on the left over an open space where they were generally fed into another long covert to the right. The keeper and his assistants beating, we told 149 that flew and ran by. The beaters then preceded us to the right and the battue commenced. But they rose so fast that very little execution was done until they rose more leisurely. We were allowed to shoot cock pheasants, hares and rabbits. Bro' Robert and Robert Hanbury shot well. Mr. Palmer preferred shooting at hares and rabbits. After getting to the end we halted and the beaters went into a small covert beyond, and we were to take them flying as they came across. I missed some capital shots, not being accustomed to pheasant shooting. Afterwards we retraced our steps towards the keeper's lodge at the Vineyard and

took another whet there. All the pheasants that had been disturbed
went into an adjoining thick preserve covered with fine large spruce
trees which was not to have a gun fired in it.

We then proceeded to the outlying coverts of the estate where the
game is not so plentiful but quite enough and much pleasanter
shooting, giving you time to load your gun for the second bird.
In the first preserve ten or more rose at once and flurried such
indifferent shots as myself.

A hot luncheon was served to which we did justice; also ale,
porter and gin. My feet were extremely wet and cold. I was very
glad of the gin altho' warm in every other part of my body. We
then continued our sport until 4 o'clock and then returned to dry
and prepare for dinner. The produce of the day was 20 brace of
pheasants, 22 brace of hares, 1 wild duck, 1 woodcock, 1 partridge,
and 6 couple of rabbits. I only shot a leash of pheasants, a brace
of hares, and 1 rabbit. But I enjoyed the sport. Had the snow not
been so deep I should have liked it much better. We often sunk
into ditches without seeing them.'

Surtees, who was a north country squire, also had little use for
the pheasant, but on the surprising grounds that 'though they run
pretty fast, yet when they come to fly, it must be an indifferent
shot who can't knock them over.'

On 15 May 1828 John Izzard witnessed a shooting match
between two of the first shots of the day.

May 15, 1828
'Went by water to the Red House at Battersea to see a match of
pigeon shooting, 30 yards from the trap—this being the first day—
to be completed in four days a week apart. Said to be for 1,000
guineas.

Morris and myself both stopped two hours and both came away
satisfied that Capt. Ross would win the match. It was between
Capt. Ross and Mr. Osbaldeston. The former was so perfectly
cool and collected and shot his birds dead. Mr. Osbaldeston was a
little nervous and did not kill his birds so completely dead as Capt.
Ross. Although both excellent shots each killing five or six pigeons
to missing one but Capt. Ross missed much the fewest this day.'

George Osbaldeston (1786–1866), 'the Squire of England',
oarsman, cricketer, boxer, marksman, Master of Foxhounds, was
15 years older than Captain Horatio Ross. In his autobiography

Osbaldeston says he never shot a match singly against Ross. But Bell's *Life* records several such matches. On this occasion Ross hit 175, and Osbaldeston 164, birds out of 250.

John Izzard used a single barrelled gun.

August 7, 1833
'I bought a single barrelled new gun at Wilkinson's in Pall Mall for which I am to pay 18 gns. and 1 gn. for a second-hand case, some copper caps, wadding and pellets.'

The Pryors always opened the season at Sandon, where the best partridge shooting was to be found. The bags seem to get progressively smaller as the years go on, although the weapons used must have been growing more efficient.

September 5, 1827
'Made a party to shoot at Sandon. Lafont and myself to shoot together and John and Morris together. Started after an early breakfast and shot our way to Sandon where we lunched. We had a wonderful day's sport shooting 36 brace of birds and a brace of hares.

viz. Lafont 14 brace and a hare

I.J.P.   <u>4 brace</u>

<u>18 brace</u>

John and Morris shot 9 brace each. They also shot a hare.'

September 3, 1828
'Breakfasted half past 7 and soon after 8 we set off on a shooting party to Sandon. Lafont and myself shot together and sons John and Morris shot together, meeting at luncheon at White's Farm at Sandon. The morning was showery and unfavourable, the birds running very much and unsettling the dogs. After luncheon the day improved. We saw a great quantity of birds which lay well and we had excellent sport. The proceeds of our day's sport was as follows. Lafont shot 10½ brace of partridges, 1½ couple of quails and a rabbit. I shot 4 brace of partridges and a couple of quails. John and Morris shot 8 brace of birds, 1 leveret, 1 quail.'

The last shoot described was on 11 September, 1851.

'A most delightful morning. A day's shooting at Sandon being proposed the party started at 10 a.m. The shooters, Richard and Thomas Pryor, John Branton in the spring cart, Camp driving, Richard's servant Joseph and Wray with the pointers in the servants' Sunday cart; sons Morris, Alfred and myself on horseback.

The day being very hot and the ground dry we had not so much sport as we expected. Mr. R. Walby accompanied us a great part of the time, and brought a capital luncheon into the field. The proceeds of the day were 2 brace of hares and 6 brace of birds.'

Throughout the winter there was sport to be had at Clay Hall, and Belle the spaniel and Sancho the pointer, and their heirs and successors, had no cause to complain that life was dull.

Poaching does not seem to have been a source of trouble. The Stevenage Bench convicted 'three great boys' for coursing a hare at Clay Hall on a Sunday *(horribile dictu)* in January 1834. At John Izzard's intercession, the penalty was reduced to 5/- 'upon their promising never to do so again.' In September of the same year three men were fined 40/- or two months in gaol for poaching at Clay Hall. Otherwise 'the Lower Orders' at Walkern seem to have been blameless. It is shocking to have to record that in the same year John Izzard caught Captain Hampson, a Deputy Lieutenant and a Justice of the Peace, and his brother shooting on Pryor land at Clothall. He told them that he did not think that 'they could have behaved so unhandsomely', a masterpiece of understatement.

There were no point-to-point races at this time. But on Easter Sunday there were horse races every year at Kimpton Hoo, the seat of Lord Dacre, near Luton. They were well attended by the gentry, but rarely provided much sport. It was quite a business to get a carriage there from Clay Hall. But John Izzard consoles his diary in 1830 with the remark that the lanes by Knebworth although rather stony 'are perfectly safe'.

His heart was in the chase, and he must have followed the Puckeridge Hounds for upwards of forty years. His hunters, King George, Lofty and Fowler, carried him many a famous day, the last named for nearly twenty years. But the glories of the Puckeridge Hunt, the epic hunts, the leaps taken, the miles ridden, the foxes killed, all these are written in the chronicles of the Puckeridge Hunt by Michael F. Berry, and need no retelling here. Three entries from his diary must suffice, the second of which should make foxhunters furiously to think.

March 9, 1833

'Engaged in my library all the morning until nearly 3 o'clock;

after which I went to take a walk in the garden, and heard the fox-hounds at St. John's. I immediately ordered my old horse King George to be saddled, and set off as I was in my trowsers to join them. I came up with them at Basset Green. Went by Ardeley and Cromer towards Cumberlow Green, when the fox headed back by Cromer to Cottered, and from there to Aulmy Wood where the hounds killed him. A very thick snow storm came on just after we had killed our fox.'

October 14, 1840

'Paid in my annual subscription £25 to the Puckeridge Hounds by check payable to N. Parry or bearer at Mr. Adams, Ware Bank.'

Mr. Parry was Master of the Puckeridge. Both the amount and the date on which it was paid are noteworthy.

March 4, 1854 (in his 80th year)

'The hounds met at Cumberlow Green, found at Cold Ash, ran their fox to ground at the Bourne near Munden, dug him out and ran him to St. John's. I rode my pony there just before, thinking they might come there, and shook hands with several gentlemen of the hunt that I used to know.'

The Pryors were fond of fishing, and the little river Bean which flows along the Walkern valley provided scope for their rods. At the foot of the hill upon which Clay Hall stood was the water mill with a pool always worth fishing, and a mile up stream, in the Rectory Grounds, was a small waterfall where trout lurked.

July 31, 1844

'Accompanied my grandson J. Eade to the ponds to try to catch some of the small fish with which they abound but could not get even a nibble.

My bro' Vickris and Mr. Randolph came up from Baldock to join Richard in trying to catch a few trout in the river after luncheon. I accompanied them and called on Garratt the miller to say we were coming. He said that we were quite welcome. They had good sport, Mr. Randolph caught three fine trout, one of them a pound and three quarters. Richard caught one, more than a pound and a half, and Vickris two, more than a pound. We dressed two for dinner and they were very good. The day was alternatively fine and cloudy with a few showers and a nice ripple on the water.'

May 30, 1849

'Arthur and Tom Pryor rode over from Baldock. They sent word
they could not get over until about 1 o'clock. Richard therefore
took his rod and walked down to Mr. Harding's waterfall between
11 and 12 o'clock and caught two brace of trout there, one of
them a pretty good one. Arthur and Tom got to Walkern about
1 when Arthur stopped at the river and began to fish whilst Tom
rode his horse and led his brother's to Clay'Hall. He stayed and
took luncheon with us as only Richard and Arthur had rods for
fishing. I rode down with Tom to see the sport. The day proving
very favourable, being warm but cloudy and a few drops of rain
occasionally falling, the trout took the worm well and they caught
altogether 9 brace, the largest weighing about 2 lbs.'

It would appear that the Pryors were not fly fishermen.

> Men may come and men may go,
> But I go on for ever

sang Tennyson of his *Brook*. In the case of numberless streams in
the south of Britain this has proved to be an empty boast. The
improved drainage of agricultural land has made possible the
enhanced yields of modern farming. But the water which the
farmer hurries off his land is by the zeal of the Drainage Boards
hastened to the sea, and is lost to the country. Springs are no
more replenished as they used to be by the gradual seepage of
water; but the calls upon them are incomparably greater than ever
before. It is not surprising that the water table in the south of the
kingdom is sinking, and that in many a spot where within living
memory trout swam in clear spring-fed water there is not water
enough to content a frog.

Nowadays, except at times of spate, the merest trickle flows
down the Walkern valley, and trout swim there no more.

XIX

TAXATION

To the modern Briton taxation means but one thing—Income Tax. But although the infant Income Tax did enter into John Izzard's life, both when he was a young man and in his old age, it was never a source of serious worry to him. It was not an Act imposing taxation which inflicted most worry on him, but one which reduced duties.

John Izzard, it will be remembered, owned the Brewery at Baldock. When he took up residence at Clay Hall, he leased the business to his elder sons, John and Morris.

March 11, 1830

'Rode over to Baldock to confer with my sons about the measure proposed by the Chancellor of the Exchequer (Mr. Goldbourne) in the House of Commons for throwing open the beer trade and granting licences to who ever may require them, which unjust and sweeping measure would ruin the publicans, victuallers and many small brewers, and seriously injure all of them.'

Goldbourne's Act empowered any householder and ratepayer to open his house as a beershop merely on payment of two guineas to the local excise office. Unlike the regular alehouse keeper, he was entirely free from the control and supervision of the local Justices. The only advantage which the alehouse keeper enjoyed over the two guinea licensee was the freedom to sell liquor between 10 o'clock at night and 4 o'clock in the morning—which even in those thirsty times was not a concession of striking value.

This measure was passed by a Whig ministry in the name of Free Trade; but it was probably inspired by malice. Most of the local Justices were Tories.

It might have been expected that a law likely to facilitate the consumption of beer would be welcomed by a brewer. But John Izzard does not seem to have looked at it in this light. Attached to the Brewery were a number of inns—what would be called

180

nowadays 'tied houses'. The virtual abolition of licensing resulted in a great increase in beerhouses, and thus depreciated the value of the Baldock Brewery's 'tied houses'.

Writing in 1869, just before licensing was reimposed, Cussans, the historian of Hertfordshire, remarks that there was one public house to less than every fifty of the male population. Taking into consideration the numbers who had no occasion for this accommodation, the number in his opinion was excessive.

From time to time John Izzard mentions his concern at the continued depreciation of Brewery property.

March 6, 1851

'Engaged the greater part of the day going over the whole of my last will making memorandum respecting some contemplated reductions in several of the legacies to meet the great deterioration in Public House property.'

This is typical of many entries. Whenever depression attacked him he would revise his will, writing down the value of the legacies. Mr. Veasey, the family lawyer, used to exercise a restraining influence. But it was the consequences of the Beerhouse Act, rather than the exactions of the Income Tax Act, which were his principal worry.

The Repeal of the Income Tax Act in 1816 removed the only direct tax which made an important contribution to the Revenue. In 1830 the Revenue was between 46 and 47 million pounds. Over 40 millions accrued from Customs, Excise and Stamps. Less than 5 million came from the so-called Assessed Taxes. These included duties on male servants, carriages, horses, hair-powder, armorial bearings, game, inhabited houses, and windows. These were taxes upon expenditure rather than income, and inflicted the maximum annoyance for the smallest return.

John Izzard wrote his diary for 1833 in Dunn's *Daily Remembrancer*. This volume included in its preface an attack upon the Inhabited House Duty which might well have come from Mr. Pickwick's friend Mr. Alfred Jingle.

The duty was leviable on the real annual value of the house, a practical test of which was the annual rental. When the mansions of the aristocracy came to be assessed, rental was little guide. Who in his senses would wish to hire Blenheim? The bigger the house, the less its attractions as a letting proposition. In a note of considerable length the writer goes through the assessment lists, county by county, enumerating the mansions and describing their splendours.

Thus Stowe—'A magnificent seat, the greatest ornament of the county, with towers, columns, obelisks, and temples; principal front 916 feet from east to west—centre wings—colonnades—Corinthian columns—pilastres—flight of 31 steps—splendid interior—noble rooms—saloon paved with marble-Scagliola columns—white marble capitals.'

This was rated at £300 per annum, and paid duty £42.10.0, which was as much as 'a Ludgate Hill haberdasher might expect to pay.' The Earl of Pembroke's seat Wilton House was rated at £150 per annum, duty £21.5.0. 'In the classic regions of Wapping, Bow, Poplar, Bethnal Green, Shoreditch and Mile End', writes Dunn acidly, 'we find 28 dwellings rated as high.'

The Inhabited House Duty did not worry John Izzard. He nowhere records what the assessment on Clay Hall was. The tax was repealed in 1835. It was re-imposed in 1851 in a modified form, to console the Treasury for the loss of the window tax.

From time to time he gives details of which he had to pay on account of the assessed taxes.

March 17, 1835
'Set off on horse-back for Hitchin to meet Chapman the Surveyor of Taxes, the purpose of my journey being to see him respecting compounding for my assessed taxes. I compounded for the same establishment as entered last year, viz.

5 servants	£12. 5. 0.
1 4-wheel carriage	6. 0. 0.
2 2-wheel carriages	6.10. 0.
5 horses exceeding 13 hands	13.18. 9.
1 horse not exceeding 13 hands	1. 1. 0.
3 dogs	2. 2. 0.
1 armorial bearing	2. 8. 0.
	£44. 4. 9.

for which I am to pay 5% and in addition window tax not compounded £23. 5. 0.'

The male servant tax was one of the few at this date which was graduated so that the richer paid tax at higher rates than the less well-off. Where one male servant was kept the tax was £1. 4. 0. per servant, and it gradually increased until an employer of eleven or more paid £3.16. 6. per head. When the employer was a bachelor the rate was higher, starting at £2.14. 0. The servants of Roman Catholic clergy were exempt—a most remarkable concession in a country so wholeheartedly Protestant.

The object of compounding for these taxes was to enable the number of male servants, carriages, horses, dogs and armorial bearings to be varied during the year without incurring liability for fresh taxation.

John Izzard had on one occasion to fight the Assessors of the window tax. This iniquitous exaction had been imposed in the reign of William and Mary to help pay for the wars which followed the Glorious Revolution of 1689, and continued to blight the lives of Britons until 1851. It was the cause of much ill-health, especially among the poor; and the damage it did must have been out of proportion to the revenue it produced. It is difficult to trace any principle behind its assessment. The theory that the rich should pay taxation at a higher rate than the poor was not one familiar at the time. Indeed, it had a surprisingly slow growth, and did not blossom until the end of the century, if that be the appropriate expression.

Houses of an annual value of £5 with 1—6 windows had to pay 3/6 until 1825 when they were exempted. A house with 8 windows was assessed at 16/6, with 9 at £1. 1. 0, with 10 at £2. 8. 0. Thereafter, the more windows a house had, the greater the incidence per window up to 40 windows, when each window was assessed at slightly more than 7/3. The incidence per window then fell until a house with 180 was assessed at £46.11. 3, or 5/2 a window. Every window above 180 was charged at 1/6. Windows were separately assessed up to 40, then in groups of four until 100, and thereafter in groups of ten. The occasional blind window to be seen, particularly in houses of Georgian date, owes its existence to the assessment of the window tax in houses of moderate dimensions by fours. The omission of one window put the house into a lower category.

October 16, 1840

'This being the appeal day at Welwyn for the assessed taxes I rode over to appeal against an additional charge of one window made by Mr. Simson the Inspector, about a fortnight ago, he having charged my house and offices at 80 windows which brings me into another class. I was before charged for 75 which are charged the same as 79, going by fours—65—69, 75—79, 80—84 etc. I argued that I had only opened one window since the year 1835, and that I was entitled to open more by the Act, and there the statute 4 & 5 Will. IV c. 4, 5 and 7 was my authority. The Commissioners, on referring to the statute, allowed I was entitled to be charged for only 79 windows.

I then appealed against being charged for 16 windows for my farm house, claiming an entire exemption for 12 of them, being in a quite separate house occupied by my bailiff for the farm and for my farm menservants, there being no communication whatever with the part containing 4 windows occupied by my gardener.

I therefore said under the head "Exemptions", to which I referred the Commissioners, I was clearly entitled to exemption for the windows. The Government Commissioner Mr. Hinde tried his utmost to set it aside, wishing to make it appear it was all one house. But he completely failed, and my claim was unanimously allowed. The gardener's house containing only 4 windows is by law exempt and I shall have nothing to pay for window tax there.

Had I not bought a small book when I was in London a few days ago viz. *A Practical View of the Assessed Taxes as altered by the last Act,* by Chas. Egan Esq. Barrister, I should not have been aware of the exemption I was entitled to and should have continued paying for 12 windows as usual. Having opened some more windows in making alterations, and being charged for 16, I was determined to get the Act or an explanation of it, which has proved of great service to me.'

The exemption which he pleaded was probably that in favour of farm houses belonging to farms of less than £200 per annum.

The first mention of Income Tax occurs on 13 January 1843. Income Tax, introduced in 1799 to finance the war against France, had been finally repealed in 1816. Peel reintroduced it in 1842 as an emergency measure to put an end to a series of deficit budgets for which Whig Governments had been responsible. He hoped that the improvement in the country's finances, which he anticipated from a reform of the tariff, would enable him to dispense with it within five years. The Victorians hated it on account of its inquisitorial character and the inequality of its impositions.

January 13, 1843

'Engaged in my library examining my notice of assessment under the Property & Income Tax Act delivered yesterday in which I am charged at a higher rate than in my statement sent in under Schedule A & B. The Assessor has evidently made a mistake as he has charged me 7d in the £ under both, whereas Schedule A ought to be 7d and Schedule B only 3½d according to the Act. Rode down to Mr. Wright one of the assessors and pointed out the error to him. He is to see Mr. Simson the inspector about it tomorrow as he has sent out most of his notices in the same manner.'

January 16, 1843

'I walked to Walkern to see the assessors of the Property & Income Tax. Mr. Wright was not at home but I saw Mr. Pearman who had been made acquainted that they had made a great mistake in filling up the notices. I found his son busy in endeavouring to rectify them.'

John Izzard seems to have taken the tax in his stride. There is no suggestion that he resented having to furnish the private information for which the Act calls. No doubt he remembered the days when Income Tax had been paid during the wars with Napoleon; and one can get used to anything. The four schedules of the modern Act have come down unchanged from that of 1803.

Letts' Diary for 1843 contained a table showing the incidence of the Property & Income Tax at 7d in the £. A gentleman with £5,000 p.a. payed £145.16.8 tax. It is not surprising, therefore, that John Izzard did not see in it a sharp-edged tool capable of transforming society and shaping it into a Socialist Paradise; and nothing can have been farther from the thoughts of the Tory Members of Parliament who passed the bill into law. Professor F. Shehab of Baghdad, the latest explorer in the somewhat arid fields of Income Tax History, points out in his *Progressive Taxation* (1953) that the doctrine of graduation, or the redistribution of income by means of direct and progressive taxation, did not begin to make its way until towards the end of the nineteenth century, and one of its earlier protagonists was Joseph Chamberlain.

XX

THE MEDICAL PROFESSION

John Izzard enjoyed exceptional health, and there is comparatively little in his diary about the medical profession. Nevertheless, there is enough to make us profoundly grateful that we have escaped the attentions of Early Victorian medical men. They had but one cure for every ailment—the letting of blood. But they were not forthcoming with the lancet. There is only one mention of 'bleeding', or cupping. When John Lafont 'was seized with an attack of paralysis, which deprived him of the use of his limbs on the left side for about two days, a skilful physician was immediately called in who cupped and blistered him and administered proper medicine.' On every other occasion of which we are told, the leech, not the lancet was used.

When John Izzard had a swollen knee in 1840—

July 12, 1840
'Mr. Evans came and applied a dozen leeches to my knee which took good hold and drew a good deal of blood.'

July 14, 1840
'Mr. Norwood came over this morning and examined my knee and thought it necessary to apply ten more leeches which did their business very well. He informs me it will be necessary to put on a blister on Thursday. Poultices were applied as before but the punctures made by the leeches did not bleed nearly so much as the first time. Confined to the sofa nearly the whole of the day.'

July 15, 1840
'My knee is in much less pain when I move.'

Evidently the treatment was to some extent successful. Two years later when Juliana 'remained very poorly and suffered violent pain in her head . . . Mr. N. accordingly came and found a good deal of fever lurking about her. He ordered twenty leeches to be applied to the nape of her neck in the evening and to take medicine every four hours. I sent over a note to Mr. Cooper of Stevenage

186

written by W. Bell [a surgeon] for the twenty leeches for which he charged 10/-. I should have had to pay more, I expect, if I had written myself. They were applied in the evening and performed their part very well.' Next day—

January 4, 1842

'My daughter Juliana felt relieved by the application of the leeches and has been more comfortable today but has not been able to get much refreshing sleep.'

January 21, 1842

'Mr. Norwood came today. He pronounces Juliana to be going on very favourably, the fever having entirely left her.'

The young lady was lucky, one feels, to get out of it without being blistered.

January 28, 1845

'Passed a bad night with scarcely any sleep and my wife being no better we concluded to call in Dr. Hicks. Mr. Hicks accordingly came and began with ordering me to take a blue pill at night and a black draught in the morning and will send other medicine for my wife. He prohibits my going abroad entirely.'

January 30, 1845

'Mr. Hicks reports that I am no worse and my wife rather better. Both are to continue to take medicine but of a different kind. Paid Mr. Hicks two sovereigns for his (two) visits to my wife and myself.'

February 9, 1845

'My wife got downstairs and we had a little dinner together in the drawing room on a tray brought in at 6 o'clock whilst the party dined in the dining room. We all drank tea and a coffee together at 9.'

Medical science can claim the merit of having introduced John Izzard to the habit of having a warm bath. (He always speaks of a warm bath, never of a hot one.) He had occasionally had a warm bath while at the seaside. Warm baths were part of the equipment of a seaside resort, and he mentions visits to them. On the other hand, prior to 1848, he never makes any mention of having a bath at Clay Hall. It would, perhaps, be unsafe to assume he never had one.

June 29, 1848

'Having a considerable eruption on different parts of my body and a very troublesome itching I thought it best to see Mr. Norwood. He pronounced it a species of nettle rash and said I must take medicine immediately and make use of a warm bath every night. I am to take two pills every night and a draught every morning and be very careful what I eat and drink—no malt liquor, but weak wine and water with my meals and only two glasses of light wine afterwards.'

Mrs. Pryor, not to be outdone, took to a shower bath. John Izzard 'went in a cab to Dean's and gave particular directions for it to be made of a larger size than common.'

The next entry of medical interest sounds a more modern note.

June 7, 1851

'Walked to No. 5 Albermarle Street to call on Mrs. Vickris Pryor who was lodging there and was to undergo a most painful operation for a cancer in her breast. We found her son Richard who had come up from Spettisbury and also her daughter Jane, son Alfred's wife, there. Mrs. Vickris was very low but had quite made up her mind about the operation. Some of the first surgeons in London were to operate.'

June 10, 1851

'Received a letter this morning from my wife mentioning that Mrs. Vickris Pryor had gone through the operation favourably. Chloroform was administered before and during the operation and she got some sleep in the night afterwards.'

Mrs. Vickris survived her operation by two years.

On 29 September 1851, it will be remembered, John Izzard broke his leg in King William Street, and was taken to the Berners Hotel at his own request, where he was attended by the head surgeon of the Middlesex Hospital. He did not return to Clay Hall until the end of November.

November 30, 1851

'I am wheeled out of my bedroom betwixt 9 and 10 into the adjoining large dressing room and take my seat in a large easy chair. There I remain and take my meals and read a little until 9 at night when I am wheeled back into the spring bed (bought at the sale at Hexton some years ago). My wife occupies the large bed. What I should do without my dear wife I cannot tell as I lay like a hog with my leg on a rest in front of my chair and cannot move any way without help.

My leg is bandaged with three layers in strips one over the other, with a coating betwixt them composed of the whites of 20 eggs mixed with flour which has become as hard as a wooden case. Whilst at rest my leg is quite easy.'

December 16, 1851

'Mr. Campbell de Morgan the surgeon who attended me at the Berners Hotel came down by the Gt. Northern, arriving at noon. My leg had been bound up for nearly a month. He came to take the bandage off which was rather a difficult job, the strips of calico with which it had been bound with the white of eggs and flour having encased it like a mummy. He examined my leg, found it going on well, and bound it up in the same manner as before. We had dinner at 4½ p.m. of which he partook, son Fred taking a walk round the garden with him after the operation.'

It was fortunate that there was a spring bed at Clay Hall. Feather beds were still usual. Air mattresses were not unknown. Mr. Jorrocks recommended one as a suitable present for a fond aunt to give to a nephew about to take up hunting.

February 8, 1852

'My leg felt relieved by having the very hard bandage cemented with the whites of egg removed and a soft bandage substituted.'

April 21, 1852

'A cheque for sixty pounds as follows.

For Mr. De Morgan making with £30 previously paid on account Eighty Gns. for his surgical attendance.	£54. 0. 0.
Middlesex Hospital—a gift.	5. 5. 0.
Bill for cradle	5. 6.
Sundries	9. 6.
	£60. 0. 0.'

The carriage accident in which John Izzard was involved resulted in inflammation of the leg which had been broken. His 'Medical Man' Mr. Foster scored a success by painting it with iodine. He seems to have been a progressive man.

May 14, 1858
'Mr. Foster recommended my having a bottle of hot water every night put into my bed to keep my feet warm. I did as he prescribed and found the hot water very comfortable to my feet.'

By the end of John Izzard's life the medical faculty had more in its quiver than lancets, leeches and blisters.

There is a solitary mention of a chiropodist.

July 11, 1835
'Immediately after breakfast I accompanied my wife and son Fred to Dr. Wolf the chiropodist in Leadenhall Street. Each underwent an operation on corns. His charge was 3 guineas which I thought very high.' So may we!

Of dentists the diary has much to say.

April 1, 1828
'Being obliged to pay my dentist in London a visit for the purpose of having a new artificial front tooth, in room of one of the same sort which would last no longer, I went to London.'

April 2, 1828 (in London)
'After breakfast paid a visit to my dentist Mr. Tho. Parkinson who was at home and soon set my mouth to rights with a new tooth for which I paid 3 guineas.'

It is noteworthy that the new tooth was to be artificial; it might well have been a 'borrowed' human tooth. It was eighteenth century practice to transplant human teeth, and it was the privilege of the Lower Orders to provide teeth, at a price, for the Quality. There is a tradition in the dental profession that Emma, Lady Hamilton, on the threshold of her career, was dissuaded from visiting a dentist who was to remove her front teeth in order to improve the appearance of an aristocratic lady.

January 29, 1830
'Called on Mr. Sherwin, Dentist, No. 9 Bruton Street respecting my mouth to supply it with some different artificial teeth. Those I have at present are always incommoding me by coming out. He took three different models of my gums in wax. In the course of three weeks I am to see him again.

February 20, 1830
'To Bruton Street again and was there punctually at 11 o'clock. Mr. Sherwin after being engaged with me for an hour and a half

said he must see me once more but should not be ready for an hour. I therefore made my way to the British Gallery to see the paintings there and returned within the hour. After being about ¾ of an hour he finished my new false teeth and fixed them very firmly without putting me to any pain. They are to be taken out every night on going to bed and replaced in the morning.'

It would seem that he still had some of his own teeth left as he speaks of the dentist 'fixing' his artificial teeth.

The English dentists had learned the art of taking wax impressions of the gums from their continental colleagues towards the end of the eighteenth century. This had resulted in a development of the craft of making artificial teeth. They were carved from ivory or bone. (A fine example of eighteenth century craftsmanship exists in the ivory dentures made for George Washington, now at the London Hospital.) When bone was used, walrus or hippopotamus was preferred on account of its hardness; but when neither was available ox bone was used. Both bone and ivory had the defect of being absorbent, and teeth made of them became highly unpleasant. To get over this difficulty porcelain teeth were introduced. But it was a difficult medium; the early models were clumsy and made a 'clacking' noise; and it became the practice to set them in a bone or ivory base. Gold teeth were similarly set. About 1857 the introduction of vulcanite by Goodyear—his name is still familiar owing to the survival of his Company—enabled dentures to be made for the million instead of the few.

It was not the making of the 'artificial teeth' which troubled the Early Victorian dentist. The difficulty was to make an accurate impression of the mouth. It was taken in wax which owing to its soft nature was liable to 'drag'. A more accurate impression resulted when plaster of Paris was introduced.[1]

On this occasion John Izzard was lucky. The impression must have been accurate. His dentures fitted and lasted him ten years. He was not so lucky again.

December 2, 1839

'Passed a good night not being disturbed by any alarm of fire. The ladies set off in the glass coach shopping in the East End of the town and called for me coming back to accompany my wife to

---

[1] Dr. Lilian Lindsay, Hon. Librarian, British Dental Association. Paper read June 23 1926 to Metropolitan Branch.

the dentist Mr. Sherwyn in Bruton Street to have a tooth stopped.
I also took my false teeth with me which I have not been able to
use since I had them principally on account of the springs which
I found disagreeable to bear.   I told Mr. Sherwyn and suggested
his taking them again and trying a different mode if it was only for
the upper jaw.   He therefore took a fresh model and is to try what
he can do.'

The procedure in making dentures at this time was to take a wax
impression of the gums, make a model from it, and to fit the dentures which were carved by hand from ivory or bone, to the model.
Unfortunately, owing to the defects of wax, the model was rarely
accurate.   The dentures did not fit properly and there was great
difficulty in keeping a full denture in place.   To assist in doing so
springs were devised which were fastened into slots in the back of
the upper and lower bone blocks. The earliest were of whalebone
sewn over with cotton.   Next springs were made of gold in spiral
form.   Sometimes when an ingenious dentist introduced a joint in
the springs they became fixed, and the mouth could not be closed
until the dentures were removed.   Springs served their turn until a
more accurate method of taking impressions of the jaws was discovered with the introduction of plaster of Paris.

June 17, 1840

'I proceeded to my dentist's Mr. Sherwin according to appointment.   He told me I must pay him another visit tomorrow and he
could then tell me how many more visits I must pay him.'

June 18, 1840

'Mr. Sherwin said he was satisfied he should make a very good job
with my teeth but that I must be with him several days next week.
It is very vexatious that I must give up so much time but there
appears to be no alternative.'

July 11, 1840

'Went to Sherwins the dentist and paid him £20 on account of
my set of false teeth.   I left them with him to alter as I cannot
articulate my words with them and find them otherwise uncomfortable.'

August 15, 1840

'Proceeded to Mr. Sherwin, my dentist, No. 14 Bruton Street.
According to his direction I slept with my false teeth in my mouth

and attempted to eat my breakfast with them. But they were so very uncomfortable and would not remain firmly attached that I was obliged to take them out again and finished my breakfast much better without them. I therefore took them with me and on arriving at Mr. Sherwin's told him that they were not only no use but positively an annoyance. After trying a variety of schemes he eventually decided he must make a fresh set. He therefore took a fresh model.'

August 26, 1840
'Paid my last visit to Mr. Sherwin and was with him for above an hour. He has made my fresh set of teeth to fit my gums much better than the first, added to which I can articulate much better and can just manage to masticate my food but very slowly and not without pain to my gums.'

February 13, 1841
'Was punctual to my time at Mr. Sherwins. He fitted in temporarily my teeth and fixed to see me in a fortnight's time.'

June 9, 1841
'I went to Sherwyn who filed my stumps of teeth in the upper jaw and fitted in the bone intended to act as teeth.'

October 20, 1841
'Called at Sherwins the dentist who, I think, will not succeed with my teeth.'

Evidently Sherwin had to admit defeat and for the rest of his life John Izzard had to get on with 'the bone intended to act as teeth' in his upper jaw. Perhaps he kept his dentures in his lower jaw.

Sherwin was well known in Hertfordshire. William Lucas of Hitchin (E. B. Bryant, *A Quaker Journal*) went to him in 1842 and 1845. 'Blustering, unpunctual Frank Sherwin', he calls him. He does not appear to have been much more successful with Lucas.

XXI

SERVANTS

January 24, 1848

I wrote to my son John and sent him over the circular I had received from Mr. Deeds respecting the Institution for a Training School for Mistresses for the purpose of educating Girls for going out as Servants by acquiring all knowledge of all kinds of Household Work as well as Reading and Writing. The Committees soliciting donations for building suitable erections are being handsomely aided by Government Funds in proportion to the donations raised. I think of giving £10 and wish to know what my son intends.'

February 3, 1848

'I wrote to Mr. Deeds saying I would give £25 and my daughter Emma £5 and Dr. Bliss £2, to be paid when decidedly required. I also mentioned I thought my son John would give £20 through Mr. Blomfield when he returned home.'

Institutions of this kind were legion in Early Victorian times. The importance which the Pryors attached to the project can be gauged from the size of their donations. It was evidently very close to John Izzard's heart. On only one occasion did he subscribe more to a cause—and that was to the Walkern school.

On moving in to Clay Hall, he had to find a new butler as his former butler elected to remain at Baldock and serve his sons. One Smith was appointed: 'I am to give him 50 Gns P.A. I do not promise to give him my left-off clothes as I do not like to be prevented giving any of them away to any object I wish. But I told him he would most likely have the greatest part of them.'

He also engaged a groom upon the following terms. The turnover in grooms was large but they were all recruited on the same conditions: 'He is to have £25 a year wages and board in the house and to find himself all his clothes, stable dress, boots etc; to be always clean and tidy for riding out with any of the family when required and to find himself for that purpose two suits of clothes and two pairs of boots every year.'

Smith the butler left after a year.

September 27, 1830

'Agreed to give John Wilson my present footman who is to succeed Smith the butler who leaves at Michaelmas 35 guineas per annum, he finding all his clothes, to be advanced 2 guineas the following year if approved.'

In Wilson's place as footman Young was engaged, John Izzard having 'finally agreed to give him 20 guineas for the first year, and 21 guineas for the following, two suits of livery, morning jackets and trowsers, and settled for him to wear breeches and knee buckles for dinner.'

With John Wilson as butler, and Mrs. Merrill as housekeeper, nearly twenty years of domestic peace ensued. Only in the garden was this peace broken. John Izzard considered that something more 'high falutin'' than a locally recruited gardener was needed to uphold the dignity of Clay Hall.

Mr. Chauncy's gardener produced 'a person of the name of Jas. Ambrose (a Scotsman by birth). After having some conversation with him as to where he had lived previously as gardener, and about wages, I finally agreed for him to come. I am to give him 25/- p. week and to find him a house or lodging, to fetch his coals and to give him a quart of skim milk a day for his family, he having a wife and two children.'

He does not seem to have been very successful. Clay Hall did not win any more prizes at the Baldock Horticultural Society's Shows than before when its record had been modest.

September 18, 1843

'We were surprised at dessert seeing some indifferent peaches and nectarines brought onto the table. Dr. and Mrs. Bliss and I had seen my gardener Ambrose bringing in some fine peaches, nectarines and pears, which determined me to make particular enquiry. The servants declared Ambrose put the fruit that was bad into the dishes himself. I shall therefore endeavour to find out what became of the good fruit.'

He did, and Ambrose was given notice. It is curious that his wages which seem to have been liberal did not satisfy him.

May 10, 1849

'My butler John Wilson left my service this morning. We were sorry to part with him, he having been with me from a little boy. He is going to marry Caroline Cross who lived as lady's maid some years with my wife. She was obliged to leave on account of ill health and go to her friends in Oxfordshire. She is now much better. J. Wilson has bought a nice cottage with a good garden in the parish of Broughton. The marriage is to take place in about a week and they are to reside there. J. Wilson has saved a few hundred pounds and I hope will do well but I tell him he will not feel so happy without employment. He thinks his health is not so good as it was and he should like to be more in the open air.'

Caroline Cross came from a family who were retainers of the Colstons at Filkins, and Broughton Hall in Oxfordshire. The latter were connected by marriage with the Pryors. Her successor in office, Wenham, was described by John Izzard on December 6 1849 as 'very unwell, and I fear consumptive.' Perhaps Caroline was.

John Wilson's health is unlikely to have been improved by a couple of decades spent in the butler's pantry, although, unlike many butlers, he slept, not in the pantry, but in his bedroom. Henry Young succeeded as butler, and Fordham as footman. Then trouble began.

June 24, 1849

'Our new cook was taken very ill and obliged to go home as she thought. She was seized with a violent fever and wished to be sent to Hertford directly, it being then 6 p.m. I ordered Camp to get the omnibus ready to take her to Hertford, Lloyd the chambermaid offering to accompany her. She did not get back until 12 at night. She saw Mr. Wodehouse, a medical man, who said she had alarmed herself too much but that she was much too delicate to think of returning to her place again, the heat of cooking on a fire being too much for her.'

June 7, 1850

'Received a letter from my wife, giving a good account of herself. I replied by return of post and informed her of the unsettled state of the three under servants who appear to have caballed together against Mrs. Merrill. I considered the last servant we took on in Lloyd's place as under housemaid had done the others much harm;

and as she will not mind what I say to her and is most careless, having gone to bed last night without shutting the window shutters, I determined to get rid of her. I therefore paid her the wages due to her this day and a month's wages more in consequence of her not having notice. Jane Baillie was her name and I sent her home in the little cart to Yardley. I had a conference with the other two and told them they should be dismissed if they did not behave better and treat Mrs. Merrill respectfully.'

February 28, 1851

'John Fordham leaves my service tomorrow as footman, having given notice. He is a very respectable good servant and I am sorry to part with him. He leaves us in consequence of a quarrel with the housekeeper. I think both were in fault, but he perhaps rather the most, and the housekeeper has lived with us about twenty years. I told him I would give him a good character.'

Soon after, Mrs. Blomfield, wife of the Bishop of London, wrote asking for a character of Fordham. John Izzard 'was very happy in giving him an excellent character.'

His successor had the unusual name of Swan Brand. Although 'not so tall as could be wished he was respectable looking', but he was misguided enough to ask for more pay and so gave way to George Studman, who had to be discharged 'at a moment's warning for his scandalous behaviour to Sarah Grubb our cook'. To him succeeded Fred Smith who 'altho' always respectful to his mistress and myself, was very impudent at times to others.' Next came Hill, who had to be 'sent in the little cart to Hitchin to go by the Midland train to Rugby. He proved quite unfit for the place and therefore we sent him back to his friends.' Then came Walton, who after some months 'gave notice to quit our service.' When asked if he had any particular reason, he said, 'No, but he thought he should like a change'. He was followed by Howell to whom John Izzard presented 10/- on his 86th birthday. A year later, on his 87th and last birthday, it was to another footman Brooks that he presented the now customary 10/-.

There was also some coming and going among the female staff.

January 27, 1854

'Three of our female servants have given notice to leave at the expiration of a month from this time viz. Hervey, Mrs. Pryor's maid, Mary the under house-maid, and the kitchen girl. The reason assigned was that they find the situation dull and wish for a livelier where they may see more company, and Hervey to see more of the world where the family travel about a great deal. The kitchen girl wishes for a housemaid's place. Hervey has been with us nearly five years but I think wishes to get a husband.'

Hervey was followed by Abrams who, although the lady's maid, looked after John Izzard until his death.

August 5, 1857

'Poor Young my butler is in a very bad state, suffering under Delirium Tremens, not fit to be left alone. We were obliged to have two men sit up all night with him in his bedroom.'

August 6, 1857

'Henry Young, my butler, died about 3 o'clock this morning. We ordered two men to be with him all the night and two men in the next room in case of his being very violent, which he was, and they were all four obliged to manage him and keep him in his bed. He expired quietly at last.'

August 7, 1857

'Son Fred superintended the getting down the corpse of poor Young after it had been screwed down by the undertaker. Our carpenter having first taken out the window from the room over the back kitchen slid the coffin down on planks from the window to the ground. It was deposited in the two-stall stable. It had already become very offensive.'

August 8, 1857

'The funeral of our butler H. Young took place about 1 p.m. A hearse and coach arrived about 12, and the coffin was deposited in the hearse. A number of the family attended, he having eight brothers. They all assembled in the farm house and partook of refreshment, John Pike superintending the whole. They left for Ardeley Church yard at 1 p.m., several of the relations in chaise carts, our housekeeper and several of our servants also.'

August 9, 1857 (Sunday)

'The greater part of our servants went to Ardeley church. Poor Young's funeral having taken place there yesterday, a sermon appropriate to the occasion was expected of the vicar Mr. Malet.'

August 20, 1857

'Gave to my house servants who put on slight mourning for my late butler H. Young, at their own cost, £3. 2. 6d.'

September 8, 1857

'W. Cooper who has lived with Mr. Baker's family at Bayford Bury came over this day. My wife and myself had an interview with him which was quite satisfactory and settled with him to come to us on the 29th Sept. His wages are to be 50 guineas p. annum, he finding his own tea. He is 50 years old but a very respectable looking man and strong and active.'

The Pryors' stipulation that the butler should drink his own tea appears somewhat surprising. It might have been expected after their recent experience that they would not mind whose, or how much, tea he drank as long as he did not punish the port. But some such stipulation was common form at the time.

October 12, 1857

'Our late housekeeper Mrs. Merrill left this day.'

Thus John Izzard records the departure from under his roof of a servant who had been with him thirty years. There is not a word of concern for her future. But he did leave her 19 gns. in his will.

Two housekeepers followed in quick succession before the household settled down again. The last three years of the diarist's life were untroubled by domestic changes.

XXII

THE FAMILY AT CLAY HALL, 1847–61

It was not until the summer following Dear Fred's ordination that his father first heard him take a service and preach.

July 11, 1847

'My son Fredk. had kindly offered to take Mr. Harding's duty for a month or five weeks to set him at liberty to go out with his wife to visit their friends, and they are to leave tomorrow. Fredk. told me he should read the prayers in the afternoon but said nothing to me about preaching the sermon in the morning. I was quite taken by surprise, when seeing him in Mr. Harding's pew, my wife told me he was going to preach, and very much gratified I was in hearing him. He acquitted himself well, his delivery being very good and his manner impressive. The sermon was good and adapted to the lesson of the day (Nathan and David). Fredk. also read the prayers in the afternoon, Mr. Harding preaching the sermon.

After dinner I proposed Fredk.'s good health with good wishes for his well doing in the holy profession he has made choice of, which was most cordially and affectionately responded to by all.'

After the Long Vacation was over Dear Fred returned to Oxford where he was now a senior Fellow of New College.

November 23, 1847

'A letter from Mrs. Bliss from Oxford respecting the vacancy likely to occur in St. Mary's Hall, the Principal Dr. Hampden being appointed Bishop of Hereford, taking the place of Dr. Musgrave who is to be Archbishop of York vacant by the death of Dr. Harcourt. The situation of Principal would exactly suit Dr. Bliss. It is in the disposal of the Duke of Wellington, the Chancellor of the University. Dr. Bliss, we hear by the letter, made early application to the Duke. Nothing is known at present, Dr. Hampden not having actually resigned yet.'

200

But then a hitch occurred. Dr. Hampden was a controversial figure. In his Bampton Lectures he had shocked Dr. Pusey and his followers by drawing a distinction between the 'Divine Facts' of Revelation, and the inference drawn from them; in the latter category he had lumped all church formularies, the Creeds included. 'That', said Newman, 'would make shipwreck of the Christian Faith.' Worse was to follow. Hampden in 1834 had recommended that the rule insisting that all young men on Matriculation should sign the XXXIX Articles should be rescinded. In 1836 Melbourne, with, it is reasonable to suppose, malicious glee, had thrust him on the Tory University as Regius Professor of Divinity.

John Izzard remembered all this; he had been in Oxford when the University had expressed its displeasure at the appointment.

May 5, 1836 (at Oxford)

'A very important day at Oxford. A convocation was held, attended by the clergy, not only in the University, but from all parts of the country, to vote upon a new statute purposing to prevent Dr. Hampden, the newly appointed Regius Professor of Divinity, from nominating the Select Preachers. His principles are not considered orthodox as exemplified in his published Bampton Lectures, and his appointment to the Professorship was obnoxious to many of the Heads of Houses. The statute was carried by a great majority.

Some of the undergraduates behaved riotously and broke into the theatre but were soon ejected when they broke several of the windows.'

Much water had flowed under Folly Bridge since then, and many of Hampden's old opponents were now in the Church of Rome. Nevertheless, his proposed elevation to the episcopate so shocked Church opinion that the Dean of Chapter of Hereford talked of ignoring the Congé d'elire.

The Blisses spent January at Clay Hall.

January 20, 1848

'Dr. Bliss is not well and refuses all invitations to dine out. He is very much worried at the delay in consecrating Hampden Bishop of Hereford after he has been elected.'

However, after the Prime Minister had reminded the Cathedral Authorities of Praemunire and the penalties attaching thereto, their ardour cooled. But it was not until 3 May 1848 that the good news reached Clay Hall.

May 3, 1848

'Received a letter from Dr. Bliss containing the gratifying account of his appointment to the Principalship of St. Mary Hall Oxford by His Grace the Duke of Wellington. I write by return of post a letter to himself and one to his wife, congratulating them both on this joyful occasion.'

St. Mary Hall which, on the death of Bliss's successor, was amalgamated with Oriel College, maintained to the last a good reputation.

Meanwhile at Clay Hall George Pemberton had been packed off to India.

January 3, 1848

'I had some conversation with Dr. Bliss respecting George Pemberton who is going out as Assistant Surgeon to India. The cost of his outfit is considerable and there are no funds with his father's agents in London, and there is no time for a remittance to arrive before he sails on the 20th of this month. The result of the conference was that I should advance £150 and Dr. Bliss £100, making £250, which we did.'

January 20, 1848

'This day my wife's nephew Geo. R. Pemberton sailed for India by a very fine vessel the Hindostan from Southampton. Fred went to Southampton, dined with him yesterday and was to see him off this morning. He goes by the overland Passage, touching at Gibraltar and Malta on the way to Alexandria. Thence they cross the desert to Suez and then take ship again.'

The Hindostan, a paddle-wheeler, 2,017 tons, 520 horse-power, was one of the early ships of the Peninsular & Oriental Line, incorporated in 1840.

The cost of outfitting George Pemberton seems high, but it probably included surgical instruments.

Dear Fred now obtained a post as curate in a parish near Henley. He also secured his father's permission to marry after he had worked a year as curate.

Shortly before the date fixed for the ceremony on

September 4, 1849

'My wife received a letter from her sister Mrs. Bliss this morning mentioning that her husband Dr. Bliss would be prevented officiating at the altar at our son's marriage on Thursday next, being a sad sufferer from a boil or rather carbuncle.'

'This', wrote John Izzard, 'affects my wife very much and sadly damps our anticipated pleasure.'

September 6, 1849

'A lovely morning after a brilliant moonlight night. We rose about 8 a.m. Took coffee and bread and butter at 9 and at half past 9 we set off in different carriages provided for the occasion by Col. West for Rotherfield Greys, where my son Fred's marriage with Louisa Mary West was to be solemnised. My son-in-law the Rev. Richard Pryor supplied Dr. Bliss's place. My wife, my daughter Emma, and Winifred Lafont, the latter one of the brides-maids, were in the first carriage, several others followed, and the bride elect with Col. West and some of her friends in the last.

Richard performed the service very well, and after the signing and witnessing in the vestry was over the parties all returned to the Red Lion at Henley and between 12 and 1 o'clock about thirty sat down to a very handsome dejeuner provided by Mr. Dixon, the landlord, in an excellent long room accommodating nearly the whole number. I sat at the top with Mrs. West and Mr. Henry West, the Colonel's son at the bottom, the bride and bridegroom in the centre on one side, and the colonel on the other side of the bride. Everything went off well excepting only my wife being sadly out of spirits.

There was good champagne and other wines, and the health and happiness of the bride and bridegroom was done justice to. They left early on their journey to the Lakes in a carriage with four horses to Reading where they took the Rail and were to proceed to Worcester and remain the night there.

Sons John, Morris, Alfred and R. V. Pryor went afterwards on the river in two boats with the ladies which they all enjoyed.

My wife was not easy without going to Oxford to see Dr. Bliss and her sister, Mr. Weatherell and her brother William accompanying her. I remained with Emma and Winifred and took a long walk with them and had a snug dinner by ourselves half past 6.'

A week later John Izzard was able to wear his 'new blue coat' at another family wedding, that of his granddaughter Marian Heathcote Lafont with the Rev. Henry Heatley, at the little church of Hinxworth.

For two more years John Izzard enjoyed unclouded happiness. Then the shadows began to fall across his life. For the time being all was serene and he was happily absorbed in an occupation which Mr. Pooter would have found congenial.

November 27, 1849
'Engaged superintending the planting of laurels and making a small elevation of old vitrified bricks on a projecting point with an ascent of wooden blocks at the end of the shrubbery which I have named The Surprise. I had the place cleared and the walk made whilst my wife was absent last week, and on showing what I had done she was quite surprised.'

The Great Northern Railway was making its way north and its progress was watched with fascinated interest by John Izzard and Dr. Bliss whenever he was at Clay Hall.

January 4, 1850
'Set off in Alfred's phaeton to see the stupendous viaduct now erecting at Digswell for the Great Northern Railway. There are nearly 40 arches, those spanning the river being 90 feet high. The piers are nearly all built, but no arches over them yet. It is a most striking and wonderful work.'

Works of art such as the Digswell Railway Viaduct have yet to attract the admiration which they deserve.

In 1851 the clouds began to gather. Mention has been made of how John Izzard fell in a London street and broke his leg, and was carried to the Berners Hotel. Worse was to befall him there.

November 24, 1851
'My nephew the Rev. R. V. Pryor, who became my son-in-law by marrying my daughter Juliana in 1843, died this day at the Berners Hotel after being extremely ill for rather more than a week. His illness for the last few days was inflammation of the brain which caused him to be delirious and was most heart rending to us all located in the house, but particularly to his poor wife. There were four medical men consulting together attending him.'

November 26, 1851
'The hearse containing the corpse of my son-in-law, the Rev. R. V. Pryor, left the Berners Hotel at 5 o'clock this morning for Baldock as his remains are to be deposited in the family vault in the chancel there.

I left the hotel at ¼ past 11, being carried into my chariot, and my broken leg being placed in an easy position on a rest with soft pillows, my wife sitting beside me. Our own horses took us to Hertford, taking them out for ¼ hour at Waltham Cross. We arrived at the Salisbury Arms at 3.15 and had a pair of horses put to the carriage, leaving our own horses with Beckwith to follow, after being well baited there. Arrived at Clay Hall at 5 p.m. and was carried into the breakfast parlour where I was deposited safely, thank God for it. Dined, and about 9 in the evening was carried upstairs to my bedroom, selecting the pink room for that purpose. The adjoining large dressing room made me a comfortable apartment to be wheeled into where I could sit and have my account books to enter up gradually.'

November 29, 1851
'The funeral of my deceased son-in-law took place this forenoon. The widow was very much overcome. She is very much to be pitied and felt for.

It appears that her deceased husband has left no will as diligent search has been made and none found. He became delirious so soon after his attack of fever that he was not in a situation to make a will the last three or four days of his existence.'

December 2, 1851
'My daughters Emma and Juliana came up from Baldock before the departure of the latter for her late residence at Spettisbury, which will now go into the hands of the patron Mr. Drax, the deceased having only a life interest in the living.

We had a good deal of conversation about her unfortunate situation. She becomes entitled to one half of the personal property and the brother and sisters of the deceased to one third each of the remainder.'

The law of intestate succession had come down unchanged from the Middle Ages. Land went to the eldest son, and the remainder was shared between the widow and all who could claim a real blood relationship with the deceased. Not until 1890 was the law amended so as to give the widow preferential treatment. Recent legislation has increased this preference to the first £5,000 where there are children and £20,000 otherwise.

December 14, 1851

'This was an important day, my son Fred preaching his first sermon as rector of Benington. My wife, daughter Emma and granddaughter Winifred went in the carriage and took luncheon with them and remained for both morning and afternoon services, the sermon being in the afternoon.

Most of our servants also attended. I would have been there but it was too hazardous to attempt it in my present state. There was a full congregation who came away well pleased. Fred read the sermon to me in the evening which I thought very appropriate for the occasion.'

April 11, 1852 (Easter Day)

'A brilliant day, very warm in the sun, but chilly in the shade. I went to church this morning after a very long absence viz. since the 29th Sept. on which day I broke my leg. I was drawn in my chair by my coachman and footman, alighting at the church door with the assistance of my two sticks walked up the nave to the Rectory pew in the chancel, having arranged with Mr. Harding to do so as I wished to return thanks to Almighty God for recovering from my accident. I afterwards partook of the Sacrament with many other communicants. I put in five pounds to the collection which I had great pleasure in doing.'

June 16, 1852

'The afternoon being fine I mounted my pony for the first time for many months and rode all round my farm and inspected my crops. I was out for about two hours. I felt very thankful for being favoured to recover the use of my leg to enable me to ride. I took Tom Aylott to walk by my side.'

During the winter of 1852, it became clear that the health of his eldest son John was failing, and on Ash Wednesday, 1853, he took formal leave of his father.

'He told me that he felt weaker, and that he was quite resigned to die when it should please God to call him. He had made his will, given up all worldly concerns, and felt great peace of mind especially since having partaken of the Sacrament. He told me he should like to see my wife for a very few moments. He spoke very affectionately to her and presented her with another little remembrance belonging to his first wife which he said was the last he had to distribute that belonged to her.'

Before Easter he was dead. It was a hard blow for John Izzard. Apart from his feelings of grief, there was the awkward fact that, without John to help him, Morris could not manage the Brewery. The Pryors had made it in the course of several generations and it was bitter to part with it. John's sons were still boys at Eton, and no attempt was made to continue the business until one or other could take it over.

May 28, 1853

'Son Morris informs me that the two Mr. Simpson (brothers) who through their uncle Mr. Jhn. Philips, brewer of Royston, have been in treaty—with my consent—for some weeks past, for the brewery at Baldock, have agreed to take the whole concern at a valuation. Half the purchase to remain on mortgage at 4% and the business to be completed, if possible, by the 4th October.'

Under the name of Simpson's this brewery flourished for another century, and then, like many another country brewery succumbed to a merger and brewed no more. Its building which for nearly two centuries lent elegance and distinction to Baldock High Street, was acquired by the Baldock Urban District Council in 1966, and despite the protests of the Georgian Group, demolished.

Nor were its claims to survival based only on architectural grounds. When in its issue of 24 May, 1969 the *Economist* discussed the newly emerging interest in industrial archaeology its first illustration was that of the Baldock Brewery.

It is to be hoped that under the protection of the Town and Country Planning Act 1968 the Brewery mansion and Vickris's house in Hitchin Street, both Georgian buildings of merit, may survive. But their present dilapidated condition does not suggest that there has been any change of heart in either the Baldock District Council or the Hertfordshire County Council.

May 3, 1854

'This day I completed my eightieth year and have great reason to thank God which I sincerely do for the enjoyment of the great blessing of health vouchsafed to me at this advanced period of my life, and for my recovery from the several most serious accidents that have befallen me, having had, at different times, both my legs broken, and a rupture of the blood vessel in the leg that was last broken, by being upset in the carriage last year.

I was surrounded by my family at dinner this day, viz. my sons

Morris, Alfred and Fred, daughter Lafont, Emma and Juliana (the latter being the widow of R. V. Pryor), son Morris's wife and daughter, and son Fred's wife; grandson Ogle Lafont and granddaughter Winifred Lafont, who with my wife and myself made the party thirteen. From them and from many others I received most kind greetings. We had a very agreeable evening together.'

Despite increasing infirmity he continued to find much in life to interest him. He followed the careers of his grandchildren with keen, if unequal, interest. At every stage of his career, Henry Maclean Pryor, John's second son, received some token of his grandfather's affection; when he entered and left Sandhurst, when he showed himself at Clay Hall in the uniform of the 60th Rifles, when he joined at Winchester, and when he left for Calcutta, on each occasion a tip was bestowed. In return the young officer sent his grandfather his photograph, the first John Izzard ever received, and which he was somewhat doubtful what to do with. The elder son John Eade was destined for the church. He had a creditable academic career at Oxford, winning a College prize. Of this John Izzard heard with satisfaction, but nothing further transpired. Reginald, Alfred's son, who won a scholarship at University College Oxford, was rewarded with a tip of staggering generosity, £20. When later he had to be removed 'in a deep decline', his grandfather was much concerned.

July 29, 1859

'Doctor George Pemberton came this day to see his aunt, my wife, and make us a visit. He has lately arrived from India and had a narrow escape, being a passenger on the unfortunate ship the Alma, wrecked on a reef. Fortunately no lives were lost.'

December 25, 1859

'I received a letter from my daughter Lafont informing me of her daughter Winifred being affianced to George Pemberton M.D. now on leave for two years from India.'

John Izzard gave the young lady a present of £50.

It was not until early in 1860 that the first hint occurs of the approaching tragedy which was for John Izzard to make calamity of so long life.

February 21, 1860

'I went with my wife in the clarence to Benington to see my son Frederick who has been very poorly lately.'

March 3, 1860
'My wife had invited Mr. Veasey to come to Clay Hall to luncheon. I wished to have some conversation with him respecting my son Frederick's affairs. I told him I had paid my son £100 and had agreed to give him £400 more to discharge some long standing debts. Fred was to send him the bills. It had pressed upon Fred's mind and made him unhappy, being so much in debt, especially as he had been so unwell.'

March 7, 1860
'Sons Morris and Alfred came up, dined and remained the night. I had a long conversation with them about son Frederick's affairs, he owing bills to a large amount. They are to be sent to Mr. Veasey at Baldock for inspection. I expect I shall be obliged to discharge them, amounting to several thousand pounds. It is a grievous affair.'

March 9, 1860
'After luncheon I went with my wife to Benington to see my son Frederick. We found him in his parlour alone, his wife having gone to Hertford. I had a long conversation with him about the sad state of his affairs, he being deeply involved in debt. I thought it had probably caused him much sorrow and had preyed on his mind. But he told me his illness had not risen so much on that account. I said, however, I would pay all his debts that his character might not suffer.'

April 16, 1860
'My wife passed a rather better night than she has had lately altho' grieving very much for our son Frederick (her only son), whose life is despaired of.'

April 26, 1860
'Son Fred and his wife left home this afternoon for Hastings. I sent them in the clarence to Stevenage whence they intended to go by train to the Great Northern Hotel, pass the night there and proceed to Hastings by rail tomorrow.'

May 20, 1860
'A telegram arrived last night about 11 p.m. containing a very sad account of son Frederick being taken alarmingly worse, so much so as to require the immediate attendance of his mother (my

wife), who arose from her bed and decided to set off as soon as she could get ready. My son Alfred who happened to be staying with us very kindly offered to accompany her to Hastings. After preparing a few things my wife and son set off in the carriage for Hitchin. It being Sunday there was no train starting from Stevenage. They left Hitchin at ½ past 5 and arrived in London about 7. But there was no train going to Hastings until 5 o'clock in the afternoon.'

May 22, 1860
'Received this morning letters from my wife. They found dear Fred very ill and no hope for his recovery. He knew them both and was very much pleased to see them, but a little wandering at intervals.'

May 24, 1860
'This morning's post brought a letter from my son Alfred giving a sad account of the decease of my dear son Frederick about 7 o'clock yesterday morning at the Marine Hotel in Hastings without a struggle. The midday post brought a letter from my wife. Frederick was not conscious the whole preceding night and appeared not to suffer much pain. The grief and affliction both my wife and Frederick's widow have gone through have been very great. The funeral is intended to take place at Hastings in a cemetery three miles distant.'

May 26, 1860
'The funeral of my dear son Frederick took place this day. This forenoon we read the burial service quietly by ourselves with heavy hearts.'

June 1, 1860
'I gathered two very beautiful roses this afternoon from the wall of the kitchen garden, which I presented to my wife.'

August 3, 1860
'I have disposed of the Benington advowson and apply the proceeds to the payment of my late dear son Frederick's debts which amount to several thousand pounds.'

The purchaser of the advowson was his grandson the Rev. John Eade Pryor, who presented himself to the living.

September 25, 1860
'Mrs. Fred Pryor left us with her two children for Tonbridge

where she has taken a small house for the benefit of her children, there being an excellent school there at moderate expense.'

December 7, 1860
'Wrote a letter to my little grandchild now with her Mamma at Tonbridge.'

December 13, 1860
'I told my wife I should be quite willing and glad to see poor Frederick's widow and children at Xmas, with which she was much pleased. She will write to Tonbridge and impart the news to them, with which they will be delighted I have no doubt.'

December 21, 1860
'There was a heavy fall of snow in the night. A cloudy morning with a little snow falling now and then. In the afternoon it snowed very much. My late son Frederick's widow and her two children came to us this day for their Xmas holiday.'

It cannot be far from the truth—his father seems to have thought so—that Dear Fred's early death was, at least partly, attributable to worry over debts incurred while still a boy at Oxford. Fred Pryor was not the only parson whose whole life was ruined by the consequences of youthful folly. Tradesmen in both University towns encouraged undergraduates (and they seem to have specialised in men going to family livings) to run into debt before they knew what they were doing.

> An thin he coom'd to the parish wi' lots of Varsity Debt.
> Stuck to his taail they did, an 'e 'ant got shut on them yet

so said Tennyson's Northern Farmer of his parson.

But a propensity to run into debt was not a weakness peculiar to undergraduates destined for the church. The novelists of the period, Trollope and Surtees, show how easy it was, particularly after a good dinner, for otherwise sensible gentlemen to put their names to bills, if not on their own, then on some friend's, account.

The undue ease with which credit was given at the University became something of a scandal during the forties. A bankruptcy case in 1848 gave the whole matter an airing, and inspired an article in *Punch* entitled 'Oxford Doings and Oxford Duns', which in the present context seems apposite enough. It purports to be a letter from Thomas Tandem of Christ Church.

'I'm a younger son with a £300 a year allowance. There's a

family living waiting for me and the warming pan is a very decent old bird who will turn out when I'm japanned. I've two horses entered for the Bicester Steeple Chase, a boat on the river, a kennel of bull dogs in Jericho, and an awful bill at Crumpets in the High Street, besides a tick as long as my arm at that infernal old Melchizedeck for claret and champagne. I'm allowed, in fact, to be a "credit to my college". How could I do this on £300 a year? Of course, I shall pay sometime or other for Sneezum Parva is worth £800 a year . . .'

Dear Fred had an allowance of £200 p.a., but he was also a fellow (modern parlance, scholar) of New College. He probably had much the same amount to spend as Thomas Tandem. But he was no horseman, and there is nothing to suggest that he rowed. He seems to have taken some interest in coursing, and to have occasionally won at Baldock Coursing Club Meets. But this is not an expensive sport. When rector he seems to have lived modestly. There are references to his 'little carriage', but, often enough, Dear Fred and his wife travelled by hired fly. What he spent his money on must remain a mystery. It is likely that what was initially a debt of small proportions became swollen as a result of the renewing of bills at extortionate rates of interest. No doubt his creditors made no difficulty about renewing 'paper'. John Izzard and his wife often stayed in Oxford with the Blisses. Enquiries from the servants would establish that John Izzard was comfortably off, and likely to 'cut up' well. Dear Fred was a good investment.

He must have longed to tell his father of his plight, but have lacked the courage to do it.

John Izzard survived him by a year—just long enough to settle his debts—and died on 5 June 1861 in his 88th year. His remains were laid to rest in that 'capacious family vault' beneath the chancel of Norton church which he and his sons had had prepared twenty years earlier.

XXIII

THE MAN JOHN IZZARD PRYOR

D espite Dear Fred's inability to confide in his father, John Izzard was fundamentally a kind character. But he was a man of his own times, and believed that as a father he possessed a wisdom not given to sons. He never doubted that he had been right in insisting on Dear Fred entering his 'Holy Profession'. It was the memory of that October evening at Clay Hall when his father had condemned him to an uncongenial calling which came between Fred and his hopes that the story of his debts might receive a sympathetic hearing.

But he must, too, have realised that his father regarded money as a trust, and spent a substantial fraction of his life keeping his accounts.

December 16, 1844

'Engaged all the remainder of the day in my Library transferring the open accounts from the old Ledger B into the new ledger C. Began with some ink I bought in London called the Registration Ink and made use for the first time of a steel pen, both for the heads of the different pages and also for the general writing. Began the ink in this diary yesterday but with a common quill pen, only using at present the steel pen for the ledger.'

The steel pen was in his hands two or three times every week. He expected his money to do its work, and made sure that it did. Long hours were devoted to his account books. It is typical of him that on his return home after breaking his leg, his first concern was to bring his accounts up to date. He had little sentiment. 'Poor Highflyer' he wrote, 'a very old and excellent servant, the finest carriage horse I ever was master of, or ever shall be, but completely done for.' After this handsome tribute, he sells him for ten guineas. (It is a relief to know that old Fowler, his hunter, was shot and buried.) Mention has been made of his personal calls on defaulting London customers of the Baldock Brewery. But it would be wrong to conclude that he had an excessive love of money. He had a hearty respect for it because, in his experience, it was earned by hard work, sober judgment, and thrift.

His attitude towards the poor was kindly, if unimaginative. Mention has been made of his attempts to temper the harshness of the Poor Law. He was always mindful of the poor in hard weather. Faggots and bread were distributed to tide them over bad times. The following entry records the first distribution of coal—probably the first time that it was burnt in Walkern cottages.

February 16, 1855
'Sent the waggon to Stevenage for one ton and a half of coals to distribute to the poor cottages. J. Pike made out a list and finds there are 103 cottages inhabited by the labourers and poor widows. I found 1½ ton would give each cottager half a bushel of coals which would be acceptable this very inclement weather.

My coals cost me 36 shillings at the station at Stevenage besides the carriage. They just held out for half a bushel to each person.'

It was no cold-hearted capitalist who stood by the Clay Hall chimney when it was swept.

December 20, 1836
'The chimney sweepers came over from Hertford. Having spoken to Mr. Pemberton last Saturday about the difficulty of sweeping the flue from the stove in the hall, they were to bring the instruments they use when boys do not go up the chimneys. But they proved quite useless as they only screwed on straight and would only pass up to the beginning of the bend over the arch. The little boy therefore went up and I stood by giving him particular orders to run no hazard and not to attempt getting up if he found any difficulty. He was a good boy and said he would try but would not run any hazard of getting fixed; and I kept talking to him as he proceeded. He said it was very small and bad getting over the turn but he could manage it by taking time; and he made his way to the top. When he came down again he found greater difficulty at the turn than when he went up. I expected he must get out at the top, but by pushing his small clothes down his legs—a thought of his own—he said he could manage. I was very glad to see him safe back again.'

He could not have been a life-long friend of Dr. Philip Bliss, had he not possessed intellectual interests. He followed the events of the day in the newspapers, and was fond of reading biography and travel—but it does not seem that he ever read a novel. Moore's *Life of Byron* he read 'or more properly skimm'd particular parts of it, and was very much amused and interested by it.' So was Lord Macaulay who published one of his celebrated essays upon it.

November 13, 1845
'Engaged on my accounts nearly the whole day. Left my library at 9 p.m. and after tea went on with my reading of Warburton's Work The Crescent and the Cross, as I like very much reading from half past 9 until 12 o'clock.'
This was a best seller, reaching 17 editions. It described the author's travels in Egypt, Palestine and Syria. Years later Admiral Lord Fisher praised its account of Nelson's victory of the Nile.

John Izzard writes of one book, that it kept him from his accounts. This tribute he paid to the Memoirs of Dr. Chalmers in 3 volumes, 'one of our Club books'. It is unlikely that he was interested in the dispute which led to the secession of the 'Wee Fraes'. But Dr. Chalmers was an authority on social problems, and it may well have been his views on the Poor Law—he held that it should be abolished, and the exercise of Christian Charity be substituted for it—which engaged John Izzard's interest.

His reading enabled him to hold his own, not only with the parsons and gentry of Hertfordshire, but also with Oxford dons. When Dr. Bliss rose to eminence as Principal of St. Mary Hall, and John Izzard was staying with him, he had to meet and dine with the Heads of Houses at Oxford.

But his chief interests were those of a countryman. He delighted in observation of bird, beast and flower—many are the entries in his diary on these subjects—and he found unceasing satisfaction in the procession of the seasons. These tastes he shared with many of his fellow squires.

To the Early Victorian country gentleman a debt of gratitude is still owing. Many of the more pleasing features of the modern countryside are to be attributed to him. The pattern of hedge and ditch, the woods and spinneys, the country roads, many of the cottages, farm houses and farm buildings, date from his days; and who shall say to what extent his care of the soil enabled it to produce the food needed to tide the nation over two deadly emergencies?

In the words of Tennyson he strove

> . . . to help his homelier brother men,
> Served the poor, and built the cottage,
> Raised the school and drained the fen.

Much, no doubt, was committed to him. It was his merit to have used it to live 'a quiet and peaceable life in all godliness and honesty'. To this modest Anglican ideal generations of English country folk have been content to aspire.

INDEX

Acts: Corn Laws, Repeal of, 170; Farm
  Drainage, 165; General Enclosure
  (1836), 162; Goldbourne's (Beershops),
  180; Highways (1835), 91, 97; Income
  Tax, Repeal of, 181, Re-enactment,
  184–5; Local Government (1888), 91,
  98; Navigation, Repeal of, 175; Poor
  Law Amendment (1834), 91, 95; Public
  Health, 100; Reform, 50; Rural Police,
  105–7; Tithe Commutation (1836), 80;
  Window Tax, 183
Agriculture see Farming
Albert, Prince: wedding, 153; shooting at
  Hatfield, 155; at Hitchin, 156
America, Minister: observer, Washington
  Irving, 100; clipper, 135
Ampthill (Beds.): 4–10
Archery: 72, 86
Architects: Pemberton, 8; Wilkins, 24;
  Burton, 111
Army: disposition of, 70; moved by rail,
  51
Art: summer Show, 112; Great Exhibition,
  117
Assembly rooms: 125
Assizes: 49, 103
Astleys: 111
Asylum: lunatic, 13; orphan, 101
Athenaeum Club: 112
Australia: 78

Ball: hunt, 94; Hatfield House, 155;
  Pryor, 84
Ballet: 109
Barclay, Edward, M.F.H.: 157
Bath, shower: 134, 159; warm, 187
Bayley, Rev. E. G.: 14
Bed, Spring: 188
Bedford, Headmaster, Twyford School: 36
Beer shops: licensing of, 180
Bliss, Rev. Dr. Philip: 11, 130, 200;
  Principal of St. Mary's Hall, 202
Blomfield, Bishop Charles: 74, 136, 143

Blomfield's Academy: 24
Bowdler, Thomas: 86
Brick Lane, Truman's Brewery at: 26
Bridge, Walkern, repair of: 98
Brighton: Butler's holiday at (1855), 124;
  Pryor's holiday at (1833), 125; dis-
  embarkation at, 130; boarding house
  (1845/1852), 130, 134; sermon at, 149
Burton, Decimus: 111

Carriage, second-hand: 20
Chalmers, Rev. Dr.: 215
Charterhouse: 139
Chartism: 50
Chauncy family of Green Elms, Munden:
  Reginald joins Indian Civil Service, 77;
  family leaves Munden, 78; suicide of
  Nathaniel, 78
Chimney sweep: 214
Cholera: attack 1831/2, 50; 1848/49, 99;
  seq. 1854, 100; death of Mrs. Pemberton
  by, 77
Christening dinners: 63, 80
Christmas: fare, 61; first presents, 62;
  tree, 63
Clarance: 116
Clarkson, William: 92
Clay Hall: 8; house-warming dinner, 10;
  planting of trees, 9; cellar, 9; water
  closets, 102
Coach: glass coach, 108; fares, 114, 124;
  journeys, 121; coachmen, 89–90
Cockayne, Thomas: Master of Harriers, 58
Colosseum: 111
Colston family: Juliana elopes, 87; Pryor's
  visit, 130; Dr. Colston, 130
Commuting: 64
Constables: parish, 93; special, 47
Constantia, South African wine: 59
Corn Laws: 54, 158
Covent Garden: 108–9
Crockford's: 111
Crystal Palace: 117

217

Dacre, Lord: 104, 177
Dances: country, 84; polka, 85; quadrilles and waltzes, 85, 155
Dental treatment: artificial front tooth, 190; fees, 190; false teeth, 181, 192–3
Dinner: Assize, 103; Conservative, 81; Christmas for farm men, 62; tenants', 172; tithe, 80; Trustees of River Lee, 82; parish, 83; time of, 60
Diorama: 110
Doctors *see* Medical treatment
Dogs: at Clay Hall, 77; worrying sheep, 158
Drainage: Acts for advancing money for, 165; tile, 165; hollow, 165; effect of, 179; house, 102; Walkern village, 102
Drunkenness: 10, 57, 58
Drury Lane: 108

East India Company: College at Haileybury, 73, 148 ; Director William Wigram, 76; Surgeon Bell, 13; Reginald Chauncy joins Civil Service, 77; Capt. George Malet, 77; Rev. William Malet, 77; Capt. John Murray, 77; George Pemberton Surgeon, 77; Lieut. William Pollard, 77
Elections: Parliamentary, 51 *et seq.*
Elopement: 87–88
Emigration: 78
Emotion: free expression of, 56; weddings, 57; sermons, 149, 141
Excursion: train, 118
Exhibition (Summer exhibition of Royal Academy): 112
Exhibition, Great (1851): 117
Exeter Change: 111

Family Prayer: 64
Farming: Corn Law, 169, 172; attempt to re-enact, 54; depression, 159–161; drainage of land, 165–6; enclosure, Walkern, 161; Sandon, 162; Dunton, 164; fatstock, 169; fertilisers, chemical, 165–6, 168; Lawes, 167; hedges, plantation of, 163; incendiarism, 47, 160–1; labourers' revolt, Luddism, 46–50; machinery, seed drill, 168; liquid manure-spreader, 168; Mr. MacCormick's reaping-machine, 168, threshing-machine, 167; potato blight, 170–1; prices of wheat, 170; Royal

Agricultural Society's show, 169; rural housing, 169, wages, 160
Fish: dominance of cod, 61; oysters, 62; turbot, lobsters, 62; salmon, whitebait, 82
Fishing: 178
Flower show: Baldock Horticultural, 81, 195; Horticultural Society's show at Chiswick, 113
Forsytes: Galsworthy's comparison with Pryors, 119
"Four Swans", Aldersgate: 110
France, tour in: 127 *et seq.*
Friday, Good: observance of, 142
Friendly society, Spettisbury: 132
Funeral pomp: 66; millinery, 67–8

Gardener: Scots appointed, 195; dismissed, 195
George IV, death, 151
Gin: 59
Goldbourne's Act (Beershops), 180
Great Northern: Hotel, 209; Opening of Stevenage line, 135
Greenwich: steamer to, 114–5; whitebait dinner, 115
Groom, appointment of: 194
Gun: John Izzard's (by Wilkinson), 176

Haileybury College: 73, 148
Hamburg: 25, 27–8
Hampden, Dr.: 11, 200
Hampson, Capt.: Yeomanry, 71; caught poaching, 177; militia, 71
Hanbury, Robert, partner in Truman, Hanbury: 82; builds new church at Thundridge, 83, 174
Hanover Square, St. George's: 65
Hansom cab: 115
Harding, Rev. John, rector of Walkern: 72, 141–46, 107
Harvest thanksgiving: 140–1, 171
Hastings: 121, 209–10
Hatfield Brewery: 28; purchased for Alfred, 31
Hatfield House: invitations to, 79; Queen's visit to, 154–6
Haymarket, Queen's theatre: 110
Heathcote, Captain, squire of Shephall Bury: 70–1
Highways Act (1835): 91, 97
Hindostan paddlewheeler: 202

Hinds, Rev., vicar of Ardeley, Bishop of Norwich: 73
Holidays: family, 124–5, 127–8; on Good Friday, 142; Coronation, 111; on cessation of Cholera, (1849), 101
Holly: used for church decoration, 142
Horticultural Society: Baldock, 81; London, 112, 113
Hospital: Middlesex, 188
Hunt: Puckeridge, 177–8

Incendiarism: 47, 160–1
Income Tax: 180, 181, 184–5
Inhabited House tax: 181

Journey, wedding: 22
Jury, Grand: 103
'Jolliffe, William': steam ship, 26

Keen, Edmund: actor, 110
Kemble, Fanny: actress, 108
King's Cross Hotel: 114
Kensington Gardens: 116

Lafont, Rev. John: rector of Hinxworth, 138, 105–6; Eliza his wife, 20; son Ogle Rev., Rector of Hinxworth, 138–9; daughters Marion, 85, 139, 203 and Winifred, 203, 206
Lee: Trustees of River, inspection by, 82; dinner, 82
Leech, John: The Rick Burner's home. 161
Leeches: 186–7
Lind, Jenny: 110
Lord's Cricket Ground: 40
Lucas, William: 153, 123, 193
Luddism: 46–9
Luncheon: 60, 89, 83
Lytton, Sir Edward Bulwer: 78

McAdam, Sir James: 99
Malet: Captain George, 77; Rev. William, rector of Ardeley, 73; differences with Lady Murray, 74–5; goes on pilgrimage, 145–7, restores Ardeley church, 147
Medical Treatment: bleeding or cupping, 186; bath, warm. 187; shower, 188; cancer, 188; chloroform, 188; chiropodist, 190; fees, 187, 189, 190; iodine, 189; lancet, 186; leeches, 186; leg broken, 133–4, 188–9; pills, blue, 187

Militia: enrolling, 69; ballot for, 69; reluctance to volunteer for, 71
Morris, Betsy: 108
Morris, Joseph: 11, 32
Murray, Major Adolphus Cottin: 74, 75
Murray, Captain John: 78
Murray, Commissary General, John: 74, 75
Murray, Sir Robert Bart: 74 *et seq.*
Murray, Lady (Susannah): 74–6
Music: after dinner, 88, 89; in church, 73, 142, 147; Jenny Lind, 110; opera, 109–10; Weippert's band, 38, 85

National Society for promoting Education of Children of Poor in principles of Established Church: 140
Navigation Acts: Repeal of, 135
New College, Oxford *see* Oxford
Newspapers: 46, 49, 55, 215; *Times* forecasts repeal of Corn Laws, 170; wedding announcements in, 66; as aid to temperance, 58; Royal train journey, 157

Omnibus: 115
Opera: 109–110
Organ grinder at Walkern Church: 142
Osbaldeston, George: 175
Outdoor servants, *see* Bailiff, coachman, gardener, groom
Oxford: coach journey to, 47; "Swing letters" at, 47; Fred goes up to New College, 41; life and habits at, 41; Finals, 42; rides home, 43; ordained at, 44; convocation against Dr. Hampden, 201; Dr. Bliss applies for St. Mary's Hall, 200; appointed Principal, 202; undergraduate credit, 211; John Eade Pryor wins college (Balliol) prize, 208; Reginald Pryor wins scholarship at University, 208

Painting: 112
Panorama: 110–11
Papal aggression: 55
Paris: 128–9
Parliament: 54
Passport: 127
Peel, Sir Robert: 50; and Corn Laws, 170
Pew, squire's: in Walkern Church, repewing of, 143–4
Photograph: 208
Poaching: 177
Pocket books: 63

Police: 104–6; at Walkern, 106–7
Pollard, Rev. John: 47–8, 73, 92
Polling: 52–3
Poor Law: 91, 93, 95–7; Poor Law Amendment Act, 94–6
Port: 10
Potatoes: 169–70
Protection: National Association for, 54
Pryor: Alfred (third son of diarist), Blomfield's Academy, 24; training at Hamburg, 25; "in detestable scrape", 29; Hatfield Brewery purchased for him, 31–2; match with Jane, daughter of Vickris, postponed owing to "particular behaviour", 33; wedding, 33–4; voting qualification, 50; ball at Hatfield, 155; escorts Mrs. Pryor to Hastings, 209; at Fred's deathbed, 210
Pryor: Arthur (son of Vickris), partner in Truman at Brick Lane, married Elisabeth Dew, 21; "Daily Breading" from Putney, 64
Pryor: Eliza (daughter of diarist), 90
Pryor: Elizabeth (spinster sister of diarist), 10, 21
Pryor: Emma (only unmarried daughter of diarist), 14
Pryor: Frederick Bell "Dear Fred" (youngest son of diarist), school at Munden, 35; Twyford, 36; founder's kin Winchester, 37–8; small pox, 39; Puckeridge Hunt, 39; Good report, 40; elected New College, 40; goes up to Oxford, 40–1; rooms in college, 41; horse, 41; Holy Orders, 41; comes of age, 42; schools, 42–3; rides home, 43; Benington advowson, 43; engaged, 43–4; ordained, 44–5; officiates, 200; coursing, 212; curate, 202; marries, 203; rector of Benington, 203; very ill, 208; debts, 208–9; death, 208–10; widow and children, 210–11
Pryor: Henry Maclean (younger son of John Pryor), joins 60th Rifles, 207–8
Pryor: Isolene (youngest daughter of Vickris Pryor), attempts to elope, 88; married, 88; in difficulties, 88
Pryor: John (eldest son of diarist), education, 24; profession, 10; negotiations for Hatfield Brewery, 31–2; marries secondly, 65–6; dying, 206–7; funeral, 68

Pryor: John Eade (eldest son of John), education, 208; rector of Benington, 210
Pryor: John Izzard *the Diarist* pedigree, 2–4; purchases Clay Hall estate, 5; adds wing and lays out grounds, 8–10; stocks cellar, 9; turns off Juliana's suitor, 15; marries her to cousin, 16–19, 21; purchase of Hatfield Brewery for Alfred, 32; insists on Fred taking Holy Orders, 41–2; Deputy Lieut., 48; opposes repeal of Corn Laws, 54; votes Tory, 51–3; progressive farmer, Lawes' chemical manures, 165–7; drains farm land, 165; improved seed, 167; machinery, 167–8; fatstock, 158, 169; endeavours to administer Poor Law humanely, 94–7; takes part in enclosure, 161–3; keen foxhunter, 177–8; partridge shooting, 176–7; carriage accidents, 89–90; breaks leg, 133; friendship with Dr. Bliss, 214, 215; pay Fred's debts, 210
Pryor: Juliana (daughter of diarist), affair with Rev. E. G. Bayley, 14–16; accepts Richard Pryor, 16–19; negotiations for larger dowry, 19; wedding, 21; husband's death, 204; consequences of intestacy, 205
Pryor: Louisa Bell (second wife of diarist), melancholia, 13; affection for Dr. Bliss, 14, 203; views on sermons, 147–8; shower bath, 134, 188; medical treatment, 116–7; nurses husband, 189; at Dear Fred's death, 208–210
Pryor: Marlborough (nephew of diarist), residence in London, 119; retires in slump, 171–2; cottage ornée, 8
Pryor: Marlborough, Robert, birth, 119
Pryor: Martha (daughter of Vickris Pryor), wedding, 57; funeral, 67
Pryor: Morris (second son of diarist), occupies Brewery House Baldock, 10; leases brewery, 180; tipsy, 11, 58, 64; Labourers' Revolt, 47; Yeomanry officer, 69–70; politics, 51; coach fares, 124; marriage, 88, 130–1; declines help purchase Hatfield Brewery, 28; puts up Alfred, 29; attends Sessions to decide on Rural Police Act, 105–6; takes share in Hatfield Brewery, 31; shooting, 175–6; at Hatfield Ball, 155
Pryor: Reginald (son of Alfred and grand-

son of diarist), scholar of University College Oxford, 139
Pryor: Richard, Rev. (son of Vickris Pryor), fishes, 179; takes Holy Orders, 16; rector of Spettisbury, courts Juliana, 16–17; accepted, 18; not satisfied with settlement, 19; wedding, 21; requires financial assistance, 22–3; death, 204
Pryor: Robert (younger brother of diarist), partner, Truman Hanbury Buxton, 4; at coronation, 152; good shot, 174; sends sherry to East Indies, 59; supports dismissal of Juliana's suitor, 15; purchase of Hatfield Brewery, 28, 31; backs Alfred, 33; funeral, 68
Pryor: Robert (nephew of diarist), marries, 66; moves to Hampstead, 119
Pryor: Thomas (son of Vickris), gives ball, 84
Pryor: Thomas Mrs. (sister-in-law of diarist), Hampstead, 108; advises on Mrs. Pryor's depression, 116
Pryor: Vickris (brother of diarist), lives at Maltings Baldock, 5; at Clay Hall, 10; buys presentation plate, 93; prevents daughter's elopement, 88; makes her ward of Chancery, 88; ill, 33; officer in Yeomanry, 71; daughter Jane's wedding, 33–4
Pryor: Vickris Mrs. (wife of above), bespeaks play, 86; interested in gardening, 113; complains of Alfred, 32–3; operation for cancer, 188
Public Health Acts: 100
Punch drink: how to make, 59
Punch (periodical): 57, 66, 70, 115, 126, 141, 161, 169, 211
Pusey Rev. Dr.: 148–9

Quakers: Halevy on, 1, 3, 153
Quebec: Panorama of, 111
Queen: coronation, 152; marriage, 153, visit to Hatfield, 154–6; at Hitchin, 156–7

Racing at Kimpton: 177, Ascot, 116
Railways: beginnings, 39; diarist's first journey, 130; opening of Great Northern, 135; effect of, 121, 124; excursion, 118; speed, 134

Ramsgate: 125
Red House, Battersea: 175
Regent Street: 116
Regent's Park: 111, 114
Rent: 172
Revenue: 181
Riding: ladies, 86; Fred at Oxford, 41, 43
-Roads: Parish, responsibility, 91; safety of, 177; turnpike, 98
Rogers, Samuel: 111
Roman Catholic Priest: 183
Rouen: 129–30
Royal Academy: 112
Royal Agricultural Society: 169
Royal Horticultural Society, 113
Russell, Lord John: 170
Russian corn: 173

St. George's, Hanover Sq.: 65
St. James's: 111
Sanitation: 100–102
Sausages: 47
Scarborough: 122
School village: 139–40, 142, 145, 89; training, 194
Scots, Bullocks: 158; gardener, 195
Sculpture: 117
Seaside resorts: 121, 124–7
Seed: 167
Sermons: 147–50, 142, 126, 140–1
Servants: Domestic, butler, 194–5, 196; death of, 198; funeral of, 198; cook goes, 80; goes sick, 196; conviviality of, 89; footman, 195; scandalous behaviour of, 197; housekeeper, 197, 199; institute for training, 194; ladies' maids, 144, 196, 197–8; misbehaviour of, 196–7; outside: bailiff, 160; coachman, 90; gardener, 195; groom, 194–5; in mourning, 68
Sheep: 158–9, 87
Sherry: 59
Ships: 208, 134–5; see also steamers
Sind: 77
Small pox: 39
Smith, Abel of Hamburg: 53, 78, 25–6, 27–8, 30
Somerset House: 112
Spettisbury: 19, 20, 22
Sport: 174 et seq.
Steamers, Greenwich: 114–15; 'William Joliffe', 26; Bankes, 27; Magnet, 127;

Austrian Lloyd, 146; P & O Hindostan, 202; Alma, 208
Stevenage, polling at: 52
Stowe: 182
Strand: 111
Strawberries: 35, 82
Suez: 202
Superstition: 61
Surgeon: 13, 77, 133
Surtees: 58, 89, 121, 103, 163, 165, 175
Swing, Captain: 47
Sydenham: 118
Syllabub: 89

Taglioni, Marie: 110
Taxes: armorial bearings, 182; carriages, 182; dogs, 182; hair powder, 181; horses, 182; income tax, 180, 185; inhabited houses, 181–2; men servants, 182–3; windows 183–4; revenue from, 181
Tea and Coffee: 10, 89; children's, 145; butler's, 199
Tenants (Farming): 52–3, 166; dinner for, 81, 172
Tennyson: 211, 216, 179
Thackeray: 112, 147
Thames: watermen, 114; steamers on, 114–15, 127; boats on, 203
Theatres: 108–10
Theatricals: Knebworth, 85–6; Malets', 86
Times, The: 49, 150; corn laws, 170; Royal train journey, 157; wedding announcements in, 66
Tithes: Act for commutation of, 80, 137; dinner, 80
Tories: 51–2

Trade factors affecting: potato blight, 169–70; bad harvest, 170; bountiful harvest, 171; slump (1848), 171–2; low corn price, 172; Crimean War, 172
Travel: *see* under coach, railways, steamers
Trollope, Anthony: 211
Trousers: 178
Turkish bath: 127
Turnips: 166
Turnpike tolls: letting of, 98–9

Uncle Tom's Cabin: 134–5
Unemployed: 94–6
Union Workhouse: 96
University of Oxford: 200–2

Veasey, Mr. family solicitor: 10, 12, 19, 50, 86, 104, 181
Vestry: Baldock Select, 91–2; Walkern on employment, 94, 95–6; on poor rate, 96; domicile, 96; apprenticeship, 97
Viaduct, Digswell: 204
Voluntary enlistment: 71
Votes: Alfred's, 50; at elections, 51

Wigram, William: 76–7
Wilkins: 24
Winchester College: 37–40
Wiseman, Cardinal: 55
Workhouse: 91–2, 95, 96
Wright, Rev. James Camper: Rector of Walkern, 48, 80, 139–40, 141

Yacht, Bishop of London's: 137
Yeomanry: 69–71
Yonge, Charlotte:
York: 122

Zoo: 111